APPLEWOOD'S
# HISTORIOGRAPHY
~~ SERIES ~~

# History of Norwich, Connecticut

*From Its Settlement in 1660, to January 1845*

Francis Manwaring Caulkins

APPLEWOOD BOOKS
*Carlisle, Massachusetts*

*History of Norwich, Connecticut*
was originally published in
1845

ISBN: 978-1-4290-2284-2

- - - - - - - - - - - - - - - - - - - - - - - - - - - - - - - - - - - - - - - - - -

For a free copy of our current print catalog featuring our bestselling books, write to:

APPLEWOOD BOOKS
P.O. Box 27
Carlisle, MA 01741

For more complete listings, visit us on the web at:
www.awb.com

**Prepared for publishing by HP**

NORWICH TOWN, FROM THE EAST

# HISTORY

OF

# NORWICH,

## CONNECTICUT,

FROM ITS SETTLEMENT IN 1660, TO JANUARY 1845.

## BY MISS F. M. CAULKINS.

" Many of these little things which we speak of are little only in size and name.
They are full of rich meaning. They illustrate classes of men,
and ages of time."

## NORWICH.

PUBLISHED BY THOMAS ROBINSON.

1845.

TO THE

## CITIZENS OF NORWICH,

INHABITANTS OF A BEAUTIFUL AND VARIED TOWN,

INTERESTING FROM ITS

HISTORICAL ASSOCIATIONS,

AND ALWAYS DISTINGUISHED FOR HOSPITALITY, ENTERPRISE, AND A MANLY
SPIRIT OF INDEPENDENCE,

## THIS HISTORY

IS GRATEFULLY AND RESPECTFULLY INSCRIBED,

BY THE

## AUTHOR.

# PREFACE.

THE sources from which the following history has been drawn, as far as regards the facts, are

I. The Town Records: these are ample and in a good state of preservation.

II. Files of the New London Gazette and Norwich Packet, from which many of the incidents related in the Revolutionary period are derived.

III. Private documents: such as letters, account-books, bills, memorandums, deeds, and justices' papers

IV. Tradition and conversation with aged persons. Tradition, it is acknowledged, is but an uncertain guide,—a glimmering light that often leads astray; for it rests wholly on memory, and memory is frequently treacherous,—an officious imagination sometimes getting firmly seated in its place. But when tradition contradicts no authentic record, and when records fail, even history may be permitted to receive its aid.

To an historical work *references* are generally considered invaluable,—stamping it with authenticity, and enabling the reader to verify each particular incident. But from the nature of the materials from which this work is composed, references would be almost entirely useless. It is not a compilation from published documents, is not founded on previous histories,—it has no predecessor, and therefore cannot appeal to works which are generally accessible. As a History of Norwich, it is an independent, original work; but it makes no claim beyond that of a faithful purpose to give a more enduring form to a mass of local information, that would be lost if left much longer in the charge of mouldering paper, fading ink, and fast dropping age.

The limits of a single volume are too narrow for the publication of original documents, which are usually technical, occupying a large space. The plan pursued is to give the results of inquiries, and condensed statements of facts, without tracing the intermediate steps, and spreading out at large the materials from which they were drawn. Neither is it practicable within these limits to enter so largely into the genealogy of families, as would otherwise have been desirable. On this point the aim has been confined to the furnishing of a few data, the earliest that could be ascertained, to assist those who may wish to pursue the subject, and trace the line of their descent from the first settlers of the town.

The great point kept in view through the whole composition of the work, was *accuracy*. It was the aim of the author to be minutely accurate. Not a fact, name, or date has been given without careful inquiry and examination. Even those sketches which may seem most like fancy pictures, are faithful copies of scenes, as they were depicted by eye-witnesses. But the information on many points was scanty, and doubtless in some cases incorrect; mistakes, therefore, will probably be discovered.

The author cannot dismiss her work without giving utterance to a deep feeling of regret, that several of those aged persons from whom many of its minuter details have been derived, and who regarded with lively interest this attempt to retrieve the events of other days from oblivion, are now no more. Among those who have passed away during the progress of the work, and are not here to welcome its publication or be cheered with its details, sentiments of personal esteem and veneration lead her to record the names of

Rev. JOSEPH STRONG, D. D.,     Capt. DAVID NEVINS, and

Dr. PHILEMON TRACY,          Deacon CALEB HUNTINGTON.

JANUARY, 1845.

# CONTENTS.

# HISTORY OF NORWICH.

## CHAPTER I.

### Introduction.

As you ascend the river Thames, in the eastern part
of Connecticut, and approach towards its head, a sudden opening of its banks, presents you with a distant
glimpse of a few fine buildings, crowning the hill-top,
or scattered along the slope of a headland that seems
to project directly into the bosom of the river in your
front. Another turn in the river, hides the scene from
your view, and when it again opens, you are near
enough to see that a picturesque town is before you,
built around the base, and on the declivity of a hill,
which is embraced by the two branches of the stream
that come winding down through the distant hills.
Around this declivity the streets rise, one above another, displaying several handsome churches and other
public buildings, some of which ascend to the summit
of the hill. The very narrowness of the view, being
circumscribed on all sides by hills, except the open
space afforded by the river in front, gives it the charm
of unity and distinctness.

This is NORWICH :—but from the river you see only
a section of the place; for the buildings are extended
on each side along the arms of the river farther than
your eye can reach, and on the other side of that ob-

2

trusive hill is a lovely and varied landscape, exhibiting avenues of venerable trees, elegant dwelling
houses and numerous gardens, scattered around the
plains and extending far onward over the hills, each
group crowned with its spire, and relieved by a back-
ground of rocky heights or dark bosomed forests.
If you land on the west side, just below the bounds of
the town, where Trading Cove, an arm of the river
almost as broad and deep as the main stream, extends
a short distance into the country, and ascend the
Mohegan highlands,—the line of vision will stretch
far to the north and west, and you will obtain a good
general idea of the situation and varied surface of the
town.   You will perhaps imagine, and with good reason, that the first English explorers beheld it from this
point, and that they were struck with admiration, not
only at the romantic scenery, but at the various advantages presented for commerce, manufactures and
agriculture.   Here they beheld a navigable river and
an easy access to the ocean; hills that would make
excellent pastures for their herds and flocks; plains
and meadows that industry might soon convert into
mowing lands and cornfields; rapid streams and cat-
aracts, affording innumerable mill-seats and sites for
future manufactories.   We can almost fancy that we
hear them exclaim, " What a noble place for a settlement!"

Nearer the city, on each side of the river, are lofty
eminences, from which the prospect is still more extensive and variegated.   The eastern summit bearing
the name of Tory Hill, from its having been the confiscated property of a royalist during the Revolutionary
war, affords a fine view of the harbor, the city, and the
valley of the Shetucket.   From *Windmill* and *Baptist*
Hills on the west, the eye surveys almost the whole

area of the town, and observes the situation of its distinct villages, the course of the streams, the rude clumps of rocks interspersed, and the circumjacent hills. The short and rapid Yantic, spreads out into a broad cove, with romantic banks beneath you, and seems to be the principal tributary to the Thames, while the Shetucket, a much longer river, of considerable magnitude and power, comes almost unnoticed into its bosom, stealing through a narrow channel, round a projecting cliff.

It is not strange, that a place possessed of such advantages by nature, when once known to the English, should have been highly prized by them; or that when obtained from the natives, it should be speedily settled; or that since its settlement, it should have grown and prospered more uniformly and extensively, than any other town in the eastern part of the state. Its increase has been gradual, but sure. It has never known any serious decline, either in numbers, or property, and though at times, laboring under disadvantages, in common with the rest of New England, it has generally been upon the advance. The spirit of enterprize has shifted from one part of the town to another, but has never wholly left its precincts. It has been greatly dismembered, for the original bounds of Norwich comprise at present nearly five towns, but the nucleus has not been injured by the division.

Norwich may be considered a beautiful type of the second class of New England towns, embodying a bright portion of the genuine old English character, and rich in traditionary lore. In some respects, it has always been a prominent place. The Mohegan tribe of Indians resided upon its immediate borders, and its early history is intimately connected with that noted race. Many remarkable individuals have, first and last, emanated from the community;—the inhabitants took a bold and determined attitude in the revolutionary war, and are famous for their early attention to manufactures, as well as for their present deep interest in them.   The scenery of the town is also remarkably picturesque : it is emphatically a place of hills and springs of water.   Copse, dingle and glen are scattered about in lavish abundance and wild variety.   These and other circumstances, have thrown a more than common degree of splendor upon the place, and rendered it more conspicuous than many others of greater numerical importance.

In its present dimensions, Norwich covers an area of twenty-six square miles, in which are six considerable sections, mainly distinct, though gradually melting into each other.   The greatest extent is from Trading Cove to Plain Hills, which measures about seven miles; its medium breadth is about three miles. Almost all its boundaries are rivers and brooks.   The Thames and Shetucket wash its eastern border, and the little stream called Yantic, divides it into nearly equal parts from the N. W. to the S. E.

By the old stage route it is one hundred and twenty-eight miles E. of New York, and eighty S. W. of Boston.   By steamboat to Greenport and thence by the Long Island railroad, New York is now reached in seven hours and a half, and by the Norwich and Worcester railroad, Boston in four hours and a quarter.

Lat. 41° 34′ N. Long. 72° 29′ W.

# CHAPTER II.

THE earliest notice that we gain of the tract of land now called Norwich, either from history or tradition, is from some incidents of Indian border warfare that took place in the year 1643. It was at that period, in the possession of the Mohegan tribe of Indians, and had originally been included in the extensive domain claimed by the Pequots. The Mohegans and Narragansetts had long been engaged in a rancorous and predatory war with each other. The early history of Connecticut is perplexed with accounts of their petty quarrels. Among the rocks and ravines of Norwich, the scouting parties of the Narragansetts often laid their snares, or found shelter when pursued; and here also was the lookout port of the Mohegans when expecting an attack from their foe. All the accounts of this contest are written with an evident bias to the side of the Mohegans, whom the English were bound by treaty to defend from aggression. Nevertheless, they made many attempts to reconcile the two tribes, and endeavored to act the part of an impartial umpire. A compact was made at Hartford, in 1638, by which it was stipulated, that the hostile sachems should not make war on each other without an appeal to the English. A spirit of rivalry and of personal hatred seems, however, to have existed between Miantino-

2*

moh* and Uncas, which was easily inflamed into open war, and neither party, when roused to the conflict, waited for the sanction of the English.

The origin of this rupture is thus related by Gov. Winthrop :

" Onkus, being provoked by Sequasson, a Sachem of Connecticut, made war upon him, and slew divers of his men and burnt his wigwams; whereupon Miantun-nōmoh being his kinsman, took offence against Onkus, and went with near one thousand men and set upon Onkus before he could be provided for defence, for he had not then with him above three or four hundred men."

Other historians, and among them Trumbull, in his History of Connecticut, trace the dispute farther back, to an attempt which was made to assassinate Uncas by a Pequot, who was suspected to have been incited to this act by the Narragansett Sachem. Of this, however, no proof was ever adduced. Miantinōmoh indignantly denied the charge, and retorted upon Uncas that he had cut his own arm with a flint, and then accused the Pequot of wounding him. But whatever might be the incident which supplied the spark of ignition, the materials had long been gathering, and the flame broke forth in the summer of 1643. The following account, more minute than is usually given of this contest, is deduced from a careful comparison of the earliest histories, with the traditions of the Mohegans.

Miantinōmoh having secretly raised an armed force,

---

* This name is variously spelt and accented. The text gives, not the most popular, but probably the most correct form. Miantinōmoh, or Miantimomy, with the accent on the penultimate, is said to come nearest to the Indian pronunciation, and is sanctioned by the authority of Roger Williams.

amounting probably to six hundred warriors,* marched against the Mohegans. He expected to take them by surprise, the season being that in which they were usually busy in their cornfields, or engaged in fishing, and he might reasonably anticipate a brilliant victory. But Uncas was a wary chieftain ; his partizans were at that very time abroad, and he soon received information of the movements of his enemies. The tradition is that the Narragansetts were first discovered as they were crossing the Shetucket at a fording place, near the junction of the Quinnebaug. The Mohegans had a look-out post on Wawekus Hill, [in Norwich City,] which hill was long afterwards known as Fort Hill, and it is not unlikely that the spies who discovered the approach of the invaders, might have belonged to a scouting party stationed here. A path, afterwards widened to a road by the English settlers, led from this hill to the Little Plain, where was the burial ground of the Mohegan Sachems. A cleft or ravine from this spot, once the bed of a rivulet, came out directly by the Indian Landing Place at the foot of Yantic Falls, from whence a canoe could glide in a few minutes to Shantok Point, five miles below, where Uncas had a fort. In this way the intelligence may have been communicated to the Sachem with great rapidity.

Uncas assembled his warriors to the number of three or four hundred, and boldly advanced to meet the foe.

---

* Nine hundred or one thousand, says Trumbull, and the warriors of Uncas four or five hundred. This is doubtless an over estimate, as an enquiry into the resources of the two tribes will show. The Narragansetts perhaps numbered one thousand warriors in all; but it is absurd to suppose that every man of all their tribes was engaged in this expedition. The Mohegans at no time had much over four hundred warriors, and it is not probable that all could be collected on a sudden emergency.

When he reached what is called the Great Plain, three
or four miles from his principal settlement, and a mile
and a half south-west of the Yantic, he learned that the
Narragansetts had crossed the fords of the Yantic, [at
Noman's acre,] and were pouring down upon him.
He immediately halted, arranged his men on a rising
ground, and made them acquainted with a stratagem,
the effect of which he was about to prove.   He had
scarcely given his warriors instructions how to act, before the Narragansetts appeared on an opposite declivity.   Uncas sent forward a messenger, desiring a parley
with Miantinōmoh, which was granted, and the two
chiefs met on the plain, between their respective
armies.   Uncas then proposed that the fortune of the
day should be decided by themselves in single combat, and the lives of their warriors spared.   His proposition was thus expressed :  " Let us two fight it out:
if you kill me, my men shall be yours ;  but if I kill
you, your men shall be mine."

Miantinōmoh, who seems to have suspected some
crafty manœuvre, in this unusual proposition, replied
disdainfully, " My men came to fight, and they shall
fight."   Uncas immediately gave a pre-concerted signal to his followers, by falling flat upon his face to the
ground.   They, being all prepared with bent bows,
instantly discharged a shower of arrows upon the
enemy, and raising the battle yell, rushed forward
with their tomahawks, their chieftain starting up and
leading the onset.   The Narragansetts who were carelessly awaiting the result of the conference, and not
expecting that the Mohegans would venture to fight at
all with such inferior force, were taken by surprise ;
and after a short and confused attempt at resistance,
were put to flight.   The fugitives and their pursuers,
with despairing cries and triumphant shouts, crossed

the river at the shallows, and swept like a whirlwind over the hills, regardless of tangled forests, rushing torrents, and precipitous ledges of rock, directing their course to the well known fords of the Shetucket.

Two of the Mohegan captains, who were very swift of foot, singled out Miantinōmoh, and pursued him with relentless pertinacity. He had nearly reached the river when they overtook him, he being encumbered and retarded, it is said, by a coat, or corslet of mail. Throwing themselves against him they impeded his motion, and when the chief recovered himself repeated the act, continuing thus to obstruct his flight, but not attempting to seize him, that Uncas might come up and have the honor of his capture. The moment that Uncas touched his shoulder, Miantinōmoh stopped, and without the least resistance, sat down, calm and silent. Uncas immediately gave the Indian whoop of victory, which collected all his men around him, and the strife ceased : the whole conflict and pursuit having occupied, according to tradition, not more than twenty minutes. About thirty Narragansetts were slain. Among the prisoners, besides the great Captain himself, were his brother, and two of the sons of Canonicus, his uncle.

Some of the early historians say, that the two captains who assisted in the capture of Miantinōmoh, were his own men, who by this treachery hoped to make their peace with Uncas, whose subjects they had formerly been. From Gov. Winthrop's account it is not clear whether it was the chief himself, or his brother, whose flight was thus treacherously obstructed. Savage, in his notes to Winthrop, understands it to be the former : Trumbull, in the History of Connecticut, the latter. In a letter written by Thomas Peters, of Pequot Harbor, now New London, in 1645, just after a visit made to Uncas at Mohegan, he speaks of "Tantaquieson, a Mohegan Captain, who first fingered Miantinōmoh."* This agrees with Mohegan tradition : the family of Tantaquieson, or Tantaquidjin, is a noble one among them, and the descendants to this day have scarcely ceased to boast of the above-mentioned exploit of one of their ancestors.

After the battle, Uncas returned in triumph to his fortress, carrying his illustrious captive with him, whom he treated with generous kindness and respect. But he soon conducted him to Hartford, and surrendered him to the custody of the English. He probably feared some desperate attempt on the part of the Narragansetts to recapture their prince; and he was moreover incited to this course by an urgent message from Mr. Gorton, of Rhode Island, who supposed the life of Miantinōmoh would be safe if he could but get him into the hands of the English. Roger Williams, the warm and constant friend of the Sachem, was then in England, and there seems to have been no other person of any influence in the country to take his part. He was imprisoned at Hartford, and Uncas consented to be governed in his future conduct towards his captive, entirely by the advice of the English. The whole affair was laid before the Commissioners of the United Colonies, at their meeting at Boston in September, and the question was there debated whether it was just and lawful to put Miantinōmoh to death. The execution of a Pequot who had given his testimony against him; his repeated attempts upon the life of Uncas by assassination, poison and sorcery; his turbulence in making war against the Mohegans without a previous appeal to the English; and his inveterate hostility to the

---

* See Appendix to Savage's Winthrop.

whites, to exterminate whom he was accused of endeavoring to bring about a confederacy of several tribes,
and of hiring the Mohawks to assist in the deadly
work, were the arguments urged against him. Nevertheless, the court still hesitated whether it would be
just to put him to death, and in this dilemma referred
the matter to ecclesiastical counsellors. Five of the
principal ministers in the colonies were consulted, and
these, considering it hazardous to the peace of the
country that the Sachem should be released, gave their
voice in favor of his execution. This decided the
question in the affirmative. It was determined, however, that the deed should be committed by Uncas, in
his own jurisdiction, and without torture.

The Mohegan Sachem was soon ordered to repair to
Hartford, with a trusty band of followers, and there the
decision of the Commissioners was made known to him,
and Miantinōmoh delivered into his hands. A band
of twelve or fourteen soldiers was also sent with him
from Hartford, to protect him from any sudden burst of
revenge on the part of the Narragansetts, and to show
that the deed was sanctioned by the English. These
were to remain a while in the Mohegan country. Two
Englishmen were also directed to remain with the
prisoner, and to see that the sentence was executed in
conformity to the decision. Uncas, having received
the captive king, promptly obeyed the directions given.
He conducted him to the very spot where he had been
taken prisoner. At the instant they arrived on the
ground, the brother of Uncas, who marched behind
Miantinōmoh, at a signal from his chief, struck him on
the head with a hatchet and killed him at a single
stroke. Uncas cut a piece of flesh from his shoulder
and ate it, saying, it was the sweetest meat he ever

ate,—it made his heart strong. *Revenge* was doubtless the *sweetness* that he tasted.

The above account coincides mainly with that of Trumbull, who derived his information from Richard Hide, Esq., of Norwich, a gentleman who through his whole life was in the habit of frequent intercourse with the Mohegans, and whose house was one of the favorite resorts of wanderers from that tribe. He related the story as it was current among them, and there is no reason to doubt the correctness of even the cannibal part of the statement. Many of the Indian tribes had a custom of tasting the flesh or blood of a slaughtered foe, believing that thereby the strength and valor of the deceased was infused into their own souls.

The unfortunate sachem was buried on the spot of his capture and execution, on the western bank of the Shetucket, a little north of where the village of Greeneville now stands. The place, from these events, took the name of Sachem's Plain, which it still bears. A heap of stones was raised over the grave, and additions made to it from time to time, by all true-hearted Narragansetts, who passed that way. For several years afterwards, a party of that nation came to the spot every September, and renewed their lamentations over the heap, casting a few more stones upon it, and consecrating them with doleful cries and frantic gestures. A citizen of Norwich still living, N. L. Shipman, Esq., remembers this tumulus in his youth, a conspicuous object, standing large and high, between two solitary white oak trees, about sixteen rods east of the old Providence road, and nearly in a line with that part of the river where the great dam has since been built. At length the owner of the land, probably being ignorant of the design of these stones, removed them to use in the undersetting of a barn he was erecting in the neighborhood. In process of time the old oak trees also disappeared, and nothing was left to designate the spot where the fallen chieftain lay.

While making excavations for the water works, on the banks of the Shetucket, about the year 1830, an Indian grave was opened, containing a kettle, a spoon, and a box, all of copper, a glass bottle, and some other utensils, together with the bones of a person, apparently of enormous size. Some have supposed that these were the remains of the Narragansett Sachem, as tradition affirms that his stature was almost gigantic, but the best authorities agree in placing the tomb of that prince a least half a mile from this spot.

Before dismissing this subject it is proper to state that Gov. Winthrop, from whom we have the oldest written account of this affair, designates an entirely different spot as the place of Miantinōmoh's execution. He says, " Onkus, taking Miantunomoh along with him, in the way between Hartford and Windsor, where Onkus hath some men dwell, Onkus' brother, following after Miantunomoh, clave his head with an hatchet, some English being present." Mr. Savage also, in his notes upon Winthrop, alluding to the variance of his account with that of Trumbull, gives a decided preference to the former, and deems it much more probable that he was slain between Hartford and Windsor than in Norwich.\* There is in truth nothing opposed to Winthrop's account but tradition; but this testimony is so minute, circumstantial and uniform, that it amounts to almost conclusive evidence that Winthrop is wrong and Trumbull is right.

The sentence of Miantinōmoh is one of the most flagrant acts of injustice and ingratitude, that stands re-

---

\* The records of the Commissioners of the United Colonies also agree in designating this place.

corded against the English settlers. He had shown
many acts of kindness towards the whites; in all his
intercourse with them had evinced a noble and mag-
nanimous spirit; had been the uniform friend and assistant of the first settlers of Rhode Island, and only
seven years before his death had received into the
bosom of his country, Mason and his little band of soldiers from Hartford, and greatly assisted them in their
conquest of the Pequods.

The Narragansetts were determined to avenge the
death of their chief. They were particularly exasperated with Uncas, as he had entered into treaty with
them for the release of the sachem, and had already
received, as they averred, a large quantity of wampum
as a ransom for him. The Mohegans, on their part,
denied that any wampum or other goods had been
received by them, except small parcels which Miantinōmoh himself had bestowed, as gratuities, upon their
captains and counsellors, or given to " Uncas and his
squaw, for preserving his life so long and using him
courteously during his imprisonment."

A harrassing and inveterate system of hostility between the two tribes ensued. The Narragansetts
were double in number to the Mohegans, but the latter
were shielded by the protecting care of the English,
so that a balance was preserved between the two
nations, otherwise unequal. In September, 1644, a
treaty was made at Hartford with the Narragansetts, by
which the latter engaged to commit no hostile act
against Uncas, until after the next year's time for
planting corn, nor until after giving thirty day's notice
either to the Governor of Massachusetts or Connecticut.
This last stipulation was an idle one, to which the
Indians could not have consented from any other

motive than to keep the English quiet. They soon gave proof that they had no idea of being bound by it.

In the spring of 1645, whether before or after planting time does not appear, under the command of Pessacus, the brother of Miantinōmoh, they invaded the Mohegan country with a large force, committed great devastation, and finally drove Uncas to his strongest fort and besieged him there. According to tradition this fort was on Shantok Point, a rough projection by the side of the Thames, nearly opposite Pocquetannok. The English had assisted Uncas in fortifying this spot. There is still a fine spring of water by the bank. The position was easily defended, and the Narragansetts had no hope of taking it by assault. Many of the women and children had fled to the other side of the river, with a part of the canoes, but of the remainder the Narragansetts had taken possession, so as to cut off retreat on the water side, and thus enclosing them on this point of land, they hoped to subdue them by famine. How long the seige continued is not known; but one night a messenger despatched by Uncas, left the fort without being discovered by the besiegers, and creeping along the margin of the river very cautiously till without the range of the enemy's scouts, he crossed the country with Indian speed, and arrived the next day at Saybrook, the nearest English settlement, where he made known the desperate situation of the Mohegans. Or perhaps Trumbull's account may be more correct,—that he fell in with a scouting party from Saybrook fort, and communicated to them the message with which he was charged by Uncas.

Capt. Mason was at that time commander of Saybrook fort, and a warm friend to Uncas; there can be little doubt, therefore, that though he afforded him no relief in his official capacity, he favored and assisted the enterprize undertaken by others. Thomas Leffingwell has hitherto been considered the only prominent person in this exploit, but some subsequent proceedings which have recently been brought to light, lead to the supposition, although they do not incontestably prove the point, that Thomas Tracy and Thomas Miner had also some share in the adventure.

The version usually given of this undertaking, and which, as there is no record to contradict it, we may assume as substantially correct, is this : Thomas Leffingwell, a bold and spirited young man, (though not then an *ensign*, as stated by Trumbull,) left Saybrook in a canoe that would carry twenty cwt., laden with beef, corn, pease, &c., entered Pequot river in the night, and had the address to get the supplies into the fort of Uncas, without being discovered by the enemy. Tracy and Miner may have been engaged in the enterprize, and were perhaps in the boat with Leffingwell, for it would require more than one resolute heart and stalwart arm to carry the bark on its way with sufficient speed. It is probable that Leffingwell had often been on trading excursions to Mohegan, and was well acquainted with Pequot river, and the position of Shantok fort. We know in general that the people of Saybrook were in the habit of coming into the river to trade with the Indians, and that *Trading Cove*, which afterwards became the southern boundary of Norwich, was a name bestowed by them long anterior to the settlement.

A fanciful legend has in later times been connected with this adventure. It would be difficult now to ascertain what degree of truth belongs to it. It is said that the expected relief from Saybrook was delayed much longer than the hungry and impatient Mohegans had anticipated ; and that each night Uncas left the fort, and skulking by the water's edge, came to a rocky and precipitous ledge which juts out into the stream, and is now called Mosier's island in the neighborhood, from one Mosier since drowned in the deep water near it. It is not, however, an island except in a very high flood. Here, under shelter of the rock, the sachem remained till nearly day-light, with his sleepless eyes upon the river, and his ear intent to catch the lightest sound of a falling oar, and it was not till the second or third night of his watch that Leffingwell arrived. A cavity or recess in this ledge, well known to the fishermen and oyster gatherers on the river, has since obtained the name of *Uncas' Chair.*

No sooner was this timely supply of provisions safely lodged in the fortress, than loud shouts of exultation were uttered by the besieged, to the astonishment of the Narragansetts, who were unable to divine the cause of this midnight triumph. At the dawn of day, however, the secret was disclosed; the Mohegans elevated a large piece of beef on a pole, and thus gave notice of the relief they had obtained.* The Narragansetts dared not assail either the persons or property of the English, but we can readily believe that they beheld the boat lying by the shore with bitter feelings of exasperation, and poured out a torrent of threats and invectives against its officious owners. That they saw Leffingwell and knew it was he that brought the supplies, is evident from Leffingwell's own testimony, as will soon appear. Finding that there was no chance of reducing the Mohegans while they were

---

* Many of the minuter circumstances of this seige rest only on *tradition*, but it is tradition gathered many years since from the Mohegans themselves, and current from father to son among both them and their white neighbors.

3*

thus supported, the Narragansetts abandoned the seige and returned home.

It is probable that Leffingwell and his associates remained at Mohegan till after the departure of the invaders. Ascending Fort Hill and beholding the pleasant hills and vallies that stretched to the north of the Indian villages, untenanted and untilled, they may have conceived the design of a plantation in that quarter. Uncas in his present situation would willingly encourage such a project, as an English colony would serve as a barrier of defence to his settlements. It is not, therefore, unlikely that he did at this time make large promises of land to his benefactors, in requital for the aid they had rendered him, and give them an urgent invitation to settle in his neighborhood. Trumbull says, " For this service Uncas gave said Leffingwell a deed of great part if not the whole town of Norwich." There is, however, no such deed on record, and no allusion to any such deed in subsequent transactions; nor does it appear afterwards, upon the settlement of the town, that Leffingwell received or claimed any larger share than the other proprietors.

In a volume of miscellaneous papers recently filed and placed in books in the office of the Secretary of State, at Hartford, is an original petition of Leffingwell to the General Court, signed by his own hand, as follows :

" To the right worshipful Court assembled at Hartford. Whereas you are by God and his people, constituted a court of Justice, and have approved yourselves in matters of justice, that I know you will be so far from obstructing amongst your people or foreigners as you have occation, that its your delight to do things which are equal, I am encouraged to recommend to your considerations a case depending between Uncas, the Mohegan Sachem, and myself. Its not unknown to him and others what damage in my outward estate I have suffered by his men, and yet notwithstanding, when he and his people were famishing, being besieged by many enemies, I did afford him provition for their relief, although it was to the hazard of all my outward comforts, the enemy knowing what supply I had and did afford him ; upon these and such like reasons, Uncas hath several times offered me some land for my recompense and just satisfaction, and hath expressed the same to the Major, who is acquainted with the truth of these things, but order requireth me to propound the matter to your worshipful considerations, desiring your approbation of the way Uncas hath propounded for my satisfaction. Its far from me to desire land in such place where my possessing of it might hinder a plantation worke, or any such public good, but providence presenting such an equal means for the relief of my family, by inclining the heart of a heathen to observe rules of justice and meete gratitude for that which he hath received, and this coming on without any importunity on my part, I hope your worships will not judge me guilty of inordynate seeking after that which I ought not, but I would not be negligent in improving the present hint of Providence. so hoping you will not reject the proposition made, but show your worshipful approbation for the most real effecting of it, and l cease giving you any further trouble, I remain your humble servant,

THOMAS LEFFINGWELL."

Norwich, May the 6, 1667.

Thomas Tracy was at that time a member of the General Court, being the deputy from Norwich, and as appears from the result, preferred a petition at the same time, of similar import, although his petition has not been found on record. The Court considered them together, and gave liberty jointly to Thomas Leffingwell and Ensign Thomas Tracy, to receive a grant of land from Uncas, to be viewed and return made of it to the Court, for their further satisfaction. This return was made at the autumnal session of the Court, the same year, and the final action upon it recorded as follows :

"October 10, 1667. This Court grants unto Ensign Thomas Tracy and Thomas Leffingwell, the sum of 400 acres of land, to be equally divided between them. And this Court desires Thomas Leffingwell, Ensign Thomas Tracy, and Sargeant Thomas Miner, to agree together and lay out, each other, their proportion, according to their grants in that land of the east side of Shetucket river."

The deed of this grant is found upon the Court Records, and also in the first book of deeds of the town of Preston, within whose bounds it lay, no part of it being within the limits of Norwich. It consisted of 400 acres, in three several parcels, viz. 130 acres of upland, lying north-east of Norwich bounds ; 40 acres of meadow and mowable land, on both sides of Kewoutaquck river ; and 230 acres of upland, abutting to the S. E. on Stonington bounds.

It is matter of regret that Tracy's claim is not more distinctly stated. We may infer from the record that he was largely, if not equally with Leffingwell, concerned in the relief of Uncas when besieged by the Narragansetts; but yet we cannot positively say but that the grant may have been made for services rendered to the Sachem at some other time, and of a different nature.*

Whatever was the nature or extent of the gift, promise, or invitation, given by Uncas to Leffingwell and his companions, it was allowed to remain dormant for nearly fourteen years.† The reason is evident. During the whole of this term, the Narragansetts, Ne-

---

* Rev. F. P. Tracy, of Williamsburg, Mass. has prepared a paper relating to this point which will probably be soon given to the public. It embraces the Leffingwell documents, in the Secretary's office, at large. Mr. Tracy is also engaged in antiquarian researches upon another point connected in some degree with Norwich history. He is collecting materials for a genealogical memoir of the descendants of Lieut. Thomas Tracy.

† Some may think that too early a date has been given to the relief of Uncas by Leffingwell, and that the time when he was besieged by Pessacus, in 1657, is the more probable era of that event. The subject is not without difficulty. Historians have usually left it indefinite. If however this seige had taken place after the English had settled in any considerable number at New London, Uncas would have been

hanticks, Mohegans, and the remnant of the Pequods,
were engaged in implacable wars. The results indeed were trifling. It was a system of marauding,
skulking and assassination, rather than of legitimate
warfare, but such a state of things rendered it hazardous for the English to advance the frontier and attempt
new settlements in that quarter. The utmost vigil-
ance, prudence and bravery, were for several years
necessary to defend the points they had already
assumed.

Uncas had scarcely recovered from the effects of that
invasion, from which the timely assistance of Leffingwell relieved him, when his foes returned in still greater
force, and threatened his entire annihilation. Making
a show of forty men only, they drew him into an ambush, from which several hundred men rose, and discharging a shower of arrows and bullets, (for they had
in this inroad thirty guns with them,) they did considerable execution, and pursued the Mohegans to the
very walls of their forts.* Fortunately a few English
soldiers were in the neighborhood, who hastened to
his assistance, and at sight of them the Narragansetts
retreated. Uncas in this engagement lost four captains and several men, besides a considerable number
wounded. During the remainder of the season, Hartford and New Haven kept a constant force at Mohegan. At length through the efforts of the English, a
cessation from hostilities was agreed upon by the two
tribes, but no permanent reconciliation was effected.

About this time, and even while the war between
the Narragansetts and Mohegans was raging with the
utmost fury, the younger Winthrop ventured to commence a settlement at Pequot Harbor, now New Lon-

more likely to apply for aid to his near neighbor, and kind personal
friend Winthrop, than to send to such a distance as Saybrook for it.

* Letter of Peters referred to before.

don.  Mr. Winthrop's family, Mr. Thomas Peters, and
a few others, were upon the ground early in the spring
of 1645, and these every year increasing, were soon
organized into a permanent town.   In 1648, the settlement contained forty families.   This enterprise was
attended with comparatively little danger, as the
friendly Mohegans lay between them and the discon-
tented tribes.   It would have been quite another thing
to have stepped beyond the Mohegans, and settled
between them and the Narragansetts.   Mr. Winthrop
performed many friendly services for his Indian neighbors.   After the last mentioned battle with the Narragansetts, he visited Uncas at his fort, and in conjunction with Mr. Peters, assisted in dressing the wounds
of more than thirty of his warriors.

So late as the year 1657, we still find the Indians
engaged in implacable wars.   Pessacus of Narragansett, could not forget the murder of his brother, and
seems to have felt that he could not die in peace while
his great enemy lived.   He therefore collected all his
forces for another onslaught.   Uncas was once more
besieged in his fortress, and only preserved from destruction as before, by the appearance of a band of
English soldiers.   This timely assistance enabled the
Mohegans to turn upon their invaders, whom they pursued with such fury, that they were driven like frightened sheep, through the woods into thickets and
streams, and cut down without mercy.   So great was
the panic of the fugitives, that they seemed literally
bereft of their senses.   Long afterwards some old
Mohegans used to boast among their English neighbors, of having found in the chase a poor Narragansett, struggling and panting in the thicket that bordered the river, and so frantic as to suppose himself
in the water, and actually attempting to *swim* among
the bushes !

It is to this rout that the traditionary legend connected with the Falls of the Yantic probably belongs. One band of the fugitives being turned out of the direct line leading to the fords of the Yantic, were chased through woods, and over rocks and hills, by the relentless fury of their pursuers, and coming upon the river where the current was deep and rapid, many of them were driven into it headlong, and there slaughtered or drowned. Others in the rapidity of their career, having suddenly reached the high precipice that overhangs the cataract, plunged, either unawares, or with reckless impetuosity into the abyss beneath, and were dashed upon the rocks, their mangled bodies floating down into the calm basin below. According to tradition, two Englishmen from Saybrook chanced to be in the track of this expedition. They were exploring the banks of the Yantic to fix upon the site of their future township, and were digging ground-nuts to satisfy their hunger, upon the side hill, near where Mrs. Daniel Coit's house now stands, when they heard the shouts of the conquerors, as they drove the Narragansetts over the river, and saw the fugitives as they came rushing through the valley, and over Sentry and Long Hill towards the Shetucket.

Notwithstanding these constant alarms, the next year ten or twelve families settled at Stonington, on the Indian frontier, and apparently open to hostile incursions. Dangers of this kind had become so familiar that they had lost their terror. The providence of God seemed to be preparing the way for the peaceable settlement of the whites, by permitting the deadly passions of the Indians to take their full scope, and make them instruments of each other's destruction. The wilderness was thus thinned of its obstructions, and prepared to receive its new inhabitants.

# CHAPTER III.

### Preparations for a Settlement.

No accurate list of the early inhabitants of Saybrook, the mother town of Norwich, can now be obtained. A fort was built at that place, and a garrison established by the younger Winthrop, in the winter of 1635, which took the form of a regular settlement, on the arrival of Mr. Fenwick with his family, and other emigrants from England, in 1639. Accessions were afterwards made to the planters from various other towns in the colonies. Many of the emigrants from the old world were long in fixing upon a permanent resting place, and we can frequently track them about from town to town, through all the New England colonies. The records of Saybrook do not reach back beyond 1660, and it was formerly supposed that the previous records had been removed, by Mr. Fitch, to Norwich. No evidence of this, however, has been found in Norwich. In the books of this town, there is not a single item which looks back beyond the date of the plantation, 1660, except the purchase deed of the town, an allusion to an agreement made at Saybrook with John Elderkin relative to a town mill, and a few marriages and births, which had taken place previously, but were recorded in connection with others of the same family afterwards.

A company for the settlement of a plantation at Mohegan seems to have been formed at Saybrook, as early as 1653 or 4. The majority of the signers were inhabitants of that place, and probably members in full communion, of Mr. Fitch's church. Whether this was the case with Capt. John Mason, the most prominent person in the company, has been doubted, but upon what grounds other than that he was a man of impetuous passions and martial deeds, does not appear. Other names were from time to time, added to the company's list, from various places, until they amounted to thirty-five in number. Capt. Mason was more conversant with Indian affairs than any other Englishman in the country. He had been the friend and adviser of Uncas for twenty-four years, and had frequently visited him in his territory, to aid him by his counsel or his arms. He was, therefore, well acquainted with the adjacent country, and may have been the first to fix his eye upon the head of the Thames, as an advantageous position for a town. It is certain that all his influence was exerted to promote the projected settlement in that quarter.

In June, 1659, Uncas and his two sons, Owaneco and Attawanhood, (alias Joshua,) appeared at Saybrook and signed a deed of conveyance, which gave to the company a legal right and title to a tract of land at Mohegan, nine miles square. Seventy pounds was to be given in compensation for the land. Previous to this, in 1640, Connecticut had purchased of Uncas all his lands not actually used as planting grounds by the tribe, so that Norwich appears to have been twice, (and if a conveyance was ever made to Leffingwell, *three times*,) solemnly transferred from the aborigines to the whites, and an equivalent each time given.

> " On just and equal terms the land was gained ;
> No force of arms hath any right obtained."

4

The oldest remaining copy of the original deed of this tract bears the date of 1663, and this appears to have been a new instrument, formally acknowledged and signed that year, and recorded at Hartford and Norwich. That it is not a literal copy of the conveyance made at Saybrook, in 1659, is evident from the phrase, "Town and Inhabitants of Norwich." At that time, and for the first year or two after the settlement, the place had no other name than *Mohegan.**

DEED OF NORWICH,—[As recorded in the Town Book.]

Know all men that Onkos, Owaneco, Attawanhood, Sachems of Moheagen have bargained, sold, and passed over, and doe by these presents sell and pass over unto the Towne and inhabitants of Norwich nine miles square of land lying and being at Moheagen and the parts thereunto ajoyneing, with all ponds, rivers, woods, quarries, mines, with all royalties, privileges, and appurtenances thereunto belonging, to them the said inhabitants of Norwich, theire heirs and successors forever——the said lands are to be bounded as followeth (viz.) to the southward on the west side of the Great River, ye line is to begin at the brooke falling into the head of Trading Cove, and soe to run west norwest seven miles—— from thence the line to run nor north east nine miles, and on the East side the afores'd river to the southward the line is to joyne with New London bounds as it is now laid out and soe to run east two miles from the foresd river, and soe from thence the line is to run nor noreast nine miles and from thence to run nor norwest nine miles to meet with the western line.——In consideration whereof the sd Onkos, Owaneco and Attawanhood doe acknowledge to have received of the parties aforesd the full and juste sum of seventy pounds and doe promise and engage ourselves, heirs and successors, to warant the sd bargin and sale to the aforesd parties, their

---

* The original deed is not now extant. The author recollects to have heard Elisha Hyde, Esq., say that he had seen it: that it was brought from Hartford, and exhibited at the time when the great Mason controversy was tried in Norwich, and was afterwards in the possession of his uncle, Richard Hyde, Esq., who was retained on the Mohegan side in that case.

heirs and successors, and them to defend from all claimes and molestations from any whatsoever.—In witness whereof we have hereunto set to our hands this 6th of June, Anno 1659.

UNKOS 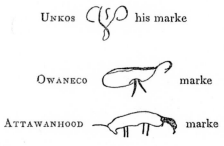 his marke

OWANECO     marke

ATTAWANHOOD     marke

Witness hereunto
JOHN MASON
THOMAS TRACY.

This deed is recorded in the Country Booke Agust 20th 1663 : as atests     JOHN ALLYN, Sec'y.

The bounds of this tract, as more particularly described in the first volume of the Proprietors' Records, were as follows :

The line commenced at the mouth of Trading Cove, where the brook falls into the cove ; thence W. N. W. seven miles to a Great Pond, [now in the corner of Bozrah and Colchester,] the limit in this direction being denoted by a black oak marked N that stood near the outlet of the " Great Brook that runs out of the pond to Norwich river ;" thence N. N. E. nine miles to a black oak standing on the south side of the river, [Shetucket,] " a little above Maw-mi-ag-waug"; thence S. S. E. nine miles, crossing the Shetucket and the Quinebaug, and passing through " a Seader Swamp called Catantaquck," to a white oak tree, marked N, thirteen rods beyond a brook called Quo-qui-qua-soug, the space from the Quinebaug to this tree being just one mile and fifty-eight rods; thence S. S. W. nine miles to a white oak marked N, where Norwich and New London bounds join; thence W. on the New London bounds two miles to Mohegan river, opposite the mouth of Trading Cove brook, where the first line began.

The southern boundary line, it will be observed, is nine miles in length, two east of the river, and seven west, without counting the breadth of the Thames, and the length of Trading Cove to the mouth of the brook, which would make this line nearly ten miles long. This seems to be little better than an imposition upon the Indians, who had granted in the deed only a tract nine miles square. Some uneasiness being produced by this, and an explanation demanded, the proprietors stated that the River and Cove were left out of the measurement, in compensation for a right reserved by the Indians, of using the waters for fishing and other conveniences.

Immediately after the conveyance of this tract to the English, Major Mason, who had that year been chosen Deputy Governor of the Colony, was commissioned by the General Court to purchase of Uncas and his brother Waweequaw, all the remainder of the Mohegan lands not actually occupied by the tribe. In this business he was successful; a deed of cession being obtained, signed at Mohegan, August, 1659, and undoubtedly made in behalf of the colony, though this fact was afterwards denied by Mason's descendants. This business kept Major Mason several weeks in the Mohegan country. The Saybrook proprietors, of whom he was one, were at the same time engaged in surveying their new township, laying out their homelots, and preparing for a removal the next year; and it was a great advantage to them, to have one at hand, to aid them by those personal services and judicious counsels, which the wisdom and experience of Mason rendered so valuable. This was the fourth town of which he had been one of the founders. The other three were Dorchester, Hartford and Saybrook.

It is not probable that the proprietors found a single white resident upon the tract. In some places the forests had been thinned of their undergrowth by fires, to afford scope for the Indians in their passionate love of the chase, and the beaver had done his part towards clearing the lowlands and banks of the rivers. A few wigwams were scattered here and there, the occasional abodes of wandering families of Indians at certain seasons of the year, who came hither for supplies of fish, fruit, or game ; and the summits of some of the hills were crowned with disorderly heaps of stones, showing where some rude defence had been constructed in the course of their wars. But in every other respect the land was in its natural wild state. It was a laborious task to cut down trees, to burn the underbrush, to mark out roads and pathways, to throw temporary bridges over the runs of water, and to collect materials for building. A highway was opened from the Yantic meadows to Mason's Swamp, at the head of the Little Plain, following the windings of the Yantic, on each side of which, the proprietary home lots were laid out, and sheds and wigwams erected for temporary shelter. A pathway was likewise cleared from the centre of the settlement, to the Indian landing place below the Falls of the Yantic, near the head of the Cove. This path coincided in part with the present Mill Lane, and was the most eligible route by which the effects of the planters could be conveyed. These arrangements were made in November, 1659. A few persons probably remained on the ground during the winter.

4*

# CHAPTER IV.

THE Town Plot* was laid out among the windings of a pleasant vale, bordered by the rapid circuitous Yantic, and overlooked by ridges of hills. The home-lots comprised a strip several acres in breadth, on each side of the Yantic, being mostly *river lands*, and consisting each of a certain portion of meadow and pasture. As these lots were afterwards registered, the names of the proprietors, and the order of their location, can be pretty nearly ascertained. Beginning at the N. W. extremity of the Town Plat, the order of settlement was as follows :—John Pease, John Tracy, John Baldwin, Jonathan Royce, Robert Allyn, Francis Griswold, Nehemiah Smith, and Thomas Howard :—John Calkins, Hugh Calkins, Ensign William Backus, Richard Egerton, Thomas Post, John Gadger ;—and on the opposite side of the town street, with no river land attached to their homelots, Samuel Hide and William Hide. Then again upon the river, Morgan Bowers, Robert Wade, John Birchard, John Post, Thomas Bingham, Thomas Waterman. Around the Plain were Major John Mason, Rev. Mr. Fitch, Mr. Simon Huntington and Stephen Giffords. From the Plain, the street made a detour to avoid a dense and

---

* In the Records, *Plot* or *Plat*, is used indifferently; sometimes it is spelt *Platt*.

miry thicket. In this section were Lieut. Thomas
Tracy, and nearly opposite to him, John Bradford :—
Christopher Huntington, Thomas Adgate, and John
Holmsted; where the street again approached the
river, Stephen Backus, Thomas Bliss, and John Ren-
alds. On the other side of the highway, more upon
the upland, were Sergeant Thomas Leffingwell and
Josiah Reed. Richard Wallis and Richard Hendys
were also among the first planters upon the ground.
Their homelots were near together, and not far from
the meeting-house plain ; but the location is not well
ascertained. This makes the number of settlers thirty-
eight, though it has been generally supposed that but
thirty-five signed the town purchase.

The impression made by the scenery upon the minds
of the planters, at their first arrival, must have been
on the whole of a hopeful though solemn character. The frowning ledges of rock, with which the
place so peculiarly abounds, and the immense preponderance of forest, chastened the landscape almost into
gloom. Many of the rocky heights were rendered im-
pervious with stunted cedar, spruce, hemlock, juniper,
savin, and the whole family of evergreen trees. The
uplands and declivities were covered with groves of
oak, walnut, chestnut and maple, and having been
partially cleared of underwood, were designated as
Indian hunting grounds. The lowlands were dense
with alder, willow, hazlenut, and other shrubs ; and
the plains, now so smooth and grassy, were rough
with bogs and stumps, mullein, thistle, and various
unsightly weeds. The inequalities of the ground
were much greater than at present. Running waters
now scantily trickling down the rocks, or murmuring
over a few small stones, were then rushing torrents,
and the little brooks that creep under the streets in

concealed channels, were broad streams, to be forded with care, or avoided by tedious circuits. Flowering plants and shrubs were comparatively abundant, and the settlers must have been regaled with a succession of scents and blossoms, from the arbutus, the shad flower, the dog-wood, the early honeysuckle, and the laurel, which at the time of their removal, were in bloom. Birds and animals of almost every species belonging to the climate, were numerous to an uncommon degree, and the hissing of snakes, as well as the howling of wolves and bears, must soon have become familiar to their ears. To complete the view, it may be added, that the streams swarmed with fish and wild fowl; in the brooks and meadows were found the beaver and the otter, and through the whole scene stalked at intervals the Indian and the deer.

On this spot, the hardy race of Puritans sat down with a determination to make the wilderness smile around them, to build up the institutions of religion and education, and to leave their children members of a secure and cultivated community. They were a fearless and resolute people, most of them being men of tried fortitude and experience, upright and devout, industrious and enterprising. Though assembled from many different places, they were bound together by a common faith, a common interest, and a common danger. They were an associated body, both in their civil and ecclesiastical capacity, and only a few weeks were necessary to give them the form and stability of a well-ordered society.

The Mohegans assisted them greatly in removing their goods and preparing their habitations. The number of the tribe at this period, cannot be precisely ascertained, but as this was about the time of its greatest prosperity, the whole number may be estimated at

2,000; the warriors at 400. For several months they kept a continual watch and guard around their white friends, and held themselves in readiness to defend them from all enemies. The Narragansetts were exceedingly irritated at the plantation, as forming an obstacle to their future inroads upon the Mohegan territories. For the same reason, it was peculiarly agreeable to Uncas, and he seems to have regarded the infant settlement with especial interest. He built wigwams on the highest hills, where he kept an advanced guard, and on the slightest alarm, would assemble his warriors on the exposed borders of the town, to protect it from danger. The situation of the place, presenting on the north and east, a naked frontier to the hostile tribes, was peculiarly hazardous. It is said, that during the first summer, a hostile band approached the settlement with a determination to break it up and expel the planters. It was a Sabbath morning, and their scouts creeping close to the town, saw the muskets of the citizens, stacked near the meeting-house, where they were assembled to worship, some of the houses fortified, cannon mounted, and Mohegan sentinels stationed on the hills; on carrying back this report to their comrades, they were intimidated, and relinquished their design.

The earliest act that has been found recorded in the town books bears the date of December 11, 1660, and is a renewal of a contract stated to have been made at Saybrook, in 1654, between John Elderkin on the one hand, and "the town of Moheagan" on the other, to erect a corn mill either on the land of John Pease, or at Noman's acre, to be completed before November 1, 1661, under penalty of forfeiting £20 in money. The toll allowed was one-sixteenth, and a tract of land was to be given in compensation for the mill.

The Indians extended the term Mohegan over the whole tract between the Yantic and Shetucket, now comprising Norwich and Lisbon. This whole territory was Mohegan, but for particular portions of it, they had individual names, each with an appropriate meaning. Thus their villages on the banks of the Thames were Shantok, Pumma-chog, and Massa-peag. This last name signifies *a place for fishing*. Some have derived the word Moheag' from a term signifying a *raspberry*, and have supposed that Norwich was originally and peculiarly, the *Moheagan*, i. e. *raspberry lands*, of the tribe, on account of the abundance of that fruit found here, and the custom of the Indians to come in bands at the proper season to obtain a supply. This explanation is derived entirely from tradition, and not from a knowledge of the meaning of the word in the Indian language. Certain it is, however, that the early settlers and their tawny neighbors used to exchange civilities in respect to their peculiar natural commodities. The English would make excursions to the Indian lands in strawberry time, while the Indians considered it their privilege to come at the proper season, with large sacks and baskets to gather raspberries and whortleberries, in the rocky glens and pastures of this their alienated territory.

The name *Norwich* was given to the place about 1662. In some old deeds recorded in New London, it is called New-Norwich. Although the name was bestowed in honor of Norwich in England, from which place it is supposed a considerable number of the settlers emigrated, this fact has not been positively ascertained, with respect to any of them but the family of Huntingtons. The original meaning of the word renders its application in this case peculiarly appropriate. In the old Saxon language it signifies North-Castle, and the formidable piles of rocks found here, might easily suggest the idea of towers and battlements.

The homelots consisted in general of five or six acres each. One of the largest portions was that of Mr. Fitch, which consisted of eleven and a half acres. His house was on the plain, fronting the N. W. He brought with him two sons, from Saybrook, of the respective ages of eleven and five years. On arriving at manhood they built houses near their father's, and soon became conspicuous men and able leaders in public affairs. The meeting-house stood upon the area of the plain, and was probably erected previous to the removal of the planters ; as otherwise we might expect some notice of its erection to have been found upon record among the town acts.

Major Mason's home lot consisted of eight acres ; his house stood near the river, not far from the place where it is now spanned by the Court-house bridge. Mr. Simon Huntington built on the corner where stands the house of the late Mr. Joseph Huntington. Thomas Tracy had a nine acre lot, east of Simon Huntington. The road around the square at that time, ran over the brow of the hill, in the rear of the Coit and Lathrop houses, and where it came out and turned south, Lieut. Leffingwell's house was situated. It stood high upon the rock, nearly opposite the present residence of John Hyde, Esq. The houses of Thomas Bliss and John Reynolds were upon the very sites where their descendants still live.

Each homestead had a tract of pasture land included in it, or laid out as near to it as was convenient. Where the street approached the river, the planters had their pasture lots, in the same line with the house lots on the opposite side of the stream.

Several farms were laid out during the first year, in

the vicinity of the town plot, and every succeeding year added to their number. New inhabitants were provided with homelots in unappropriated lands, and at intervals, public divisions were made of certain portions of the tract, among all the accepted inhabitants or freeholders. In April, 1661, the first division land was laid out, (this included the Little Plain;) in 1663, the second division land, which lay towards Lebanon, and in 1668, the third, upon Quinebaug river. After a few years, almost every citizen owned land in eight or ten different parcels. For the first eighty or one hundred years, very few of the homesteads seem to have been alienated. They passed from one occupant to another, by quiet inheritance, and in many cases were split into two or three portions, among the sons, who settled down by the side of their fathers. In many instances, they have remained in the same family and name to the present day. The first alienation of a home lot, on record, is that of Robert Wade, who soon after the settlement, transferred his right to Caleb Abell, having first obtained the consent of the town.

The first child was born in August, 1660, viz.: Elizabeth, daughter of Samuel Hide and Jane Lee, who had been married the preceding year at Saybrook. The house in which this child was born stood on a declivity, sloping to the town street, in the rear of the spot where the house stands which was the residence of Elisha Hyde, Esq., deceased. At that time there was an open space a few rods square in front, since occupied by a house and garden. Here were the home lots of the two Hides, and here their immediate descendants, fathers and sons, lived. Capt. William Hide, the son of Samuel, built around this space three houses for his three oldest sons, reserving the homestead for his fourth son.

The second birth was also a female, Anne, daughter of Thomas Bliss, born in September.

The first born male child was Christopher, son of Christopher and Ruth Huntington, Nov. 1. There is no record of any other births during the year 1660. In 1661 five births are recorded, viz. :

Elizabeth, daugter of Jonathan Royce and Deborah Calkins, . . . . . . January.

John, Son of William Backus, . February.

Sarah, daughter of John Burchard, . May.

John, son of John Calkins, . . . July.

Abigail, daughter of Thomas Adgate, August.

Christopher Huntington, the first born male, lived to a good old age. The broad and venerable head-stone to his grave states that he exercised for forty years the office of deacon in the church. One of his grand-children, who held the same office for almost as long a period, Deacon Caleb Huntington, died in 1842, aged ninety-three.

This brings the whole duration of Norwich into the compass of three generations. It diminishes the time since the settlement to a narrow compass, and seems to place our ancestors distinctly before us.

The earliest death on record is that of Sarah, wife of Thomas Post, who died in March, 1661, and was buried in a corner of her husband's home lot, " adjoining Goodman Gadger's lot." From these two lots an area of about ten rods square, enclosing the grave of Sarah Post, was afterwards laid out by the town as a place of public interment.

The first marriage has not been ascertained. It is doubtful whether there was a wedding in Norwich till Thomas Post married again, in 1663.

Most of the proprietors were men of mature years, and several of them had large families. Others among

5

them had long been wanderers and pilgrims seeking
a home ; having emigrated from the old country in
youth, and since that period passing from place to
place, till they collected at Saybrook and joined the
company that was forming for a new township.   In
anticipation of the settlement several marriages had
taken place at Saybrook within two or three years
previous ; but still it is inferred that six or eight of the
proprietors were bachelors, as their marriages are subsequently recorded without reference to any former
connection.   The Rev. Mr. Fitch was a widower.

The affairs both of the town and society, civil and
ecclesiastical, were all recorded together, until the
year 1720.   The volumes are labeled, Town Books of
Acts, Votes, Grants, &c.   They contain also an account
of the freemen, strays, cattle-marks, lost goods, and
occasionally a record of a justice's court.   Afterwards
the town and society affairs were separated, and the
latter kept by themselves in a volume entitled " The
Town-Plot Society Records."   In the first books,
dates are confounded and subjects intermixed with a
strange degree of negligence.   Some of the records
seem to have been made promiscuously, with the book
upside down, or upright, as it happened ; and forward
or backward, wherever there was a blank space.   The
earliest notices relate to the granting of lands, appoint-
ing fence-viewers, erecting public pounds, gates and
fences, *stating* highways, felling trees, and regulating
the running at large of swine, rams, and other domestic
animals.   These were the first subjects of legislation,
and the first officers were Townsmen, sometimes called
Overseers, and afterwards Selectmen.   They were at
first only two in number, and the first whose names have
been found mentioned, were Hugh Calkins for the west
end of the town, and Christopher Huntington for the

east. They were empowered to call public meetings, to take cognizance of all offences against law, order, and morality ; to settle differences, and try cases of small value. Some of the earliest entries are the following.

Jan. 6, 1661. " Chosen by the town, Thomas Tracy, Thomas Leffingwell and Francis Griswold, with the Townsmen, to end all disputes value of forty shillings, and their power to adjudicate is according to the power the Court usually grants in cases of that nature, Voted."

Aug. 2S, 1661. " It is ordered by the town, that the survaiers have power to call men out to work in the high waies, and if any refuse to go at their call to hire another in his room, and pay him 3s. 6d. y$^e$ day. And the survaiers have also power to destrain the goods of such as refuse to worke, for the payment of those that workes in their room, Voted."

The regulation of swine was a subject brought up at almost every public meeting for a number of years. Innumerable were the perplexities, the votes and the reconsiderations respecting them. Sometimes they were ordered to be *rung* and *yoked*, at others not : sometimes strictly confined, and then again suffered to go at large. There is no municipal act of those early days introduced with such prosy solemnity as the report of a committee on this subject, accepted and confirmed by the town, the substance of which was, that " in the time of acorns, we judge it may be profitable to suffer swine two months or thereabouts to go in the woods without rings."

Yokes for swine were to be two feet in length, and six inches above the neck.

The following entry is from the Records of the Gen. Court, at Hartford, May 10, 1679.

" Whereas, Uncas his son hath damnified Thomas Tracy, Jun., in his swine, and Uncas is willing to make him satisfaction for the same in land, this Court grants him liberty to receive of Uncas to the value of 100 acres of land for the said damage, if he see cause to grant it him, provided it be not prejudicial to any plantation or former grant made by the Court. Lt. Thomas Tracy and Lt. Thomas Leffingwell are appointed to lay out this grant to the said Thomas Tracy, Jun., according to this grant."

The recording of cattle marks was a work of no small labor, and one which the increasing herds made every year, more and more arduous. The pasture lands being mostly held in common, and private fences often rude and insecure, and therefore strays frequent, it was absolutely necessary, that each man's cattle should bear a peculiar mark, and that this mark should be made matter of public record. These marks were made on the ear, and were of this kind—a cross, a half-cross, a hollow cross, a slit perpendicular, horizontal or diagonal, one, two, or three notches, a penny, two pennies, or a half-penny, a crop or a half-crop, a swallow-tail, a three-cornered hole, &c.

All public affairs were transacted town-wise; and of course some mistakes were made in their legislation, which experience or mature deliberation corrected. Occasionally, under a town vote, which had been recorded, an endorsement, to this purport, is found: "Ondon next meeting."

The grist-mill—after many attempts to erect one in the Town Plot, upon waters which either failed in summer, or ran off furiously with all incumbrances at the spring freshets, was finally established upon the Cove below the Falls. Forty acres on the south side of the Little Plain side hills, upon the cove, were given to the mill, " to lye to it with the Landing Place, for the use of the town," and to be improved by John Elderkin, the miller. A tract of land along " the Mill River," above and below the Falls, was granted to

Elderkin, and in 1680, the town also voted to him
" the island that lyeth before his house at the Mill
Falls."

Elderkin's grant covered the Indian burying-place,
which had been guarantied to Uncas by the town.
In the first division of the common lands, April, 1661,
" *the Indian Graves*" was included in the grant to
Thomas Tracy; upon which the town, by way of ex-
·change, gave him eight acres of pasture land in another place. And though the same spot was afterwards
granted to Elderkin, it was stipulated that the Indians
should always be allowed to pass and repass up the
cove and ravine to their burying-place, and to cut
wood, if they chose, half-way up the side hill. These
privileges were reiterated in succeeding acts of the
town, and the land is still held with this reservation of
the Indian right.

Though Norwich was a place of frequent resort with
the Indians, and anterior to the English settlement,
their hunting field and battle ground, very few memorials of the red race have been found within its precincts. That race indeed seem to have lived and died
from generation to generation, without ever passing
out of themselves, and stamping an evidence of their
existence, either upon the material forms around them,
or the annals of time. They pass over the earth like
the wind, or melt away like a dream, and leave no
vestige behind, or if any, it is but the names that they
bestowed on the hills and streams. These still linger
among us, and always have a wild and melancholy
sound, recalling the dark history and sad fate of the
departed owners of the land.

The only aboriginal relic of any note left in the town,
is the Sachem's Burial Ground above mentioned. A
few skeletons, supposed to have belonged to Indians,

5*

have, at various times been disinterred in other places, but nothing of interest has been discovered.

There were three places within the bounds of Norwich, where, if any dependence is to be placed upon traditionary names, we may locate an Indian fortification : viz. upon Waweecos Hill, at the Landing, which was called by the first settlers, Fort Hill—on Little Fort Hill near the Great Plains—and on the south side of the Yantic, in the town plot, on a rugged and woody. height, south-east of the place where the Hammer Brook comes in. It is difficult to conceive for what purpose a fort could have been erected upon this barren and secluded spot; but a tradition has always been current among the inhabitants on the opposite side of the river, and particularly among the Hides and Posts, who first owned the spot, that here was an ancient Indian fortress. It consisted merely of a stone wall, enclosing an area upon the brow of a hill. The stones were removed about the year 1790, and used in the building of a cellar, and for other purposes, by the owner of the land.

# CHAPTER V.

### Houses. Books. Schools. Food

THE first houses were generally of one story; the better sort two stories in front, ending in a very low story in the rear. Two rooms in front, viz. a *great-room* and kitchen, with a bed-room and pantry in the rear, was the usual plan of the ground floor. It seems formerly to have been the fashion of our country to have the houses cover a large area, but they were seldom thoroughly finished, and the upper rooms of course were cold and comfortless. A snug, well-finished house, adapted to the family and circumstances of the owner, is an improvement of modern times. Our ancestors appear to have had no conception of such comfort.

Towns were not built in those days like a factory village at the present time,—all at once, and after one model. The houses were, in fact, unpainted, mis-shapen and patched, with crooked, heavy chimneys of stone, that occupied a large space in the centre of the building. Frequently on one, two, or three sides, they presented additions or leantos, that were made from time to time.

At intervals through the town, three or four houses were fortified; that is, a rude stone wall was built around them; port-holes were prepared to fire through, and they were perhaps furnished with a small field piece. One of these fortified houses was the old Gro-

ver-house, still standing, and supposed to be the oldest
building extant in the place.   In later times, during
Philip's war, the house at Huntington's corner was
fortified.   This was an important station, as was also
Leffingwell's corner, for the old Indian track from Narragansett to Mohegan, over Ox-hill, led down to these
points.   A block-house was also erected during Philip's war :—can any one tell where ?

The rooms were generally large, and agreeably to
the taste of the old colonists, well supplied with little
cup-boards, closets, and other receptacles of rubbish
and vermin.   The windows were small and few ; most
of them furnished with panes of diamond glass, cased
in lead.   As late as the year 1810, windows of this
kind were remaining in the old Post house.

Fire-places were enormously large ; from six to
eight feet wide, and two or three feet deep.   Wood
was cut four feet in length, and the rolling in of a log
was a ponderous operation, that made all the timbers
creak, and crushed the bed of burning coals upon the
hearth into cinders.   The reduction of chimneys and
fire-places is a great improvement of modern architecture, promoting at once, comfort, economy and sym-
metry.   In new countries, where wood is so abundant
that it is an object to destroy it, there may be a convenience in a large fire-place, where any quantity of it
may be stowed away and consumed.   But such a fire-
place requires more air to force the smoke up the
chimney than any common room can furnish, and of
course the room is filled with smoke unless a door is
kept open.   As it is usually inconvenient to keep an
outer door open, recourse must be had to the cellar
door, which in old houses usually opened into the
kitchen, and as fast as the air is drawn from the cellar,
just so fast the cellar is replenished with cold air from

abroad. Consequently our ancestors had their cellars filled with frost during the winter.

The kitchen was the principal sitting room of the family. Blocks for children's seats, were placed in the ample corners of the fire-place; a large settle kept off the air from the door; a tin candlestick with a long back, was suspended on a nail over the mantel, and the walls were adorned with crook-necks, flitches of bacon and venison, raccoon and fox skins, and immense lobster-claws. Afterwards, as fears of the Indians died away, and weapons of warfare were less used, occasionally a musket or an espontoon might be seen, suspended transverse from beam to beam, and bearing as trophies, strings of dried apples, chains of sausages, and bunches of red peppers. A small open recess for books was usually seen on one side of the fire-place, a little below the ceiling, where even the cleanest volumes, soon acquired a dingy hue. Venerated were these books, for they came from the fatherland, and were mostly of that blessed Puritan stamp whose truths had inspired the owners with courage to leave the scenes of their nativity, to find a home in this distant and savage land. This little recess, displaying its few books, often appears in the back ground of ancient portraits; for example, in that of Col. Dyer, of Windham, formerly among the pictures in the Wyllis mansion at Hartford.

In these houses the Family Bible was never wanting. It occupied a conspicuous station upon the desk or best table, and though much used was well preserved. It came from *home*, for so the colonists loved to call the mother country; it had voyaged with them over the billowy waters, and was revered as the gift of Heaven. One of these blessed volumes, long preserved as a precious relic in the Lathrop family, and now

deposited in the archives of the American Bible Society, merits a particular notice. It is in the old English
text, and of that edition usually called Parker's, or the
Bishop's Bible. It was brought from England by the
Rev. John Lathrop, who reading one night in his
berth, fell asleep over the book, when a spark escaped
from his lamp and falling upon the leaf, ate its way
slowly through a large number of pages, committing
sad havoc in the sacred text. He afterwards with great
neatness and patience, repaired the ravage.

Some few of the proprietors were men of education,
but the greater part had but little of what is called
school learning. Some of the most active and judicious among them, could not write their names. Eight
of the first thirty-five, it is ascertained by actual inspection of deeds and conveyances, affixed their marks
for signatures instead of hand-writing; yet among
them were men who acted as townsmen, deacons,
constables, and arbitrators. But they all alike sought
to obtain the advantages of education for their children.
The establishment of a school was the next object after
that of a church. John Birchard is the first school-
master mentioned; he was engaged for nine months
of the year, to receive £26 in provision pay. Each
child who entered for the whole term, was to pay the
value of nine shillings; and others in proportion : the
town to make up the deficit. In 1678, it was voted
that "Mr. Daniel Mason should be improved as a
school-master for nine months;" terms as before, except that nothing was said about *provision pay*.

In 1680, a special meeting was called for the settlement of a town school, and the whole matter delivered
into the hands of the select men, with a solemn charge
that they should see, " 1st. that parents send their
children ; 2d. that they pay their proportion, accord-

ing to what is judged just; 3d. that they take care
parents be not oppressed, espeshally such who are disabled; 4th. that whatever is additionally necessary
for the perfecting the maintenance of a school-master,
is a charge and expense belonging to all the inhabitants of the town, and to be gathered as any other rates;
5th. whatever else is necessary to a prudent carrying
through this occation, is committed to the discreshon
of y᷎ sd select men.''

There is no account that the planters ever experienced any scarcity of food, or were deprived at any time
of the real comforts of life. Though their modes of
cooking were more simple than those now in vogue,
the variety of sustenance was nearly as great. To
obviate the necessity of going often to mill, pounded
maize, called by the Indians *samp*, was much used.
Another dish which the Indians taught them to make,
was *succatash*, a mixture of tender Indian corn and
new beans, forming a delicious compound, still a great
favorite all over New England. They also learned of
the natives to bake corn-cakes on the hot hearth, under the ashes, forming a sweet and wholesome ban-
nock ; and to pound their parched corn and eat it with
milk or molasses. This was called in their language,
*Yo-kè-ug*. The first planters were also famous for
baked beans and boiled Indian puddings; dishes
which have been kept up by their descendants with
such constancy and spirit as to become characteristic
of the place. The beans were put into the oven early
in the morning, crowned with a choice portion from
the pork barrel, and having been kept all day seeth-
ing and browning, appeared upon the supper table, hot
and juicy, and with their respectable accompaniment,
the slashed and crispy pork, gave dignity to the best
tables. This was the universal Saturday night treat;

so that wits would say the inhabitants knew when Sunday was coming only by the previous dish of baked beans; and that if the usual baking should at any time be omitted, the ovens would fall in. Bean-porridge was also, in those early days, a frequent breakfastdish. The name of Bean-hill was bestowed on that part of the town plot now called West-ville, from the preponderance of these customs. With respect to the *puddings*, it is reported that they were frequently made of such size and solidity as to carry ruin in their path if the pyramid chanced to fall. An extra-good housewife would put her pudding in the bag at night, and keep it boiling until dinner-time the next day. The carving commenced at the top, and as the pile lowered to the centre the color deepened to a delicious red. One cannot help being curious to know whether these local customs could be traced back to those parts of England from which the planters came.

In addition to the flesh afforded by the flocks and herds which they fed, the bounty of Providence furnished them with rich supplies. Deer at the time of the settlement were not infrequent; wild fowl, especially pigeons, were at the proper season very abundant; all the smaller game, such as squirrels, foxes, wood-chucks, and rabbits might be caught in snares at the very doors of the houses, and the rivers and brooks around them, furnished first rate bass, innumerable shad, fine lobsters, delicate oysters, and highly-prized trout. Such were the dainties spread upon their board.

# CHAPTER VI.

Grants of Land. Highways. Fences. Boundaries. Selectmen. Innkeepers.
Town Clerk.

LAND at this early period was given away with a
lavish hand.  Grants were often made in this indefinite
manner,—" where he can  find it"—" over the river"
—" at any place free from engagement to another"—
" at some  convenient place in the common lands"—
" a tract not included in former grants"—" what land
may be suitable for him"—" as much as he needs in
any undivided land," &c.   A man obtains a lot, " for
the conveniency of joining his lands together,"—another five or six acres " in order to straiten his line"—
and frequently in lieu of *a lap*, of somebody else, on
his land.  These *laps*, owing to imperfect surveys,
were very numerous.  Every new inhabitant, publicly
accepted as such, obtained a grant of land, comprising
a building lot, pasture ground and wood land, sufficient
for a family; frequently in three parcels.  No one was
permitted to settle in the town  without the consent of
the majority.

Grants were uniformly made by a town vote.  Examples.

1669.  " Granted to one of Goodman Tracie's sonnes 100
akers of land in y<sup>e</sup> division of y<sup>e</sup> out lands.
" Granted to Sergent Waterman liberty to lay down
twenty acres of upland over Showtucket river, and take it
up again on the same side of the river, against Potapaug
hills, adjoining to some other lands he is to take up, and the

6

town leaves it to the measurers to judge respecting any
meadow that may fall within the compass of it, whether it
may be reasonable to allow it to him or not."

"Granted to Mr. Brewster and John Glover two bits of
land on the east side of Showtucket river, near their own land,
they two with the help of goodman Elderkin to agree peace-
ably about the division of it between them, and in case they
cant well agree about the division then it falls to the town
again."

"Granted to Ch$^r$. Huntington, Sen$^r$. an addition to his
land at Beaver Brook to the quantity of seven or eight acres
to bring his lot to the place where the great brook turns with
an elbow."

1684. "Granted to Capt. Fitch, a gusset of land from
the S. E. corner of the old meeting-house to the corner of
his father's homelot."

The earlier grants being thus indefinite in situation
and extent, and imperfectly recorded, after the lapse
of a few years great perplexities began to be experienced, and more were apprehended. Several votes were
passed by way of providing remedies. Additions were
inserted in the records here and there, or new surveys
recorded, so contradictory to the old, that the confusion was every day increased. In 1681, a resolution
passed, that if no other date could be ascertained for
the grant of any inhabitant, it was to take date from
that period, and the title remain good and firm. Committees were frequently appointed, to ascertain dates
and add them to the old book of records. In 1683,
one hundred acres of land,—"where he can find it,"
—is granted to Capt. Fitch, "for being helpful to the
town Recorder, in making a new record of lands."
This gentleman commenced a register of the proprietary lands, in a volume distinct from the town books.
It is endorsed thus, "Norwich Book of Records of the
River Lands. Capt. James Fitch writt this booke."
This register was afterwards partially copied and continued by Richard Bushnell and others, Clerks of the

Proprietors, until the year 1740, when the final division of the common lands was made, the accounts of the Proprietors closed, and their interests merged. in those of the town.

Every enterprize which had any tendency to promote the public convenience was patronized by a grant of land.  Hugh Amos, who first established a regular ferry over Shetucket river, received one hundred acres of land by way of encouragement.

1671.

John Elderkin was repeatedly remunerated in this way for keeping the town mill.  A blacksmith was induced to settle among them by a similar reward. A miller, a blacksmith and a ferryman were important personages for the infant settlement.  Saw mills met with the same liberal patronage.  In 1680, two hundred acres were granted to Capt. Fitch, on condition that he built a saw mill in a certain place : he to have the benefit of the stream and the timber near it, and no other person to set up a saw mill on the same stream to his damage.  This mill, however, was not erected and the privilege, according to contract, reverted to the town.  A person who proposed to establish a fulling mill was promised a large grant of various immunities if he succeeded.  The project, however, failed, and there was no fulling mill in the place till at a much later period the town had one erected at the public expense.  Competent workmen in this trade were then scarce in the country.  Before the year 1710 there was but one clothier in the whole colony of Connecticut.

The planters were often deceived in their first estimation of the quality of the land.  Some bog meadows in the interior of the township, the Podgeum and Wequanock lands, and other tracts of inferior quality, were eagerly taken up, from an idea that when drained,

they would make good mowing land.    Experience has
proved the fallacy of this opinion.    The more a man
does to them, the poorer he grows.    Among other
grants is one of the *island in Wequonuk river*, to
Thomas Leffingwell, 2d., for which he preferred his
petition, as though it was of some considerable value.
No such island is at present known.    Grants in the
Cranberry Pond and Swamp, were considered advantageous, but whether for the fruit or the land is now
doubtful.    In an agricultural point of view, some parts
of Norwich have disappointed the expectations at first
formed.    That part of it which is restricted within its
present limits, would have made, on the whole, but
indifferent farms; much of the sward being thin and
loose, the pasturage rocky, and of little value.

Most of the highways at first laid out, began at the
meeting-house plain, and branched out diverse ways
into the farms; but they were, at this period, little
better than cart paths.    In 1699, mention is made of
the *path* to New London, and the *path to Connecticut*.
The town street had been left from the first, four rods
wide in the narrowest part.    It was afterwards much
straitened and improved.    The present road from Huntington's corner to Strong's corner, is of comparatively
recent origin.    On this path at the time of the settlement, there was a bold and almost impassable ravine,
twenty feet deep, with a gurgling stream in its bed,
just beyond the dwelling house of the late Deacon
Caleb Huntington.    Another rivulet came down the
hill near the house of Dr. Daniel Lathrop, both passing
into the meadow below, which was then a dense alder
swamp.    It was to avoid this swamp and other obstructions, that the town street made a detour at this place.
A path was early laid out along the margin of the river,

and though fenced in, it was well understood to be a highway.   The following is the first notice of it.

Aug. 1661.—" Memorando : the footway six foote broad which goes through the homelot of Mr. Fitch, John Holmstead and Steven Backus was laid out by Towne order and agreement for the use of the towne."

Between the Little Plain and the Town Plot, there was a very thick swamp, known then, and for many years afterwards, as Capt. John Mason's Swamp.   A foot-path led through it.

The sheep walks were laid out at some distance from the Town Plot.   Two, of five hundred acres each, lay on the eastern and western borders.   One of them covered a part of Long Hill and Wequonuck plains, bordering on " the White Hills and Pople Swamp."   The other spread over " Wolf pit-Hill," in the western part of the town.   Chelsea formed another sheep-walk-pasrure of nine hundred acres ; and a fourth is described as lying " between the Great River and Great Plains, beginning at the brook below the clay banks, and so running down to Trading Cove."   In these *Walks*, the sheep of the town plot residents, as distinguished from farmers, were to be kept, and among the appointments made by the town, we sometimes find that of a shepherd to oversee the flocks.

Labor on the town lands was usually accomplished in the same way as highway work.   Laws were made which provided for the clearing of the commons by degrees.   A certain quantity was every year laid down to grass, the hay-seed being procured at the town charge.   Every citizen, excepting those who lived on remote farms, between the ages of fourteen and seventy, were required to cut bushes two days in the

6*

year, alternately, on the hills and in the town.   This
was done by a general turn out.

The winter was the period for making fences.   It
was repeatedly ordered that all front fences should be
*done up* by the first of March, and the general fences
by the first of April.   The front fences were to be " a
five rayle or equivalent to it, and the general fences a
three rayle or equivalent to it."   Afterwards a lawful
fence upon plain ground was thus defined.—" A good
three rail fence, four feet high ;  or a good hedge, or
pole fence, well staked, four and a half feet high."
Two pounds were erected in 1669, one at each end of
the town, which appear to have had plenty of occupants ;  for cattle, swine, sheep and goats, often roamed
at large, and trespasses were frequent.

All the effective males turned out at certain seasons
of the year, to labor on the highways, or to build and
repair bridges.   Two horse-bridges were very early
erected over the Yantic, at each end of the town plot ;
and before many years, six bridges over the same river
were maintained by the town, being all within her
limits.   Wood's bridge, at Portipaug, was the most
northerly of these ;  the bridge at Noman's acre the
most southern and last built.

The inhabitants being principally employed in agricultural pursuits, their trading must have been chiefly
in the way of barter.   Clothing and provisions formed
the circulating currency.   Loaded boats, however, frequently passed up and down the river, and the beginning of commerce was soon beheld at the old Landing
Place.

In 1682 we find the following entry :—

" It is voted y$^t$ there shal be a book procured at town
charge for the recording of lands, and allso a boat cumpas

and y$^t$ there shall be allowed to any of the inhabitants of this towne to make a new survey of their land provided they take their neibors with y$^m$ whose land lyeth adjoining to them."

To the confusion produced by contradictory deeds, grants without date, and careless surveys, was added that of undefined town limits. This led to ceaseless and long continued disputes with the Indians, and afterwards with the neighboring towns. The Selectmen were obliged to perambulate the bounds, in company with a Committee from the adjoining towns, every year, and to see that the boundaries and meres were kept up. The preservation of boundaries however, both public and private, was extremely difficult, where the only marks were a white oak tree, or a black oak with a crotch,—a tree with a heap of stones around it,—a twin tree,—a very large tree,—a great rock,—a stone set up,—a clump of chesnuts,—a walnut with a limb lopped off,—a birch with some gashes in it, &c. If a man set up a stone in the corner of his grant, with his initials marked on it, he was much more precise than his neighbors. A strip of land, about three miles in breadth, lying between the northern boundary of New London, and the southern of Norwich, gave rise to much litigation and controversy, not only among individuals, but between the two towns, and the whites and Indians. Three parties claimed it, and each was officious in selling and conveying it to individuals, so that a collision of claims and interests was inevitable. It was long before this affair was satisfactorily settled. Many committees were appointed; and the town hoped to arrange the difficulty by referring it, as far as they were concerned, " to the worshipful Samuel Mason and the Rev. Mr. Fitch." This tract is now included in Montville.

It has already been observed that no inhabitant was permitted to exchange or sell his homelot, without the consent of the town. Thomas Rood and some others violated this regulation, and the sales were declared null and void. Great care was taken to admit no inhabitants that were not industrious and of good moral character. Transient persons, and those who had no particular way of getting a livelihood, were quickly warned out of town. The overseers made a presentment of every such person, and the sentence of expulsion was forthwith recorded against them. The following is a specimen of the solicitous guardianship of the freemen over their beloved town :—

"1692.—Whereas Richard Elsingham and Ephraim Philips have petitioned this town that they may live here one year, the town do agree that they may dwell here the year ensuing, provided that they then provide for themselves elsewhere."

The townsmen were uniformly selected from among the oldest and most influential inhabitants; but many of the inferior officers circulated pretty generally among the citizens. The townsmen were at first two, but they soon increased to eight in number.

Innkeepers were considered as town officers. Deacon Simon Huntington is the first person on record, as keeper of " the house of entertaynement."

" Dec. 11. 1679. Agreed and voted by y$^e$ town y$^t$ Sergent Thomas Waterman is desired to keepe the ordynary. And for his encouragement he is granted four ackers of paster land where he can convenyently find it ny about the valley going from his house into the woods."

Under date of 1694, is the following, verbatim et literatim :

" The towne maks choise of calib abell to keepe ordinari or a house of entertaynement for this yeare or till another be choosen."

This was surely inserted by some occasional amanuensis, and not by one of the Huntingtons, the regular town clerks, who appear in general to have been correct and faithful scribes. Some very odd orthography occasionally occurs in the records, such as Cota, Coram and Potemporary, for Quota, Quorum and pro-tempore.

Some of the earlier records are in the hand-writing of John Birchard and Capt. James Fitch, but the first town-clerk and recorder, whose appointment is noted, is Christopher Huntington, chosen to office in 1678. After him, the office was held for a time by Richard Bushnell, and then by Christopher Huntington 2d, from whom it descended in regular succession first to his son Isaac, and from Isaac to Benjamin, and from Benjamin to Philip, and from Philip to Benjamin again, who held it in 1828, when the records were removed to Chelsea, and a clerk chosen from that society. Mr. Isaac Huntington held the office for nearly sixty years. At the annual meetings, the question was regularly put by the moderator—Will the town now proceed to the choice of a clerk? and uniformly decided in the negative; it being understood that the then incumbent was to be continued until a successor was appointed. This venerable man died in 1764.

1680. Mr. Arnold accepted as an inhabitant, and a grant of several acres of land bestowed on him gratuitously. This gentleman is elsewhere called "Mr. John Arnold, merchant." He is supposed to have been from Boston and to have opened the first stock of merchandize in town. In 1688, he purchased the homestead of Jonathan Jennings, consisting of a new dwelling-house, barn and eight acres of land. He then disappeared from the records, having removed, it is supposed, to New London. In 1698, the widow Sarah Knight was one of the principal shopkeepers.

# CHAPTER VII.

THE Mohegans were eager to exchange their services for the food, clothing and other comforts which
they received from the English. Many of them erected wigwams in the vicinity of the settlers, and some
even in their homelots. The plantation soon swarmed with them, and the whites found them rather
troublesome neighbors. Their habits of indolence,
lying and pilfering were inveterate. At first, a strong
hope of converting them to christianity, was very generally entertained, but the major part of the planters
soon relinquished the task in despair. It was now
found a work of no small difficulty to shake them off,
or to keep them in due subjection and order. Laws
were repeatedly made for their removal from the town,
but still they remained. Restrictions of various kinds
were thrown around them : a fine of 10s. was
imposed on every one who should be found
drunk in the place ; the person who should
furnish an Indian with ammunition of any
kind, was amerced 20s., but they were neither driven
away, nor their morals improved.

June 17,
1662.

1678.　Peremptory orders were at length issued to
remove every Indian found dwelling upon the Town
Plot.　Twelve days warning was given, and if
after that, any person should suffer them to remain
upon his homelot, or pasture near the town, he should
pay a fine of 20s.　Nevertheless, a certain number did

remain some years longer, and these, in succeeding town acts, are denominated *listed surrenderers*, a term perhaps denoting that they had claims upon the lands which they had formally surrendered to the planters, on certain conditions.

Those who were dislodged by the above order, knew not where to go. They had partially given up their roving habits, and it seemed harsh to turn them forth again into the wild woods. The Rev. Mr. Fitch, ever their kind friend in temporal as well as spiritual things, compassionating their forlorn condition, obtained permission for them to occupy Waweekus Hill, for a few years, rent free, " that they might have a comfortable living till such time as some other way may be made open for them." How long they continued there is not known. A division of lands upon the hill, 1696. was soon afterwards made among all the accepted inhabitants ; the first purchasers to have three acres to the hundred more than others.

A few families of resident Indians continued in the town until they slowly melted away. Several wigwams remained far into the next century. One of the last that decayed was on the hill not far from the spot where the *Marsh* house stands. It had probably been the residence of a sentinel.

In 1673, upon some hostile manifestations from the Dutch of New York, the militia or train-bands of Connecticut were ordered to be ready for service, and 500 dragoons raised, who were to be prepared to march on an hour's warning, to defend any place in the colony. Of these dragoons, New London county was to raise a company of one hundred : James Avery, [of New London,] Captain : Thomas Tracy, [of Norwich,] Lieut.: John Denison, [of Stonington,] Ensign. The number

of privates apportioned to Norwich, was seventeen.
Of these men no list has been obtained.

During Philip's war, Norwich was a frontier town,
and of course open to the depredations of the enemy:
yet there is no record of its ever having been invaded.
The inhabitants were frequently alarmed with rumors
that bands of hostile Indians were bending their course
towards them. A watch was stationed day and night
upon Sentry-hill, and men kept their arms by them at
their daily work.

Norwich was a convenient place of rendezvous for
troops who were collecting for expeditions against the
enemy. Major Treat at one time, and Major Talcott
twice, marched from this point with their bands of two
and three hundred soldiers, and their Indian allies,
amounting to nearly as many more. In the New London accounts, under date of 1676, are various charges
against the colony, for arms and provisions, sent to the
army at Norwich, or furnished to the Mohegan warriors, per order of Major Talcott, and Captains Mason,
Denison and Avery.

"The Mohegans," says an old writer, "were particularly friendly to Norwich when an infant settlement.
They were of great service in watching and spying, so
that it happened that there never were but two men
killed in said town by the Indian enemies, and one
boy carried away captive, who soon was returned, by
the help of a friendly Indian."

This is the only case any where recorded of Indian
aggression upon the town. The occurrence must have
taken place during Philip's war, and the attack was
doubtless upon some exposed dwelling, distant from
the town plot.

The Mohegans, from the earliest period of the settlement to the present day, may be called favorites

with the people of Norwich. They have been looked after with almost parental care, and the men of most influence in the town, on all public questions, have taken their part, whether right or wrong, against the state and against opposing tribes.

Quarrels frequently took place among the natives, within the bounds of the town, and in this case the magistrates interfered, to see justice done. There is a tradition that one Indian killed another on Bean-hill, soon after the settlement, in 1662. The criminal was arraigned, and being found guilty, was delivered over to his own people for punishment. They assembled on the spot where the deed was done; the prisoner was brought forth, placed in a kneeling position, and the gun put into the executioner's hand, by one of their chief men. This executioner was probably a near relation of the deceased. For some time he flourished his weapon in the air, then aimed at the criminal and made the motion of discharging its contents, but instantly wheeled about and pointed to some other object. At length, when the attention of the spectators and the prisoner was in some measure distracted, he suddenly fired: the victim uttered a single cry of *ahwah!* and fell dead. The executioner threw down his gun, fled to the woods and returned no more to his tribe. This was their custom, in order to avoid the avengers of blood. In another affray which happened near one of the English houses, murder was committed, but the criminal escaped. The Indians held a court on the spot, pronounced the sentence, and put the avenging knife into the hand of the son of the slain, who immediately set off in pursuit of the offender, but in vain, he had reached Oneida, and was there protected.

7

# CHAPTER VIII.

1668.   A rate was granted for "repairing and heightening the meeting-house."   The next year a grant of land was made " to Samuel Lotrop in consideration of his heightening the meeting-house."   This edifice had probably been built in November, 1659; hastily constructed, and expected to answer only a temporary purpose.

In 1673, a contract was made with John Elderkin and Samuel Lothrop, to build a new meeting-house, upon the summit of the hill, at the foot of which the present church stands.   It was to be furnished " with a gallery and trough to carry the water from the roof." Elderkin, who was the builder, completed it in about two years.   He had engaged to do it for £428, but the expense exceeding his estimate, he presented in town meeting the following petition :

" CHRISTIAN FRIENDS AND NEIGHBORS,

Your humble petitioner pleadeth your charitie for the reasons hereafter expressed.   Gentlemen, it is well known that I have been undertaker for building of the meeting-hous, and it being a piece of work very difficult to understand the whole worth and value off, yet notwithstanding I have presumed to doe the work for a sertain sum of money, (to wit,) 428 pound, not haveing any designe thereby to make myself rich, but that the towne might have there meeting-hous dun for a reasonable consideration.   But upon my experience, I doe find by my bill of cost, I have dun said work very much to my dammage, as I shall now make appear. Gentlemen, I shall not say much unto you, but onely if you may be made sencible of my loss in said undertaking, I pray for your generous and charitable conclusion toward me, whether it be much or little, I hope will be well excepted from your poor and humble petitioner.

JOHN ELDERKIN."

The town declared themselves to be at this time greatly burdened by the necessity of raising the £428; but as a compensation for the gallery of the new meeting-house, they granted Elderkin a tract of land " at Pocketannuk's Cove's mouth."

Mr. James Fitch having provided nails for this meeting-house, to the value of £12, " wherein his forwardness for the use and benefit of the town, is owned and accepted," liberty was granted him to take two hundred acres of land, as a satisfaction for the same, viz. " 100 in the crotch between Quinebaug and Showtucket, and 100 as convenient as he can find it, on the other side of Showtucket river."

The lofty site of this meeting-house, rendered it very difficult of access. We can scarcely imagine that the old or infirm ever reached it. It was chosen through fear of attack, and for the convenience of keeping watch. Another motive was, that the people beyond the ridge, as well as those below, might see their church. It was now the centre of vision to all the inhabitants, and presented a formidable and secure aspect; a barrier of perpendicular rocks on one side, and stony declivities on every other. This was about the period of Philip's war, and a time of unusual alarm. A better look-out post than the gallery of this church furnished, could scarcely be found in the vicinity.

In 1689, this meeting-house was found too small to accommodate the congregation, and Thomas Leffing-

well and others were appointed a committee "to consider, contrive and effect an enlargement" of it.   This
was done so as to answer the temporary emergency,
but the whole building was rough, uncouth and clumsy ; yet perched as it was like a citadel upon its rocky
height, the effect must have been imposing.

To this church the people used to repair with fire-arms
upon their shoulders, which were not, however, carried
into the house, but stacked without, in some convenient position to be watched by a person at one of the
windows.   Swords were customarily worn when in
full dress, by all the earlier settlers of New England,
both in a civil and military capacity.   Hats were at
that time made of wool : perhaps two or three at the
church door, reverently took off a " black beaverett,"
though that was a costly article, in those days.   The
poorer sort of people wore only a buff-cap, knit from
woollen yarn.   The coat was made with a long,
straight body, falling below the knee, and with no
collar, so that the band, or the neckcloth of spotless
linen, fastened behind with a silver buckle, was fully
displayed.   It is not probable that any one of the inhabitants assumed such a degree of state and dignity
as to wear a ruff, though that article was in vogue
among people of rank.   The waistcoat was long.   It
is uncertain whether the small clothes had then begun
to *grow*, so as to reach below the knee, and to be fastened with knee-buckles or not.   The earlier mode
was to have them terminate above the knee, and to
be tied with ribbons.   The common kind were made
of leather.   Red woollen stockings were much ad-
mired.   The shoes were coarse, clumped, square-toed,
and adorned with enormous buckles.   If any boots
made their appearance, prodigious was the thumping
as they passed up the aisles, for a pair of boots was

then expected to last a man's life. The tops were short, but very wide at the top ; formed, one might suppose, with a special adaptation to rainy weather ; collecting the water as it fell, and holding an ample bath for the feet and ancles !

Wigs were not then common; but long hair was getting into vogue. It was combed back from the forehead, and gathered behind into a club, or a queue, wound with a black ribbon. A congregation of such men, with their brave, manly brows, fronting their minister, worshipping God upon the high rock that overlooked their settlement, must have been a solemn and majestic sight to superior beings.

But our great grandmothers are also here : they come decently, but not gaudily dressed. They have finery, but they leave it at home on the Sabbath. The more respectable matrons have all a full dress of flowing brocade, embroidered stomachers, and hanging sleeves, but it is reserved for feasts and great civic occasions. They are dressed on the Sabbath, perhaps, in short gowns and stuff-petticoats, with white aprons of linen or muslin, starched stiff. The gown sleeve is short, and they wear mittens extending to the elbow, and leaving the fingers with a part of the thumb bare. The cloak was short, with a hood to cover the head, and was called a riding-hood. The hood was thrown back in meeting, and those who wore bonnets took them off. The matrons wore caps, and the young women had their hair curled or otherwise dressed.

Distinctions of rank and dress, titles of respect, and customs of deference and precedency, were carefully preserved, but they formed no bar to social intercourse, and every year diminished their influence. Among the first proprietors, very few at the period of the settlement, ranked so high as to be called Mr.

7*

The Rev. Mr. Fitch and Major Mason always received this title. Others afterwards, by age, character, or office, arrived at the distinction. Old men had the title of Gaffer, others that of Goodman, which was considered a respectful appellation, and is often used in the records. Women in like manner were respectfully addressed as Gammers and Goodwives.

Difficulties were soon experienced with respect to collecting the minister's rates. It had been arranged that every inhabitant should carry in himself his proportion annually, on or before the 20th of March, and for a time this mode answered well. This excellent community hoped to make the support of Christian instiutions wholly a voluntary business. Every thing was to be done according to law and order, at the same time that religious contributions were to be the spontaneous offerings of the heart and conscience. It was not till 1686, that collectors were appointed to gather the salary, one third of which was to be paid in wheat at 4s. per bushel, one third in rye or pease at 3s. per bu., and one third in indian corn at 2s. per bu., or in that which was equivalent and acceptable to the minister. This vote has a solemn preamble, setting forth the necessity of " doing what the laws of God and man, and duty obliges, to wit, the discharge of that obligation which we lie under with respect to the maintenance of our Rev. Minister, and it appearing that the great lenity of the Rev. Mr. Fitch towards some is much abused, and many are got into a way of slightness and remissness in making due payment, now therefore that we might all be more thorough so as the work of God may not fall amongst us, it is ordered,'' &c. In some cases monthly contributions were resorted to in order to make up the deficiency of the minister's salary.

In 1694 the Rev. Mr. Fitch was disabled from preaching, by a stroke of the palsy. This fact is adverted to in the preamble of a town act, in these terms,—"Inasmuch as it hath pleased Almighty God to lay his afflicting hand on our reverend minister," &c. Mr. Jabez Fitch, then pursuing his studies at New Haven, was invited to take his father's place, and the town passed a vote, "to pay the charge of sending for him from the Collidge." After a year's experience of his ministry, they passed another vote, declaring themselves well satisfied with him, and publicly inviting him to settle. His answer is not upon record, and indeed nothing farther appears respecting him. Mr. Fitch afterwards settled at Portsmouth, N. H., and there died, in the year 1746. The pulpit was now supplied by various other candidates, none of whom stayed longer than two or three Sabbaths at a time, so that new ones were continually to be sought, and a special rate was granted to defray the charge of "sending hither and thither for ministers."

At length Mr. Henry Flint was obtained, and at first was so highly acceptable and useful, that a record was made in the town books, acknowledging him as a special gift of Providence, in the following words :

"The good providence of God succeding our endeavours hath sent Mr. Flint unto us, for which we have reason to bless God, and doe desire he may abide with us half a year more or less, that he may have further tryall of us, and wee of him ;—and that he may stay as long as may be judged expedient for probation."

An agreement was made with him of the following purport :—"Dec. 15, 1696. At a meeting of the Committee with Mr. Henry Flint, minister, the Com. doe agree to allow him 20s. per week, so long as he shall continew to be our minister, and also to defray the

chardge of his board and hors meat." The next April
he was unanimously invited to settle with them, and
the following terms proposed, viz. : a grant of one
hundred and fifty acres of land on Plain hills ; a salary
of £52 per year and his board.   This was to continue
while he remained single.   If he should marry, his
salary was to be increased to £70, and sixty loads of
wood given him annually.   Mr. Flint, however, did
not accept these offers, and the preamble of a vote the
next year alludes to the melancholy fact, that they
" are still without a preaching minister."

During this interval, measures were again taken for
enlarging and repairing the meeting-house.   A *Leanto*
was added, in which several new pews were made,
and these not being sufficient to accommodate the
increasing congregation, leave was given to twelve
persons, who petitioned to that effect, " to build a seat
on the Leanto beams, for their convenient sitting on
the Lord's dayes."   All these improvements being
completed, in March, 1698, the Townsmen and Goodman Elderkin, the carpenter, were engaged to arrange
the pews into eight classes, according to their dignity.
This being done, five of the oldest and most respected
inhabitants, viz : Lt. Thomas Leffingwell, Lt. William
Backus, Deac. Simon Huntington, Thomas Adgate,
Senr., and Serg. John Tracy, were directed to seat the
people with due regard to rank : "the square pue to
be considered first in dignity; the new seats and the
fore seats in the broad ally next, and alike in dignity,"
and so on through the eight classes.

Mr. Joseph Coit was now engaged to supply the
pulpit, and after a few months probation, he was invited to settle.   The Committee who communicated this
resolution to Mr. Coit, received from him an answer,

which they reported in town meeting, in the following words.

" We have received a writing from Mr. Coit, in which he doth expressly declare his disagreement from Norwich church, and consequently he cannot walk with them, for how can two walk together, if they be not agreed ?__But he that in matters controversial doth set up his own opinion in opposition to the Synod Book, and a cloud of witnesses, will be in great danger to wander from the way of peace and truth. But as for us, let us please one another, in that that is good, and may be for edification."

Mr. John Woodward was their next candidate, and a vote was passed to "call him to office." He accepted this call and was ordained in October, 1699. A powerful opposition was nevertheless arrayed against him, excited by his opinions with respect to ecclesiastical discipline, which partook less of the congregational spirit of independence, than the notions which the old proprietors had brought with them from Saybrook. Two parties and a spirit of acrimony were beginning to appear in the church, which afterwards led to serious disturbances, and an ultimate separation. Of this, however, nothing appears on the records. The town voted to build Mr. Woodward a house, and contracted with Goodman Elderkin to do it for £140. But they afterwards purchased Mr. Samuel Huntington's house and homelot, at a less expense. Out of the lot an acre and a half was reserved for a burying place. This was soon afterwards open for interments, and is the Society burying yard, which, with an adjoining lot since purchased and added to it, is still used.

# CHAPTER IX.

The Patent.  Major Fitch.  Number of Inhabitants.

TOWNSHIPS in America were established with all their various privileges as independent communities, as early as 1650.  This was before the division into counties, before the formation of states, before even the union of settlements.  These townships are justly considered as the foundation of American liberty, furnishing a species of municipal independence and citizenship, which forms a solid basis for all other free institutions.

Counties in Connecticut were not regularly laid out, nor county courts organized, till 1666.  Norwich was then assigned to New London Co.  The counties were Hartford, New London and Fairfield.  The towns in New London Co. were New London, Norwich, Saybrook, Stonington, Killingworth, Groton and Preston.

In 1672 the Proprietors commenced a new record of lands, from which we obtain a list of the inhabitants "so far as copies of said lands were brought in by the said inhabitants."  The number is 78.

By the year 1680 Norwich had become the centre of several flourishing towns of more recent date.  After the conclusion of Philip's war, when all fear of Indian aggressions had died away, the settlements advanced rapidly, and it could no longer be said, as it had been, that in a northerly course there was not a single white settlement between Norwich and Canada.  Deeds were recorded in Norwich for several neighboring towns, and in some instances cases of trespass were brought there for decision, from Stonington, Preston, Woodstock, Killingly and Lebanon. Mr. Birchard and Lt. Thomas Tracy, the first Commissioners of the Peace, were of course men of considerable note in the country round about.

In 1684, the list of estate as returned to the General Court was £6,265. Number of taxable persons 115.

In 1685 a patent was obtained which confirmed to the town the original tract of nine miles square, to be an entire township, " according to the tenor of East Greenwich, in Kent, in free and common soccage, and not in capite, nor by Knight's service."

## PATENT
### OF THE TOWN OF NORWICH, A. D. 1685.

Whereas the General Court of Connecticut have forever granted unto the proprietors and Inhabitants of the Towne of Norwich all those lands, both meadows and uplands, within these abuttments (viz.) from the mouth of Tradeing-cove Brooke the line to run as the Brooke to the head of the Brooke to a white oake marked N : and from thence west northwesterly to a great pond to a black oake marked N : which stands neere the mouth of the great Brooke that runs out of the pond to Norwich river, which is about seven miles from the said Tradeing Cove ; and from thence the line runns North noreast nine miles to a Black oake standing by the river side on the south of it, a little above maumeagway, and from thence the line runs south southeasterly nine miles to a white oake standing by a brooke marked N : and then the line runs south southwesterly nine miles to a white oake neere Robert Allyn and Thomas Rose's Dwelling houses, which tree is marked N : and from thence westerly as New London Bounds runs to Mohegan river, the whole being nine miles square, the said land haveing been by purchase or otherwise lawfully obtayned of the Indian natives proprietors.— And whereas, the said Inhabitants and proprietors of the s^d Norwich in the Colony of Connecticutt have made application to the Governo^r and Company of the s^d Colony of

Connecticutt assembled in Court May 25th, 1685, that they may have a patent for the confirmation of the afore$^{sd}$ land, so purchased and granted to them as aforesaid, and which they have stood seized, and quietly possessed of for many years late past, without interruption.  Now for a more full confirmation of the aforesd unto the present proprietors of the s$^d$ Towneship of Norwich in their possession and injoyment of the premises, know yea that the s$^d$ Governour and Company assembled in Generall Court according to the Commission Granted to them by his magestie's charter, have given and granted and by these presents doe give, grant Rattifie and confirme unto Mr. James Fitch sen$^r$, Capt. James Fitch, Mr. Benjamine Brewster, Lieut. Thomas Tracy, Lieut. Tho. Leffingwell, Mr. Christopher Huntington, Mr. Simon Huntington, Ensign Wm. Backus, Mr. Thomas Waterman, Mr. John Burchard and Mr. John Post, and the rest of the said present proprietors of the township of Norwich, their heirs, suckcessors and assigns forever ; the aforesaid parcell of land as it is Butted and Bounded, together with all the woods, meadows, pastures, ponds, waters, rivers, islands, fishings, huntings, fowleings, mines, mineralls, quarries, and precious stones, upon or within the said tract of land, and all other proffitts and comodities thereunto belonging, or in any wayes appertayning ; and Doe also grant unto the aforesd Mr. James Fitch sen$^r$, Capt. James Fitch, Mr. Benjamin Brewster, Lieut. Thomas Tracy, Lieut. Thos. Leffingwell, Mr. Christopher Huntington, Mr. Simon Huntington, Ensign Wm. Backus, Mr. Thomas Waterman, Mr. John Birchard, and Mr. John Post, and the rest of the proprietors, Inhabitants of Norwich, their heirs, successors and assigns forever, that the fores$^d$ tract of land shall be forever hereafter deemed, reputed and be an intire towneship of itself—to have and to hold the said tract of land and premises, with all and singular their appurtenances, together with the priviledges and immunities and franchises herein given and granted unto the say$^d$ Mr. James Fitch sen$^r$, Capt. James Fitch, Mr. Benjamine Brewster, Lieut. Thomas Tracy, Lieut. Thomas Leffingwell, Mr. Christopher Huntington, Mr. Simon Huntington, Ensign Wm. Backus, Mr. Thomas Waterman, Mr. John Birchard and Mr. John Post, and other the present proprietors, Inhabitants of Norwich, theire heirs successors, and assignes for ever, and to the only proper use and behoofe of the sayd Mr. James Fitch sen$^r$, Capt. James Fitch, Mr. Benjamine Brewster, Lieut. Thomas Tracy, Lieut. Thomas Leffingwell, Mr. Christopher Huntington, Mr. Simon Huntington, Ensign Wm. Backus. Mr. Thomas Waterman, Mr. John Birchard and Mr. John Post, and other proprietors, inhabitants of Norwich, their heirs, successors, and assigns for ever, according to the Tenor of East Greenwich in Kent, in free and comon soccage and not in capitte, nor by Knite's service, they to make improvement of the same as they are capable according to the custom of the country, yielding, rendering, and paieing therefore to our sovereign Lord the king, his heires and successors, his dues according to Charter. In witness whereof, we have caused the Seale of the Colony to be hereunto affixed this twenty-first of May, 1685, in the first year of the reigne of our sovereigne lord James the Second, by the grace of God, of England, Scotland, France, nnd Ireland, King, Defender of the faith.

ROBERT TREAT, Governor.

{ SEAL. }  March 30th, 1687, pr order of Govr. and Company of the Colony of Connecticutt.

Signed pr

JOHN ALLYN, Secrety.

Entered in the pub. records, Lib. D : fo. 138, 139, Novr 27th, 1685 : pr

JOHN ALLYN, Secrety.

Twelve Patentees were chosen by the town; but from some cause unknown, Thomas Adgate, who was one, is not named in the instrument as recorded on the town books. They will all be recognized as belonging to the original band of proprietors, with the exception of Capt. James Fitch and Mr. Benjamin Brewster.

Capt. Fitch soon afterwards removed to a large tract of land that he had obtained on Quinebaug river, and commenced a plantation at a place then known as Peagscomsuck, now Canterbury. The first framed house and barn in that place were built by him. In 1688, he tendered " his accommodations in Norwich" to the town, for a parsonage, and again in 1694. But his offers were not accepted. Four years afterwards his house and homelot upon the plain were purchased by the two brothers, Simon and Samuel Huntington.

Few persons of that period had more influence in this part of the colony than Capt. or as he was afterwards styled, Major Fitch. He was a noted friend and patron to the Indians, and after the death of Maj. Mason, possessed more sway over the Sachems than any other individual, not excepting their other distinguished advocate, Capt. Samuel Mason. The signature of Owaneco, subsequent to the year 1680, was considered of no value unless countersigned by Capt. Fitch; the Sachem, with the consent of the General Court, having authorized him to act as his guardian.

Capt. Fitch, with his brothers Samuel and Daniel, were highly esteemed as brave soldiers and experienced partizans in Indian warfare. The early inhabitants of Norwich were a spirited and enterpising people, ever ready to sally forth on emergencies, to protect themselves and their neighbors from the savage foe. An instance occurred in the summer of 1696, when a band of Mohawks committed some depredations on the western towns in Massachusetts. A rumor having reached Capt. Fitch that a party of them had been seen skulking about Woodstock, he hastened from his farm to Norwich, collected a band of whites and Mohegans, and plunged into the forests in pursuit of the enemy. From Woodstock, he sent a part of his force under his brother Daniel, to range the woods farther to the west, which they did, scouring the country as far as Oxford, Worcester and Lancaster.

At the close of the century, an act was passed relative to a new division of the common lands, which led to an enumeration of the inhabitants. The number of accepted inhabitants enrolled, was eighty-three; other male residents, twelve. Either this list was never thoroughly completed, or the population had decreased since 1684, which is not very probable. From the list of cattle marks, and the new names at intervals appearing upon record, we may conclude that at the commencement of a new century, the town contained at least one hundred and twenty-five or one hundred and thirty, full grown men. Of the first proprietors a remnant still lingered to enjoy the social and religious institutions which they had founded. Rev. Mr. Fitch, Lieut. Leffingwell, Deacon Simon Huntington, Thomas Adgate, Lt. William Backus, Thomas Post, John Post, John Reynolds, and Morgan Bowers, are enumerated in the above act, as the remaining survivors of the first thirty-five. To them we may add John Tracy and John Gager, who were still living, though not mentioned in this enrolment.

# CHAPTER X.

### The Thirty-five.

WE now approach the period when the first class of settlers disappear from the scene. One generation has passed away, and another is rapidly verging towards the down-hill of life.

Before dismissing this venerated band to their last resting-place, the few facts which have been ascertained respecting each proprietor and his immediate family, will be briefly stated. It would render the work too voluminous to trace the genealogy through their descendants, and in most cases it would not be practicable. Many of the names are not now to be found in Norwich proper, but are scattered over the nine miles square, and in the adjoining towns of Canterbury, Windham, Mansfield and Lebanon, which in their origin may be considered as colonies from Norwich.

### REV. MR. FITCH.

This excellent man was born at Boking, in the county of Essex, Eng., in 1622. His early education was attended to with great care, so that he was well skilled in the learned languages, when he came to America. He was then only sixteen years of age, being one of a band of thirteen youths, all designed for the ministry, who came over at the same time. He was placed, after his arrival, under the instruction of

Messrs. Hooker and Stone, at Hartford, where he remained seven years. In 1646, a church was formed in Saybrook, of which Mr. Fitch was ordained pastor. Mr. Hooker was present at his ordination, but the imposition of hands was by two of the brethren, appointed by the church to that office. This was a congregational ordination in the strictest sense of the term. The same form was also used at the same place fourteen years afterwards, at the ordination of the Rev. Thomas Buckingham. When a part of Mr. Fitch's church decided, in 1660, to remove to Norwich, it was a subject of some contention between the two parties whether he should stay with those who were to remain, or go with those who should remove. He was greatly beloved by all, and each side claimed him. After solemn prayer and long deliberation, Mr. Fitch decided that it was his duty to keep with the majority, and this brought him to Norwich. Soon after his removal thither, the people of Hartford invited him to become their minister, thinking, probably, that the hardships of a new settlement, and the prospect of extensive usefulness in a wider and more elevated sphere, might induce him to leave his flock. The only reply he sent to their invitation was this: "With whom then shall I leave these few poor sheep in the wilderness?"

The oldest Election Sermon of which any record has been discovered, was preached by Mr. Fitch, in 1674, from this text: "For I, saith the Lord, will be unto her a wall of fire round about, and will be the glory in the midst of her."

As a pastor, Mr. Fitch was zealous and indefatigable. Seeing the Indians around him sunk in darkness and stupidity, his heart was touched with pity, and he spared no pains to alleviate their condition, both in a spiritual and temporal point of view. His house was

8*

open to their roving parties, and he never failed to dispense to them, according to his ability, food, raiment and instruction. He learned their language, and often went among them, endeavoring to enlighten their minds, and win them from vice and degradation. The legislature of the State particularly requested him to teach Uncas and his family christianity. But little impression was, however, made on the minds of the chiefs, though many of the common people listened with attention, and some, as has been already stated, gave evidence of true conversion.

The Mohegan Sachems, notwithstanding their disinclination to christianity, were warmly attached to Mr. Fitch and his family. Large tracts of land, conveyed to them either in trust, or as absolute grants, attest their friendship and confidence. A part of the town of Lebanon, five miles in length, and one in breadth, was bestowed by Owaneco on Mr. Fitch and his friend, Capt. Mason. This tract was for a time under the jurisdiction of Norwich, and was familiarly called *The Mile*. In Mr. Fitch's share of this tract, there was a large *Cedar* Swamp, which by the principle of association suggesting to the mind of its accomplished owner the Cedars of Lebanon, led him to bestow the name of *Lebanon* on the whole tract.

Mr. Fitch was highly esteemed by his contemporaries as a penetrating and solid preacher, an enterprizing, energetic, and holy man. He was disabled from performing public service in 1694, but the town still continued to supply him with a comfortable maintenance, voting him an annual present, varying from £30 to £50. He died in 1702, among his children at Lebanon, he being then about eighty years of age. His tomb-stone, with a Latin epitaph, is at that place and in good preservation.

By his two wives Mr. Fitch had fourteen children, whose births are all recorded in Norwich, though a part of them were born at Saybrook, previous to his removal. His first wife was Abigail, daughter of the Rev. Henry Whitefield, by whom he had two sons and four daughters, viz :

| James, | born | 1649. | Hannah, | born | —— |
| Abigail, | " | 1650. | Samuel, | " | 1655. |
| Elizabeth, | " | 1652. | Dorothy, | " | 1658. |

Mrs. Abigail Fitch died at Saybrook, in 1659. Mr. Fitch married for his second wife Priscilla, daughter to Major Mason, in 1664, by whom he had seven sons and one daughter, viz :

| Daniel, | born | 1665. | Anna, | born | 1675. |
| John, | " | 1667. | Nathaniel, | " | 1679. |
| Jeremiah, | " | 1670. | Josiah, | " | 1681. |
| Jabez, | " | 1672. | Eleazer, | " | 1683. |

Mr. Fitch had a brother, Thomas, who came to this country with him, settled at Norwalk, and was father to Thomas Fitch, Governor of Connecticut.

Elizabeth, the second daughter of Mr. Fitch, married Rev. Edward Taylor, of Westfield, Mass. Among the collections of the Connecticut Historical Society is an original letter written by him to Miss Fitch during his courtship, which, from some expressions in it, would seem to have been despatched by a true carrier pigeon ; but perhaps these allusions may be explained by supposing the image of a dove stamped on the seal. The daughters of Mr. Fitch were beautiful in person, and highly accomplished for the period. A letter like this of Mr. Taylor's would scarcely have been written to a person of ordinary attainments. A part of it may be quoted as a specimen of the quaint and metaphorical taste of the age.

" This for my friend and only beloved, Miss Elizabeth Fitch, at her father's house in Norwich.

" WESTFIELD, 8 day of 7th month, 1674.

" My Dove,
" I send you not my heart, for that I trust is sent to heaven long since, and unless it hath wofully deceived me, it hath not taken up its lodgings in any one's bosom on this side of the Royal City of the Great King, but yet the most of it that is allowed to be layed out upon any creature doth safely and singly fall to your share.

" So much my post pigeon present you with here in these lines. Look not, I entreat you, upon it as one of Love's hyperboles, if I borrow the beams of some sparkling metaphor to illustrate my respects unto thyself by, for you having made my breast the cabinet of your affections, as I yours mine, I know not how to offer a fitter comparison to set out my love by than to compare it unto a golden ball of pure fire, rolling up and down my breast, from which there flies now and then a spark like a glorious beam from the body of the flaming sun. But alas! striving to catch these sparks into a love-letter unto yourself, and to gild it with them as with a sunbeam, I find that by what time they have fallen through my pen upon my paper they have lost their shine, and fall only like a little smoke thereon instead of gilding them, wherefore, finding myself so much deceived, I am ready to begrudge my instruments, for though my love within my breast is so large that my heart is not sufficient to contain it, yet they can no more make room to ride into, than to squeeze it up betwixt my black ink and white paper. But know that it is the coarsest part that is chouchant there, for the purest is too fine to clothe in any linguish huswifry, or to be expressed in words."

The writer then proceeds to show "that conjugal love should exceed all other love," but in illustrating this point he runs into the style of a sermon and the lover is almost lost in the theologian.

Mr. Taylor was a man of great erudition, and left a large number of MSS. behind him. One of his daughters was mother of President Styles.

The descendants of the Rev. Mr. Fitch are exceed-ngly numerous; eleven of his children, if not more, lived to have families. Capt. James Fitch, already mentioned, was the father of nine sons, only one of whom died young.

## MASON.

Of the original band of proprietors, Capt. Mason was the second laid in the grave. He died amid his family n Norwich in 1672, in the 73d year of his age. His last hours were cheered by the prayers and counsels of his beloved pastor and son-in-law, Mr. Fitch. Two years before, he had requested his fellow citizens to excuse him from all further public services, on account of his age and infirmity; so that the close of his life was tranquil and unharrassed by care and responsibil-ty. He was buried about half a mile from his dwell-ng in a spot which the early planters had selected for a grave yard, but which was never used for that pur-pose after the year 1700. In that primitive cemetery, the only memorials erected in honor of the dead were a grassy hillock, and a block of unhewn granite at the head and foot of the grave. No squared pillars or chis-elled inscriptions ever decorated this humble spot. The stones gradually sunk into the earth, or were removed by those that knew not they had any watch to keep; the graves wore away to a level with the field, and then a little below it, and long before the end of another century, the ploughshare and the seedsman passed over and obliterated every vestige of grave and monument from the place. Tradition alone determines the spot where the noble Captain, and probably the greater part of the first band of planters were buried.

Mason was a man of great prudence and sagacity,

wise in council, and heroic in the field of action.  The
natural ardor of his mind, fostered by early military
adventures, and continually called into exercise by
great emergencies, made him a fearless leader in war.
Sturdy in frame, and hardy in constitution; regardless
of danger, fatigue or exposure, he was invaluable as a
pioneer in difficult enterprises, and a founder of new
plantations.    He was also a religious man and a
patriot; of virtuous habits, and moderate ambition.
Though he sustained many high and honorable offices
in the infant colony, he is best known by the simple
title of *Captain*.   There is a tradition that after he had
retired from the public service, and was quietly residing
with his family in Norwich, intelligence was received
of some disturbance among the Indians, either at Groton or Stonington.   Mason immediately collected about
sixty volunteers, who hastily throwing their wallets
over their shoulders, containing provisions for two or
three days, started for the scene of action.   They
crossed the Shetucket by fording, a little higher up
than where the Greenville factories now stand, marched
directly to the spot where the Indians had fixed their
camp, chastised them, destroyed their fortifications and
many of their huts, and returned in three days without
losing a man.   It was for promptness and decision like
this, that Mason was ever characterized.   Trumbull
comprises his peculiar traits in these few words.   " He
was tall and portly, full of martial fire, and shunned
no hardships or dangers in the defence and service of
the colony."

The Pequot war commenced at a time when Connecticut had only two hundred and fifty inhabitants,
comprised principally in the three towns of Hartford,
Wethersfield and Windsor.   Out of these Mason gath-

ered a band of seventy men, and passing down Connecticut river, landed in the Narragansett country, and being joined by a band of friendly Indians, marched directly into the heart of the hostile territory, assailed the Pequots in their strongest fortress, destroyed it, laid waste their dwellings, and killed nearly half of the whole nation. This expedition occupied just three weeks. The skill, prudence, firmness and active courage displayed by Mason in this exploit, were such as to gain him a high standing among military commanders. Viewing his conduct at this distance of time, we are disposed to 'charge him with cruelty to the vanquished foe ; but the same taint lies on all the early colonists. He only shared in the ferocious character of the age, and we may add, in that misconstruction of the spirit of Christianity, which devoted its enemies to immediate and vindictive destruction.

Among the various offices held by Mason, was that of Major General of the militia of Connecticut; a duty which obliged him to call out and exercise the militia of each town ten times a year : salary forty pounds per annum.

When Mr. Fenwick arrived from England with a few persons, to make a plantation near Saybrook Fort, Capt. Mason was induced to join them, and accordingly removed thither. The government of the town was entirely independent of the colony for ten years, Mr. Fenwick and Capt. Mason acting as sole magistrates. Nevertheless the latter continued to hold and exercise his military command in the colony. When the fort passed into the hands of the colony, Mason was appointed to receive the investment, and at the special request of the inhabitants of Saybrook, he was made commander of the station. During the winter of 1647–8, the Fort in some unknown way took fire, and

together with the buildings attached to it, was burnt to
the ground.   The Captain, with his wife and child,
very narrowly escaped.

The people of New Haven were not entirely satisfied
with their location, and formed a design of removing to
a tract of land which they had purchased on the Delaware river.   In 1651, they proposed this matter to
Capt. Mason, urgently requesting him to remove with
them, and take the management of the company.
This invitation is a proof of the high opinion his contemporaries had formed both of his civil and military
talents.   The offers they made him were liberal, and
he was on the point of accepting, when the legislature
of Connecticut interfered, entreating him not to leave
the colony, and declaring, that they could by no means
consent to his removal.   Finding that his presence was
considered essential to the safety of Connecticut, he
declined the offers of New Haven.   If he went, there
was no one left, who could make his place good;
neither had New Haven any person in reserve, who
could fill the station designed for him, and therefore
the projected settlement never took place.   The active
disposition of Mason, however, never lacked employment.   There was scarcely a year in which he was not
obliged to go on some expedition among the Indian
tribes, to negotiate, or to fight, or to pacify their mutual
quarrels.   At one time, his faithful friend Uncas, was
in danger from a powerful league of the other tribes.
but the seasonable preparations of Mason for his relief,
frightened the foe into peace and submission.   At
another time, he was sent with arms and men to the
assistance of the Long Island Indians, against Nini-
grate, the powerful Sachem of the Nehanticks, who
threatened them with extirpation.   This service he
gallantly performed; but only two years afterwards

was compelled to appear again on that Island with a
band of soldiers, in order to chastise the very Indians,
mischievous and ungrateful, whom he had before
relieved.

We find him, at the same time, and for several
years in succession, holding various public offices, all
arduous and important. A member of two deliberative
bodies, the Connecticut Legislature, and the Board of
Commissioners of the United Colonies—Major General
of the militia at home, and the acting commander in
all expeditions abroad; his whole life seems to be
given to the public. In 1660 he was chosen Deputy
Governor, to which office he was annually re-elected
for ten years, five under the old form, and five under
the king's charter, which united Connecticut with
New Haven. The same year he was actively employed in conjunction with Mr. Fitch and others, in
effecting the settlement of Norwich, and also in pur-
chasing of the Mohegans a large tract of land, in behalf
of the colony. The jurisdiction of these lands he publicly surrendered to the General Court, March 14,
1661, receiving from them at the same time, an order
to lay out these lands into plantations, with permission
to reserve a farm for himself.

Capt. Mason continued to reside in Norwich until
his death; though his public duties kept him absent
from the place a great part of the time. His three
sons were,

| | | | | |
|---|---|---|---|---|
| Samuel, | born | . | . . | 1641 |
| John, | . " | . | . . . | 1646 |
| Daniel, | . " | . | . . | 1652 |

His family continued to reside in Norwich for some
years after his death. His widow, Mrs. Abigail Mason,
was living there in 1681. The sons ultimately settled

9

in neighboring towns.   Between the years 1704 and 1712, they were all three residing in Stonington.

### ADGATE.

Thomas Adgate was one of the two deacons of Mr. Fitch's church, ordained to office in Saybrook, 1659. Nothing is known of him previous to this event, but it is supposed that he was the only one of his family who emigrated to America, and that he came direct to Saybrook, and there resided till the settlement of Norwich. By his first wife, he had two daughters, born in 1651 and 1653.   Previous to leaving Saybrook, he married the widow of Richard Bushnell, she having at that time two sons and two daughters.   Their children born in Norwich, were three daughters and one son. Deacon Adgate died in 1707.   His son, Deacon Thomas Adgate 2d, born 1669, lived to be nearly ninety-two years of age.   He had two sons, Thomas and Matthew.   The line of Thomas, in the male branch, is believed to be extinct, and the descendants of Matthew, (who had seven sons,) have removed to other parts of the country.

### ALLYN.

Matthew and Robert Allyn, the former found at Cambridge, in 1632, and the latter at Salem, in 1637, are supposed to have been brothers, and to have soon removed to Connecticut.   Matthew settled at Hartford, and Robert at Saybrook.   The latter removed with Winthrop, to New London, and subsequently became a proprietor of Norwich.   His name is not found on the list of inhabitants after 1672, and the homelot passed into the hands of his son John, of New London, who in 1692, exchanged it with Joshua Abell, and Simon Huntington Jun., for two considerable tracts of land "east of the Great River," [the Thames,] and within the bounds of New London. In this district, afterwards included in Groton, and now in Ledyard, Robert Allyn, the son of John, and grandson of the proprietor Robert, had previously settled.

In the Norwich Patent of 1685, the S. S. E. corner of the nine miles square is designated by "a white oake neere Robert Allyn and Thomas Rose's dwelling houses." The descendants of Allyn removed nearer the river, and lived upon the Point, where the station house of the Norwich and Worcester Railroad Company has been recently erected. Allyn's Mountain and Allyn's Point, are names still retained in that quarter.

Timothy Allen, who settled in Norwich about 1670, was of another family, and his descendants have used a different orthography for their name.

### BACKUS.

The relationship between William and Stephen Backus, has not been accurately determined. They were probably brothers. One of the first settlers of Saybrook, was a Backus; the name is found there as early as 1637. It is not improbable that William and Stephen Backus, proprietors, of Norwich, were the sons of this man, by a first marriage; that his second wife was Mrs. Ann Bingham, and that he having died at Saybrook, previous to the removal, his relict came to Norwich, with Thomas Bingham, her son by a former marriage. The death of Mrs. Ann Backus, the mother of Mr. Thomas Bingham, is recorded in Norwich, in 1670. This statement, though partly conjectural, harmonizes the few facts that have been gleaned. William Backus was an active man in town affairs, and is generally mentioned as Ensign or Lieut.

He was married May 11, 1660, but the record does not state where, or to whom. The children of this marriage were

John, born February 9, 1661.
Sarah,               1663.
Samuel,           1665.
Joseph,            1667.
Nathaniel,        1669.
Hannah.          ——

This must have been a second marriage ; for William Backus Jr., whom the Lieut. in certain documents styles " my eldest son" was married in 1681. One of the wives of the Lieut., and most probably the second, was the " daughter of Lieut. William Pratte, of Seabrooke."

William Backus Jr., known as Sergeant William Backus, in 1692, sold his house, homelot and three other parcels of land, in Norwich, to his father, for £55, and removed to " the nameless new town lying about ten miles N. W. of Norwich." [Lebanon.]

Lieut. William Backus, was doubtless *the last* of the proprietors, to leave earth. He was living in 1718. His death is not recorded in the town books, but a conveyance made in 1721, speaks of him as " late of Norwich, deceased."

Stephen Backus married Sarah Gardner, of East Hampton, Long Island, in 1666. This lady was the daughter of Capt. Lyon Gardiner, first lord of Gardiner's Island.

Their sons were Stephen, born 1670.
                   Timothy,     1682.

No record has been found of the death of Stephen Backus. Mrs. Sarah Backus, his widow, was living in 1700. About that period, Stephen, the eldest son, sold his property in Norwich, and removed first to Plainfield, and afterwards to Canterbury.

### BALDWIN.

Several persons of the ancient name of Baldwin, (derived from Baldwinus, a bishop of Great Britain, A. D. 672,) are found among the early emigrants to Massachusetts. It is not ascertained whether the Baldwin who early settled at Saybrook, came direct from England or not. Farmer, in his Genealogical Register, observes that he may have been the Richard Baldwin that was in Braintree, in 1637. In that case, John, who removed to New London, and from thence to Norwich, was probably his son, but must have been of transatlantic birth, as John Baldwin Jr. was of man's age previous to 1678. John, the proprietor, had two sons : 1, John, who died in 1700, and as far as appears, without leaving any sons : 2, Thomas, who married, in 1684, Sarah, daughter of John Calkins. The children of this marriage were all daughters. By his second wife, Abigail Lay, Thomas had three sons :

Thomas, born 1701.     Ebenezer, born 1710.
John,     "     1704.

The name is still a common one in the towns around Norwich. The late Judge Baldwin, of New Haven, born in 1761, was a native of Norwich, and descended from this stock.

### BINGHAM.

Nothing has been ascertained respecting Thomas Bingham previous to the settlement. He married Mary Rudd, Dec. 12, 1666. Their children were

| | | | | | |
|---|---|---|---|---|---|
| Thomas, | born | 1667. | Abigail, | born | 1679. |
| Abel, | " | 1669. | Nathaniel, | " | 1681. |
| Mary, | " | 1672. | Deborah, | " | 1683. |
| Jonathan, | " | 1674. | Samuel, | " | 1685. |
| Ann, | " | 1677. | Joseph, | " | 1688. |
| | | | Stephen, | " | 1690. |

9*

Thomas Bingham 2d. married Hannah, youngest daughter of Lt. William Backus, and settled in Windham. The name is no longer to be found in Norwich, but is still common in the vicinity.

### BIRCHARD.

John Birchard was a man of considerable note among the proprietors, and perhaps the best clerk in the company. The earliest records are supposed to be in his hand-writing. He officiated also as townsman and constable, and was the first Commissioner of the Peace. Hence he was always designated as Mr. Birchard. His origin has not been traced. The orthography of those times was so uncertain, that he may have been of the same family with Edward *Bircher*, who arrived in Plymouth, 1623. He married Christian Andrews in 1653, by whom he had a large family of sons and daughters. The sons were all born in Norwich, viz.,

| | | | | |
|---|---|---|---|---|
| Samuel, | born | 1663. | John, | born | 1671. |
| James | " | 1665. | Joseph, | " | 1673. |
| Thomas, | " | 1669. | Daniel, | " | 1680. |

The name is still found in Norwich, Mansfield, and perhaps other towns of this vicinity.

### BLISS.

It is probable that most of the families of this name scattered through New England, may be traced back to George Bliss, who removed from Lyme to Sandwich in 1637. Admitting that this man was the father of Thomas, who was one of the first settlers of Rehoboth, in 1643: of Nathaniel, who was at Springfield, in 1646, and John, at Northampton, in 1658, the genealogy loses its intricacy. Thomas may have removed from Rehoboth to Saybrook, for the purpose of joining the company then projecting the settlement of

Norwich.* In the history of Rehoboth, (a very valuable work, by Leonard Bliss Jr.,) the name of Thomas Bliss does not appear after 1650; that of Jonathan
Bliss, perhaps another brother, supplies its place.

Thomas Bliss, of Norwich, died in 1700, being about
80 years of age. His two sons were

   Thomas, born 1651, deceased, 1681.
   Samuel,  "   1657,   "    1709.

He had six daughters, viz. : Elizabeth, Sarah, Mary,
Dolinda, Anne, Rebecca. The descendants of the
male branch in a right line, still reside upon the homelot of their ancestors. The house, though in good
preservation, is one of the oldest in town. Seven generations have dwelt in it, and though often repaired
and modified, it is supposed not to have been entirely
rebuilt since its erection by the first proprietor. This,
and the old Grover and Post houses, are probably the
only dwellings in the town, any part of which can look
back beyond the year 1700.

### BOWERS.

Very little is known of Morgan Bowers. He appears
to have been illiterate and thriftless. In the year 1700
he was still living, but so poor and infirm as to be in
part supported by his neighbors and townsmen ; apparently the first case of penury that had occurred in the
community. As the name continued in the town at a
later date, it is inferred that he left children, but no
record of them has been found.

### BRADFORD.

John Bradford was the son of Gov. William Bradford

---

* That Thomas Bliss, of Rehoboth, and Thomas Bliss, of Norwich,
were the same person, is a conjecture, resting only on identity of name
and coeval existence.

of Plymouth, by his first wife, Dorothy. He was left either in England or Holland, when his parents came out in the May Flower. His mother fell overboard and was drowned, Dec. 7, 1620, while the vessel was anchored in Plymouth harbor, before they had fixed on a place for settlement, and while her husband was absent in the shallop, exploring the coast. It is not ascertained when John Bradford arrived in this country. Very little is known respecting the early part of his life ; for neither Morton, nor Prince, the earliest authorities respecting Plymouth colony, give any hint of the existence of this son of Gov. Bradford. He lived first in Duxbury and afterwards in Marshfield and was the Representative of both places in the Plymouth Court.*  "He married Martha Bourne, daughter of Thomas Bourne, as is proved by Thomas Bourne's will, and by deeds of John Bradford's farm, in Marshfield, which he sold in 1663 and 1664, which deeds are signed by Martha, his wife."†  He appears next at Norwich, where his homelot was laid out with those of the first purchasers, in Nov., 1659. His name is often found on committees requiring prudent counsel and integrity of character, and though sometimes styled simply *Goodman Bradford,* he is usually distingished as *Mr.* Bradford, which was then an appellative of respect.

He died in 1678. His widow shortly afterwards married their near neighbor, Lieut. Thomas Tracy. This we learn from an instrument dated Feb. 20, 1679, wherein Martha, the wife of Thomas Tracy, styles herself executrix of the estate of her late husband, Mr. John Bradford. It is not ascertained that Mr. Bradford

---

* Farmer.        † F. P. Tracy, of Williamsburg, Mass.

left any posterity, the presumption is to the contrary. His nephew, Thomas Bradford, was an inhabitant of Norwich in 1678, and probably a member of his uncle's family, and inheritor of a part of his estate.

Mrs. Martha Tracy is supposed to have died in 1689. In an instrument dated at Norwich April 12, 1690, Maj. William Bradford, of Plymouth, conveys to his son Thomas Bradford, of Norwich, one ninth part of all the real and personal estate " of my loving sister Martha, the wife and late the relict widow of my well beloved brother, John Bradford, late of Norwich, deceased," which the said Martha, by her last will and testament, had bequeathed to him.   In 1691 Thomas Bradford sold his property in Norwich, which included the homelot that had belonged to his uncle, and removed to a farm in the vicinity, though not within the bounds of Norwich.   He died in 1708.

William Bradford, another grandson of Gov. Bradford, married Anna Fitch, the youngest daughter of the Rev. James Fitch.

### CAULKINS.

Two of this name, Hugh and his son John, were among the thirty-five proprietors.  Hugh was one of the first deacons of the church, and it is inferred, from the various offices he held, a man of sound discretion, and considerable experience and activity.   He was admitted a freeman of Lynn, Mass., in 1642 ; but removed the next year to Gloucester, of which town he was a representative in 1650 and 1651.   In 1654, if not earlier, he was an inhabitant of New London, where he had a homelot in the town plot, and a farm at Nehantick, laid out to him.   It does not appear that he ever resided in Saybrook, though he must have been there at the gathering of the church which was to accompany Mr. Fitch to the new plantation, as he was chosen one of its deacons. His name is found on the list of inhabitants at New London, until 1660. He had two sons, John and David. The latter succeeded to his father's property in New London. John, who seems to have resided previously at Saybrook, removed with his father to Norwich. Deacon Hugh died about 1690, leaving " his accommodations in Norwich" to his grandson Hugh, oldest son of John.

The name is variously spelt, both with and without the *u* and the *s*. In the earlier records it is generally *Calkin*. The family tradition is that Hugh came from Wales. Though an illiterate man himself, his sons appear to have been well educated for that period. It is a singular fact, that neither of the two deacons of Mr. Fitch's church could write. Both Thomas Adgate and Hugh Calkins invariably affix a mark instead of hand-writing to their documents. Others of the proprietors,—as Stephen Backus, John Pease, John Gager, Thomas Howard, John Reynolds, and Richard Edgerton, were in the same predicament.

John Calkins, the proprietor, brought with him to Norwich a young wife and infant son. He died in 1703, and his wife in 1711. They had seven children : the sons were—

Hugh,     born    .     .     .     .     .     1659.
John,      "    at Norwich,     .     .     .     1661.
Samuel,   "    "    "    .     .     .     1663.

Hugh 2d married for his first wife, Sarah, daughter of Thomas Sluman deceased, and step-daughter to Solomon Tracy, by whom he had four sons. His second wife was Lois Standish. One of his sons was the father of Solomon Calkins, from whom the various families of the name afterwards found in Lebanon and Sharon, descended.

### EGERTON.

Nothing antecedent to the settlement at Norwich can be ascertained respecting Richard Edgerton, except the date of his marriage, viz, 1653.

He had two sons, Richard and John ; the latter born June 12, 1662. The name is still a common one in Norwich and the adjoining towns.

### GAGER.

William Gager, "a right godly man, and a skilful chyrurgeon," came to America with Gov. Winthrop, in 1630. After his arrival, he was elected deacon of the church at Charlestown, but died the same year, together with his wife and two children, from a disease contracted by ill diet at sea, which swept off many of the emigrants. John, the son of Dr. William, removed to Saybrook with the younger Gov. Winthrop, and from thence accompanied his patron to New London, where his name is found on the oldest list of inhabitants extant. The elder Gov. Winthrop remembered him in the following item of his last will and testament. " I will that John Gager shall have a cow, one of the best I shall have, in recompense of a heifer his father bought of me, and two ewe goats, and ten bushels of indian corn." He joined the company of Norwich proprietors and removed to the new plantation, in 1660. He had nine children, whose births are recorded in Norwich, though most of them were born before the settlement. Only three of them were sons, viz :

John,   born 1647.   William, born 1660.
Samuel,   "   1654.

He died Dec. 10, 1703. His descendants are still

found in the place.    Othniel Gager, the present
Town Clerk, is the sixth in descent from the first proprietor.

### GIFFORD.

Very little is ascertained respecting Stephen Giffords.
His immediate successors were Stephen and Samuel
Giffords, and Samuel Giffords, Jr.    Stephen the 2d
was a deacon of the church at West Farms.

### GRISWOLD.

Lieut. Francis Griswold was one of the most active
and enterprising men in the first company of settlers.
He was probably the same Francis Griswold, who was
in Cambridge, Mass., in 1637, and admitted a freeman
in 1645.    His wife was Mary, and their daughter Hannah was born March 1, 1644. [See Farmer's Genealogical Register.]    He died in 1671.    Thomas Adgate
and John Post Sen., appear to have been guardians to
his orphan children, an accurate list of whose names
has not been obtained.    His daughter Mary married
Jonathan Tracy, in 1672.    His oldest and perhaps his
only son, Capt. Samuel Griswold, was born in 1665,
married Susannah Huntington in 1685, and died 1740.
The sons of Capt. Samuel were Francis, Samuel, John
and Joseph.    Joseph, born in 1706, lived to his 90th
year; was a deacon of the church, and venerable, not
only for age, but for piety.

### HIDE.

The Hides or *Hydes* of Saybrook, appear to have
been older emigrants than those of that name in Massachusetts.    They may have come direct from the old
country in company with Fenwick.    The name is an
ancient and honorable one  in the annals of England,

By the marriage of Anne Hyde, daughter of the earl of Clarendon, with the duke of York, afterwards James II., the stock was ingrafted into the royal family.

William Hide, the proprietor, was undoubtedly of much humbler origin, but a man of discretion and integrity. He often served as townsman of the West end.

In a deed of 1679, he is mentioned as " old Goodman Hide." He died in 1681. No reference has been found to any of his children, except Samuel and a daughter Hester, the wife of John Post. His grandson William succeeded to his homestead.

Samuel Hide and Jane Lee were married in Saybrook, 1659, and their daughter Elizabeth was the first born of Norwich. The record of their children stands thus :

Elizabeth, born Aug., 1660.  William born 1669.
Phebe,        "          1662.  Thomas,   "   1672.
Samuel,       "          1665.  Jabez,    "   1677.
John          "          1667.

Samuel died in 1677, leaving his seven children, all minors; Mr. Birchard became their guardian.

This is one of the familes that have become numerous and been widely dispersed. In 1779, there were more than twenty families of Hydes, numbering over 150 persons, in the western part of the Town Plot, and the societies of West Farms and Portipaug.

### HOLMSTEAD.

John Holmstead or Olmstead, has not been traced beyond the era of the settlement. His wife was aunt to Joseph and Richard Bushnell, and most probably by their mother's side, in which case she must have been the daughter of Matthew Marvyn of Hartford. Mr. Holmstead died before 1679, as a deed of that date

10

mentions " the widow Olmsted." He left no children; the homestead passed into the hands of the Bushnells. In 1686, Elizabeth Holmstead who styles herself the sole heir to her husband's estate, and executrix of his will, relinquished a two thousand acre right " in the plantation above Norwich," belonging to her late husband, to his near kinsmen, Lt. James and Ensign John Holmstead, of Norwalk.*

### HOWARD.

Very little is known of Thomas Howard; it is even doubtful whether he was one of the original thirty-five; but his home lot was laid out with the others. He married Mary Wollman, in 1666. He appears to have owned lands east of the Shetucket, a part of which he sold to Greenfield Larrabee, in 1671. He died in 1696. His widow married William Moore.

### HUNTINGTON.

The numerous families in New England, of the name of Huntington, may all be traced back to one common ancestor, viz: Simon Huntington, an emigrant from Norwich, in England. He had a brother Samuel, who was a Captain in the King's Life Guards; but he himself being a noted Puritan, and of course exposed to persecution, united himself to a small, but devoted company, who for the sake of unmolested worship, had resolved to emigrate to America. With these he embarked in 1639 or 40, for Saybrook, Conn., where Mr. Fenwick, who accompanied them, proposed to effect a settlement in behalf of the original patentees of the colony. Mr. Huntington, brought with him his three sons, Simon, Christopher and Samuel, he being

---

* QUERE. Are not Holmstead and Hempstead, originally the same name?

about fifty years of age, and his sons in the bloom of youth. He fell sick on the voyage, and died just as the vessel entered the mouth of Connecticut river, and came in sight of the port to which they were bound. The vessel anchored in the river, and he was buried upon the shore. His son Samuel afterwards settled at Newark, in New Jersey, but Simon and Christopher, after residing 20 years at Saybrook, removed to Norwich.

Simon was born in 1629; married Sarah Clarke 1653. He was for many years deacon of the church at Norwich, and a man of great respectability and influence. He died in 1706. Six sons survived him, viz:

Simon, born, 1659.     Nathaniel, born 1672.
Joseph,    "    1661.     Daniel,    "    1676.
Samuel, "    1665.     James,     "    1680.

Joseph settled in Windham, and was the ancestor of Gov. Huntington: Samuel in Lebanon; the others continued in Norwich.

Christopher Huntington, the proprietor, was married at Windsor, in 1652, to Ruth Rockwell. There is no account of but three children of this marriage, viz:

Christopher, born Nov. 1, 1660.    John, born, 1666.
Thomas,     "       1664.

Thomas settled at Mansfield.

It is not ascertained when the first Christopher died. The second Christopher, the first born son of Norwich, had a noble family of twelve children, most of them sons. The two wives of deacon Christopher, were Sarah Adgate, and Judith, widow of Jonathan Brewster. His daughter Ruth was the mother of Dr. Eleazer Wheelock, the founder of the Indian school at Lebanon, and first President of Dartmouth college.

In the early part of the next century, there were perhaps no more distinguished men in town, than the three Huntingtons, Mr. Isaac, Ensign James, and Capt. Hezekiah ; the latter afterwards deacon and Col. The Huntingtons, although extensively diffused in other towns, have always been numerous in the neighborhood of their first settlement. The homesteads of their ancestors have never been alienated to other names. From an enumeration made in 1779, we learn that there were at that time fifteen families of this name, comprising about one hundred persons in what was called the east end of the town plot, or First Society.

LEFFINGWELL.

Thomas Leffingwell, usually mentioned with the military prefix of Serg., Ensign, or Lieut., denoting the rank he held in the train-bands after he came to Norwich, was a native of Croxhall, England, and one of the earliest planters of Saybrook. In his testimony before the Court of Commission at Stonington, in 1705, he says he was acquainted with Uncas, in the year 1637, and was knowing to the assistance rendered by the Sachem to the English, then and ever after, during his life. It may be inferred from this, that he was personally engaged in the Pequot war. He also belonged to Capt. Denison's volunteer company of English and Mohegans, during Philip's war. Only three of his sons have been traced, viz : Thomas, Nathaniel and Samuel. He died about the year 1710. Mary, his wife, Feb. 6, 1711. The name, *Thomas*, descended in a right line, for five generations, each that bore it, living to a good old age.

Thomas Leffingwell 2d., born 1649, married Mary Bushnell in 1672; died 1724. His pious and venerable partner, survived him more than twenty years, living to be ninety-one years of age.

Thomas the 3d, born 1674, died 1733.

Thomas the 4th, born 1704, died 1793.

Thomas the 5th, died unmarried, in the year 1814, aged eighty-two.

The staff of the venerated Lieutenant, brought with him from his native place in 1637, and bearing his initials on its silver head, is in the possession of one of his descendants, N. L. Shipman, Esq.

Lieut. Leffingwell, was one of the last survivors of the proprietors. He had lived to see a great alteration take place in the nine miles square, since he first viewed it from the Mohegan heights. The dwellings of upright, intelligent, and industrious men, were scattered at intervals, over the surface ; the pleasant meadows upon the banks of the rivers, were reclaimed and cultivated, the uplands were cleared for grazing, the rocky pastures were clothed with flocks, and extensive fields in the suburbs, now comprised in other towns, were planted with wheat and Indian corn. The wilderness and solitary place had blossomed as the rose.

### PEASE.

Of John Pease, little is known. We find him with Gov. Winthrop, at New London, in 1650, and ten years afterwards, trace him to Norwich, where his homelot was at the extreme west end of the town. We do not find his name after 1673. The conjecture may be hazarded, that he was son of Henry Pease, mentioned by the elder Winthrop, in a letter to his son at New London, dated at Boston, June 14, 1648 :— "Henry Pease, my old servant, died this day senight." [See Winthrop's Journal.]

10*

### POST.

This family is supposed to have been of that original band of planters of Saybrook, who came direct from England, in 1639. Thomas and John, who removed to Norwich, were brothers; others of the name were left at Saybrook. Thomas was married in 1656, to Mary Andrews. She died at Norwich soon after the settlement, leaving a daughter Sarah, who afterwards married a Vincent. The second wife of Mr. Post, was Rebecca Bruin, whom he married in 1663. They had two sons,—Thomas, born 1664, and Joseph; perhaps others. Mr. Thomas Post died in 1704. His son Joseph married Mary Post, of Saybrook, by whom he had one son, Joseph, born 1747, and seven daughters.

John Post married Hester Hide, who died in 1681. His second wife was Sarah Reynolds, deceased, 1685. He had two sons, John and Samuel; the latter born in 1668. Mr. Post died in 1704. The house built by Samuel Post, on the town street, is still standing, though the name of Post is no longer to be found in the place. The two large elm trees that throw their shade over it, were planted by his son, Samuel Post 2d., about the year 1750.

### READ.

John Read obtained a grant of land for a homelot in New London, soon after 1750. It is probable that Josiah, of Norwich, was his son. The marriage of Josiah Read and Grace Halloway, took place in 1666. They had eight children. The sons were Josiah, William, John and Joseph. Josiah Read senior, was living in 1699. Josiah jun. married Elizabeth Armsden, in 1697. He died in 1717. This family appear to have removed at an early period to Newent Society, now Lisbon. The above-mentioned John died there in 1768, aged about ninety.

### REYNOLDS.

John Reynolds appears to have removed to Saybrook from Massachusetts; and probably came to this country as early as 1635. He died in 1702. He had eleven children, of whom three sons lived to the age of manhood : John born anterior to the settlement in 1655 ; Joseph, in March, 1660; the very period of the removal; Stephen, 1682.

### ROYCE.

Jonathan Royce was married at Saybrook, March, 1660, to Deborah, daughter of Hugh Calkins. The births of two children are recorded : Elizabeth, born January, 1661; John, 1663. The death of John in 1720, is mentioned, and the name then disappears from the records.

### SMITH.

We learn from Winthrop's letters to his son, the younger John Winthrop, that a Henry Smith was with the latter at Saybrook, in 1636. In 1652, Nehemiah Smith was an inhabitant of New London, whither Winthrop had removed, and continued there long after the plantation of Norwich. The Nehemiah Smith of the latter place, may have been son of the former. Only two children of Mr. Smith have been traced ; Obadiah, who married Martha Abell in 1700, and a daughter married to Joshua Abell. January 12, 1684, Nehemiah and Ann Smith made over their homestead and other property to their son-in-law, Joshua Abell, stip-

ulating only for a maintenance during life, they being
"in an infirm and weakly state."

Capt. Obadiah Smith died in 1727. His grave-stone
bears this quaint epitaph :—

> And now beneath these carved stones,
> Rich treasure lies,—dear Smith, his bones.

### TRACY.

In January, 1637, Thomas Tracy, "ship-carpenter,"
was received as an inhabitant of Salem, Mass. He is
supposed to have removed to Saybrook as early as
1639. His name frequently appears upon the records
of the General Court at Hartford, after 1644. In the
company of Norwich proprietors he ranked high, having more education than most of them, and being in
ability, enterprize and integrity, equal with the first.
He officiated on all important committees, and as surveyor, moderator, and townsman; and between Oct.,
1662, and July, 1684, was twenty-seven times chosen
Deputy to the General Court. He was also ensign of
the train-band, and after 1678, in the Commission of
the Peace. Even in those days of simplicity, Mr.
Tracy is usually mentioned with some adjunct indicating respect or the possession of office ; but as "Lieft-
anant Thomas Tracy," he was best known. This title
was acquired from the rank he held in Capt. Avery's
company of dragoons, raised in New London County
in 1673. He died Nov. 7, 1685.

Mr. Tracy brought with him from Saybrook six sons
and one daughter, but as no reference has been found
to his wife, it is inferred that she was then dead. In
1679 he married Martha, the widow of John Bradford.
His children were John, Jonathan, Thomas, Solomon,
Daniel, Samuel and Miriam. He and his six sons were

for several years all active men together. The order of his children, as to age, has not been ascertained.

John, being ranked as a proprietor, and having a homelot laid out with the others in 1659, was undoubtedly the eldest. If, however, all the children of Mr. Tracy were born at Saybrook, as seems most probable, we can scarcely reckon him more than twenty years of age at the era of the plantation. He was made a freeman by the General Court at Hartford in 1671; his brother Solomon in 1685. Young men at that day were not qualified to vote as soon as they attained their majority. They were obliged to acquire a character, and possess a certain amount of property, before they could become electors.

John Tracy married in 1670, Mary, daughter of the Hon. Josiah Winslow, of Plymouth—a stately and beautiful woman, according to tradition. He died in 1703. His widow in 1721. A deed conveying a parcel of land to his son, John Tracy jun., was signed by him Dec. 30, 1702. Their children were,

| | | | |
|---|---|---|---|
| John, | born 1672. | Joseph, | born 1682. |
| Elizabeth, | " 1675. | Winslow, | " 1689. |

Jonathan and Thomas Tracy settled upon a tract of land east of the Shetucket, purchased by their father from the Indians. It was afterwards included in the town of Preston, of which town Jonathan was the first Town Clerk. He married in 1672, Mary, daughter of Lt. Francis Griswold.

Solomon Tracy, whom we conjecturally reckon the fourth son of Lieut. Thomas, was married in 1678, to Sarah Huntington, who died in 1683. His second wife was Sarah, the widow of Thomas Sluman, whom he married in 1686. Mr. Solomon Tracy died in 1732.

Daniel Tracy married in 1682, Abigail Adgate, sister by the mother's side, to Joseph and Richard Bushnell.

Mr. Tracy was killed in the year 1728, with several others, by the falling of the frame work of a bridge, which the inhabitants were engaged in building over Shetucket river. He was then in the 76th year of his age, which gives 1652 for the date of his birth. This is the only one of the family whose age has been ascertained.

Samuel Tracy died in 1693, unmarried.

The descendants of Lieut. Thomas Tracy are very numerous, and widely dispersed. In 1779, there were twenty-four families of the name in Norwich, numbering about one hundred and eighty persons.

### WADE.

Robert Wade, very soon after the settlement, transferred his homelot to Caleb Abell. His son married Abigail Royce, in 1691. The family has not been traced any farther.

### WATERMAN.

There was a Thomas Waterman at Roxbury, Mass. in 1641, who died there in 1676. The identity of name leads to the conjecture that Thomas Waterman, of Saybrook, and afterwards of Norwich, was his son. He married in 1668, Miriam, daughter of Lieut. Thomas Tracy, by whom he had ten children. The sons were Thomas, born 1670, John, 1672, and Joseph, 1685. Both father and son are successively styled in the records, *Ensign* Thomas Waterman. The name was soon extensively spread in the vicinity of the town plot.

### WALLIS.

Of Richard Wallis and Richard Hendy, nothing certain has been gleaned. The latter died soon after the settlement. His children are mentioned as orphans in 1672.

# CHAPTER XI.

### BREWSTER.

MR. BENJAMIN BREWSTER was a grandson of the venerated elder William Brewster, of May Flower memory. Jonathan, the third son of the Elder, removed to New London, where, in 1649, he was acting as one of the townsmen. His son Benjamin was old enough to convey a tract of land by deed in 1654, and in 1659 was married, at New London, to Anna Dart. He removed to Norwich very soon after the settlement. The birth of his daughter Anne is recorded there Sept. 1662. His sons were

Jonathan, born 1664.     William, born 1669.
Daniel,    "    1667.     Benjamin, "    1673.

Mr. Brewster was an active and highly respected member of the infant plantation. In 1693, he succeeded Mr. Burchard as Commissioner of the Peace. His descendants are still to be found in Norwich and its vicinity. In 1779 there were eleven families of this name in East Society.

The venerable Mr. Seabury Brewster, now living in Norwich City, and one of the patriarchs of the place, is not, however, descended from *Benjamin*, but from *Wrestling*, the second son of Elder Brewster. He was born at Plymouth, in 1755, and emigrated to Norwich when about twenty-two years of age. He is the father of Sir Christopher Brewster, an eminent dentist who has resided a number of years in Paris and Petersburg, and has been knighted by the emperor of Russia.

## LATHROP.

Samuel Lathrop was an inhabitant of New London in 1648, and perhaps earlier. He and John Elderkin appear to have been in partnership as master builders. The second meeting-house in New London and the first in Norwich were built by contract with them. Mr. Lathrop removed to Norwich in 1668, having purchased the homelot of Elderkin. He is found on record as constable the same year, and acted afterwards in various public capacities.

Mr. Lathrop was the son of the Rev. John Lathrop, of England, a man of great piety and varied adventures. He was minister of Egerton, in Kent, before 1624, and afterwards preached in London, as successor to Mr. Jacob, in the first Congregational church organized in England. After suffering two years imprisonment in England for non-conformity, he was released, and came to America in 1634. In this country he was highly esteemed, being the first minister of Scituate, and afterwards of Barnstable. Four sons came with him from England, of whom Samuel was the second. Samuel had nine children. His sons were—

John,    born 1646.        Israel,  born 1659.
Samuel,  "    1650.        Joseph,  "    1661.

Mr. Lathrop died Feb. 19, 1700. His wife, Abigail, [her maiden name has not been ascertained,] survived him nearly thirty-five years, having lived into her 104th year. On the completion of her century, Jan. 13, 1732, the Rev. Mr. Lord preached a sermon in her room, at the house of her son.

This name is frequently spelt in the records Lotrop;

an orthography about on a par with that occasionally used for Leffingwell, viz : Leppinwell.

In 1779 there were twenty four families of the name of Lathrop in the Town Plot society, and that of West Farms.

### ELDERKIN.

John Elderkin, carpenter and miller, the first proprietor of the Cove, emigrated to America in 1637. He came first to Lynn, and went from thence to Dedham. We next find him at New London, where, in 1650, he had a houselot, and a tract of meadow and upland laid out to him.

In 1654 he entered into a contract with the Saybrook company, who were planning the settlement of Norwich, to erect a mill for them. This was subsequently renewed, and the stipulations on both sides performed. He was accepted as an inhabitant of Norwich in 1663, and a homelot laid out to him next to Mr. Adgate's. This he alienated to his friend and partner, Samuel Lathrop, and removed to the vicinity of the Mill. Though residing in Norwich, he still continued occasionally both to *build* and to *grind* in New London, as the early records of that town testify. He died June 18, 1716, aged 95. His sons were—

John, born 1664. Joseph, born 1672.
James, " 1671.

John Elderkin the second died in 1737, leaving three sons, Jedidiah, John and Joshua. One of these was the keeper of the first public house at Chelsea. The name has since been a noted one in Windham. One of the last who bore it in Norwich was a pilot, who died in 1821, aged 82.

11

Settlements were early made east of the Shetucket. Some of the first planters in that quarter were Samuel Starr, Robert Roath, Samuel Andrews, Josiah Rockwell, John Glover, and Grinfield Larrabee.    Mr. Rockwell came from Windsor, and is supposed to have been brother to Ruth, wife of Christopher Huntington.    He died in 1675, about three years after his removal.    His son, Josiah Rockwell 2d, on arriving at manhood, obtained a grant of land, which is described as lying "east of the Great River;" and in 1718 an additional tract was given him by the town, " on account of his sheep concerns."    He was married in 1688, to Anne, daughter of Thomas Bliss, by whom he had two sons, Daniel and John.

The name of Capt. Josiah Standish appears upon record as early as 1686, as owner of a farm east of the Shetucket.    He was a son of Miles Standish, the famous hero of New Plymouth.    He is supposed to have had in his possession the sword of his father, and though the house in which he lived was destroyed by fire, this relic was preserved.    After several times changing hands, it was obtained by the late T. W. Williams, Esq., of Lebanon, and by him deposited in its most appropriate place, Pilgrim Hall, in Plymouth. Mr. Williams took great pains to trace the history of this sword, and was satisfied that he had established its claims to be the genuine weapon, both hilt and blade, with which Capt. Standish was accustomed to do battle with the Indians.    But the same honor has been claimed, and it is said upon as good authority, by another sword, preserved among the collections of the Mass. Hist. Soc.    It is not improbable that a person who had so much fighting to do as Capt. Standish, both in the old and new world, might have had two swords, that passed as heir-looms to different branches of his family.

The marriage of Greenfield Larrabee to Alice Youngs, is recorded in 1673. Their sons were Thomas, John and Nathaniel. Mr. Greenfield died in 1739.

Samuel Andrews probably came from Saybrook, and may have been brother to the wives of John Birchard and Thomas Post. In 1779 there were eight families of this name in East Society.

Robert Roath was from New London, where either himself or father had a houselot and other land granted him in 1650.

John Glover married in 1682. His descendants remained in the town for a century or more, but have since dispersed. The Hon. James Glover of Ottawa, Illinois, was of this family, and a native of Norwich. He removed in early life to Illinois, and aided in the first settlement of that State. He died in 1840, in the 73rd year of his age.

Other names which occur at a very early period, are Thomas Sloman or Sluman, Thomas Rood, Caleb and Joshua Abell, Jonathan Rudd, Jonathan Crane, Stephen Merrick, Hugh Amos, Jonathan Jennings, Caleb Forbes, David Knight, Owen Williams, Edward Culver, Timothy Allen, John Hough, Frederick Ellis, Richard Cooke, Peter Cross, Benjamin and Jonathan Armstrong, Matthew Coy, William Moore. These all appear within the first ten or twelve years of the plantation, and may be ranked as first settlers. Most of them were farmers, and settled in those parts of the town now included in Bozrah and Franklin.

Joseph and Richard Bushnell may be reckoned among the first class of planters. They belonged to the company of proprietors, though at the period of the settlement they were minors in the family of John Holmstead, whose wife is supposed to have been sister to their mother. Mrs. Bushnell's maiden name was Mary Marvyn; she was the daughter of Matthew and Elizabeth Marvyn, who came to New England in 1635, and settled at Hartford. She was six years of age at the time she arrived with her parents, and in 1648 married Richard Bushnell of Saybrook, by whom she had two sons, Richard and Joseph, the former born late in 1651, and the latter early in 1653. Mrs. Bushnell afterwards married deacon Thomas Adgate, by whom she had several daughters and one son.

Richard Bushnell married in 1672, Elizabeth, daughter of Mr. Adgate, by a former marriage. They had two sons, Caleb, born 1679, Benajah, in 1681.

Joseph Bushnell was married in 1673, to Mary, daughter of Thomas Leffingwell. Their sons were Joseph, born 1677, Jonathan, 1679, and Nathan, 1686.

Mrs. Mary Bushnell died March 31st, 1748, in the ninety-second year of her age.

Mr. Joseph Bushnell died Dec. 23, 1748, in the ninety-sixth year of his age.

In the earlier part of the eighteenth century, Richard Bushnell was one of the most noted and active men in Norwich. After arriving at man's estate, we find him taking a prominent part in almost every enterprise that was set on foot in the place.

In 1686 he obtained a grant of privilege—"to take fish in Showtucket river, and to make weares there, for that purpose." This privilege extended from the mouth of the Shetucket to the crotch of the Quinebaug, and was to continue for seven years. He managed a farm also upon the Great Plains, but had his residence in the town plot, where he performed successively, if not contemporaneously, the duties of townsman, constable, school-master, poet, deacon, sergeant, lieutenant and captain, town-agent, town deputy, court-clerk, and justice of the peace.

As a school-master he was highly esteemed. The school continued only during the winter months, and whenever the payment received from his scholars was represented deficient, the town remunerated him with a piece of land.

As a military man, it is probable that he had seen some actual service in scouting against the Indians, and was useful in exercising the train-bands. The first Mondays in May and September were days of general militia muster, or training days, as they were usually called. These in Norwich, as elsewhere, were always days of festivity. No one was so poor as not to regale his family with training-cake and beer at those times. In 1708 a new start was taken in improving the appearance and exercise of the trainers. " Drums, *holbarts*, and a pair of colours," were purchased for them.

As a clerk, Mr. Bushnell exhibited an improvement upon the old forms of writing and spelling ; and as a justice, he decided numerous cases of debt and trespass, both for Norwich and the neighboring towns. The fine at this time for profane swearing, was ten shillings, or to sit two hours in the stocks  In 1720, there is a record which shows that Dr. Samuel Law was presented for using an oath in conversation, and obliged to pay the penalty. The next year Henry Holland, of Plainfield, was proved guilty of the same trespass, and adjudged in the same manner to pay the fine and cost ; the latter amounted to 2*s* 2*d*. The same Henry Holland was also bound over to appear at the

11*

next County Court, and answer for breaking the peace and the law, by saying " in a tumultuous violent threatening manner, yt he would take the head of Jona$^n$ Tracy off his shoulders."

An Indian being found drunk, was brought before Mr. Justice Bushnell, and sentenced according to the statute, namely, to pay a fine of ten shillings, or receive ten lashes on his naked body. The Indian immediately accuses Samuel Bliss of selling him that afternoon that which made him drunk, to wit, two pots of cider. The fine for selling cider or ardent spirits to an Indian, was twenty shillings, one half to go to the complainant. The Indian thus obtained just the sum requisite to pay his own mulct, and set his body clear. The record of this affair is as follows :

" Feb. ye 7—1722-3. Apenanucsuck being drunk was brought before me R. Bushnell, Justice of ye peace. I do sentence ye sd Apeonuchsuck for his transgression of ye law to pay a fine of 10s. or to be whipt ten Lashes on y$^e$ naked body, and to pay y$^u$ cost of his prosecution, and to continue in y$^e$ constable's custody till this sentence be performed.

Cost allowed is 6s 6.

John Waterman promises to pay 6s 4.

Apeanuchsuck accused Samuel Bliss y$^t$ he sold him 2 pots of cider this afternoon. Mr. Samuel Bliss appeared before me and confessed he let sd Indian have some cider and I do therefore sentence sd Bliss to pay y$^e$ fine of 20s. for y$^e$ transgression of y$^e$ law one half to y$^e$ town and one half to complainant.                    R. BUSHNELL, Justice."

Some other extracts from Mr. Bushnell's record may here be given.

" 3rd of June 1708. Joseph Bushnell of Norwich complained against himself to me Richard Bushnell, Justice of the Peace, for y$^t$ he had killed a Buck contrary to law. I sentenced him to pay a fine of 10s. one half to y$^e$ county treasury and one half to complainant."

"July 20, 1720. Samuel Sabin appeareth before me R. B. Justice of the Peace, and complaineth against himself that the last Sabbath at night, he and John Olmsby went on to Wawwecoas Hill, to visit their relations, and were late home, did no harm, and fears it may be a transgression of y<sup>e</sup> law and if it be is very sorry for it and dont allow himself in unseasonable night-walking."

"An inferior Court held at Norwich y<sup>e</sup> 19. Sept. 1720. Present R. Bushnell Justice of y<sup>e</sup> Peace. Samuel Fox juror pr. complaint, Lettis Minor and Hannah Minor P'ts. for illegally and feloniously about y<sup>e</sup> 6 of Sept<sup>r</sup> inst. taking about 30 water-milions which is contrary to Law and is to his damage he saith y<sup>e</sup> sum of 20s. and prays for justice. This Court having considered y<sup>e</sup> evidence dont find matter of fact proved, do therefore acquit the Dts. and order y<sup>e</sup> Ptf. pay the charge of presentment."

Mr. Bushnell died in 1727, aged 75. His son, Capt. Caleb Bushnell, was also an active and enterprizing citizen, though he did not reside upon the town plot. Glimpses of his course are now and then obtained from the records; as—

"Dec 28, 1714. Granted to Capt. Calib Bushnell a convenient place for building vessels on the west side of the river opposite the old landing place."

"1723. The town grants liberty to Capt. Calib Bushnell to set up and maintain two sufficient cart gates across the high-way that goeth to the Little Fort."

His grave-stone says—

"Here lyeth what was mortal of that worthy gentleman, Capt. Caleb Bushnell, son to Capt. Richard Bushnell Esq. who died Feb. 18, 1724, aged 46 years, 8 months and 23 days."

# CHAPTER XII.

THE town expenses at this period were usually for
perambulating and stating bounds, laying out highways, plank for bridges, and the bounty on killing
birds and snakes.  Exclusive of this last item, the annual demands upon the treasury, frequently fell below
£10.  The expenses arising out of the difficulties that
existed with neighboring towns, on account of boundaries, added some years greatly to this amount.  There
was an ever open quarrel respecting a tract of land
south of the Norwich and north of the New London
line, with the Indians or individual settlers.  The disputes with Preston were still more perplexing and
acrimonious.  They commenced in 1695, and continued for nearly a century, being a constant source of
litigation, trouble and expense ; but as it would neither
be interesting nor profitable to enter into these harass-
ing affairs, the whole will be passed over with only
this slight notice.

### List of Town Debts.    Dec. 30. 1718.

|  | £ | s. | d. |
|---|---|---|---|
| To John Tracy for killing 4 snakes, - - | 0 | 0 | 8 |
| Th. Leffingwell Jr.      6   do -      - | 0 | 1 | 0 |
| Elisha Waterman 67 birds -      -      - | 0 | 2 | 9½ |
| John Rood         24   do      -      - | 0 | 1 | 0 |
| Jabez Hide 5 snakes -      -      -      - | 0 | 0 | 10 |
| Th. Bingham 4 snakes and drumming | 1 | 0 | 8 |
| Th. Leffingwell Jr, one day to meet New London Committee      -      -      - | 0 | 5 | 0 |

|  | £ | s. | d. |
|---|---|---|---|
| Joseph Reynolds for a plank  -  - | 0 | 1 | 0 |
| Solomon Tracy one day on Committee | 0 | 5 | 0 |
| Charges about Preston Line  -  - | 6 | 13 | 10 |
| Several persons for perambulating at 3s. pr day each. | | | |

Public improvements were usually made by the general labor of the citizens, or by individuals who assumed the job and were compensated by a grant of land.

In 1704, Eleazer Burnham, set up a fulling mill " near Showtucket, by the Chemical Spring," and had twenty acres of land given him for his encouragement. From some cause or other, this enterprize did not succeed. The same year, Mr. Edmonds of Providence, a blacksmith, was formally invited by the town, to remove thither, and a place to work in and coals provided for his use, one blacksmith being then insufficient for the town's convenience.

Occasionally, we find a town expenditure for military equipments, and for " ammunition, with the charge of bringing it up from New London."

In 1720, John and Simon Tracy, were appointed by the town, " to make search for the Towne Armes, with their magazeans of amunition and other accotrements for war, injoyned by law," who reported as follows :

At Lieut. Tracy's, two guns and two pair of snow shoes.
" Samuel Fales', one gun.
" Lieut. Bushnell's one gun, one barrel of powder, and seventeen lbs. of lead.
At Lieut. Backus', 344 lbs. of bullets.
" Ensign Leffingwell's, one barrel of powder.
" Deacon Simon Huntington's half barrel of powder, thirty-one lb. bullets, and 400 flints.
At Simon Tracy's, one pair of snow shoes, and 4 pr. of maugosuns.
" We ware also informed, (say the Committee,) that there

was formerly lent to Mr. John Leffingwell, pr Lieut. Bushnell, seventy-one lbs. of Led, which said Leffingwell was
obliged to pay in Bullits, y<sup>e</sup> same quantity.   All y<sup>e</sup> Led and
Bullits 523 pound.                          JOHN TRACY,
                                            SIMON TRACY."

Very rarely at this period, do we find any person
so poor as to require the assistance of the town.   There
is however, now and then, such a charge as " a pair
of shoes for alice Cook, 5s.," " a coat and leather
breeches, for old Russell 12s.," " a sheet to bury John
Nickols in 10s.," duly entered in the town books.   In
1723, great amazement seems to have been excited in
the townsmen, by what they designate " the extraordinary charge of Henry Wallbridge Jr. for entertayneing
Christian Challenge in her late sickness and distraction
at his house."   Yet the whole charge for eight weeks
" nursing, diet, and strengthening salve," going for
doctors, four days waiting and tending, and finally conveying her to Windham, amounts only to £3 5s. 6d.
Dr. Calib Bushnell's bill "tords the cure of Christian
Challenge," stands thus, and will show what a physician's fees then were :

|                         |          |
| ----------------------- | -------- |
| To 3 travells           | £0 7 6   |
| to Lusisalig Bolsum,    | 0 4 0    |
| to 3 times bleeding     | 0 1 6    |

This poor woman appears to have been a traveller,
tramper, or transient person, as wandering beggars are
indifferently called in New England, who was " rode
over by Solomon Story on the Sabbath day, either wil-
fully or carelessly," and being very much hurt, was
for some time a burden on the town.

At one time the town seems to have been greatly
bothered with the trouble and expense of maintaining
a poor *Ediote*, or as it is spelt in another place, *Edj-*

*nuett*, named Peter Davison, but the case was at last aid before the General Court, and relief obtained.

Down to the period of 1730, a rate of half penny on the pound, was sufficient to liquidate all the current expenses.

It may be interesting to note the prices of a few articles in the earlier part of this century :

| | |
|---|---|
| Wheat 5s. pr. bushel. | Cheese 4d. pr lb. |
| Rye 3s. " | Tallow 5d. |
| Indian corn, " | Sugar 6d. and 8d. |
| Oats 1s 6. " | Molasses 2s. 4d. per gall. |
| Turnips, 1s. 0. " | Quire of paper, 2s. |
| Milk 1½d. pr qt. | pane of glass, 2s. 3d. |
| Wool, 1s. 4d. per lb. | pair of shoes 5s. and 5s. 6. |
| Beef 2d. per lb. | day's work of laborer 2s. and |
| Pork 3d. and 3½. | 3s. |
| Butter 6d. | day's work with a team 6s. |

Town Clerk's salary, £1. 10s.
A meal of victuals at a tavern 6d. or 8d.
A bowl of toddy, 6d.
A bell rope, 3s.
A barber's charge for once shaving, 2d.—a year's shaving, £1.
" A fals tail," (copied from a Barber's account,) 3s.

In 1702, the town ordered that the Law Books on hand, should be sold for 18d. a piece.

Benajah Bushnell sent by the town to New Haven, to appear in their behalf, before the General Court, absent twelve days, his whole account amounted to £2 10.

The following memorandums are in some degree illustrative of this period :

" Sarah Vincent of Norwich, her portion of the property of her father John Post, who died in 1704."

Here is mentioned sundry parcels of land at Connecticut Plains and elsewhere, neither extent nor value expressed.

Received as her marriage portion £5.
at his death 1 spade,      3s.      iron ware      5s.
            2 augurs      2s.      an old Bible 2s.
            one platter   4s.      pewter          4s.

The account of Thomas Blythe, 1726, for tending of Josiah Guiller.
        12 dayes tendaning, [3s. 6. per daye, £2,2 0

Benjamin Slam's Sheriffs Bill of Charge on Nathaniel Otios.
        To my travell 18 miles at 3½d.   £0 5 9
        To my tendence at cort,              0 1 0
        To the Corts fees, 2s. 8.              2 8
                                              ————
                                          £ 0 9 5
            allowed, R. B. Justice.

Constable's Bill.    Abiall Marshall contra Nath¹. Gore.
        To yᵉ writt                      £0 0 8
            yᵉ constable's fees           0 3
            yᵉ Courts fees                0 2 8
            yᵉ plaintiffs attendance      0 1
                                         ——— —
                                         £0 7 4
This bill of cost is allowed, R. Bushnell, Justice.

The following is a sample of simplicity and disinterestedness, in making out a bill :

"Dec. 16 day 1745.  The town is Dr. to me Jacob Hide for 208 feet of 2 inch plank improved to make and mend bridges by order of the surveyor of highways.  The price of said 208 feet of plank I think must be about 30s. more or less as the town thinks fit."

Voted, that the selectmen pay Jacob Hide what is just.

# CHAPTER XIII.

In addition to their droves of neat cattle and swine, and flocks of sheep, the inhabitants at one time turned their attention to the keeping of goats. Herds of these troublesome animals roamed at large, until they became an intolerable nuisance. No law of the colony then existed for their restraint. Joseph Tracy, in 1722, having taken up a herd of fifty-four goats trespassing upon his land, impounded them : whereupon their owner, Joseph Backus, bought a suit against him before Mr. Justice Bushnell, which was decided as follows :

"This Court having heard and considered the pleas on both sides in this action, and also the law quoted to, and finding in the last paragraph in said law it is said, ' all neat cattle and horses taken &c. shall pay 8d. per head, and swine 12d. and sheep 1d. per head' and nothing in said law concerning goats, this Court cannot find any thing allowed in the law for impounding of goats and therefore this Court consider that the plaintiff shall recover of the defendant his cost of prosecution."

The defendant appeals from this judgment to the County Court to be holden at New London in June next.

Nothing further appears upon record respecting goats, but the following item :

"At a General Court at Hartford May 15, 1725, the representatives of Norwich, having laid before this court, that
12

the act respecting Goats, October last, is very grievous to
their town, this Court grants liberty to said town to except
themselves out of said act :—This town do now by their
vote, except themselves out of said act."

The lands upon the Yantic, at the time of the settlement, were greatly infested with wolves and foxes.
Settling in the midst of them would very soon lead to
their extirmination, or expulsion; and this is said to
have been one motive which actuated the proprietors
in their choice of the first location. Long after the
settlement, a bear or a wolf were occasionally seen,
coming from the woods towards their old haunts, and
on finding themselves near the habitations of man,
they have rushed forward, terrified and causing terror,
till they found a secure refuge in the uncleared swamps
that still in some places skirted the river.

In the early stages of the settlement, therefore, the
craft of the hunter, the trapper, and the sportsman,
was pursued from necessity instead of pastime. Depredations upon the fold and the barnyard were often
made, not only by the animals named, but by another
popularly called the *Woolleneeg*, or Sampson Fox, which
is still occasionally seen in the wilder parts of New
England. But these and all the smaller mischievous
quadrupeds, were in a few years either entirely driven
away or reduced so greatly in number as to be seldom
troublesome. Birds and snakes were not so readily
vanquished, and it was necessary to offer rewards and
bounties for their destruction.

A half penny per head was first granted for each
and every blackbird and crow killed; their heads to be
exhibited by the claimant to one of the townsmen;
and two pence a piece for all rattlesnakes killed between the fifteenth of April and the first of May, the
tail, and a bit of the bone to be received as evidence.

The last fifteen days of April was therefore the season appropriated to hunting the rattlesnake, and the people turned out for this purpose in large parties.

Notwithstanding the smallness of the bounty, so many birds and snakes were killed every year, that it became a considerable item in the town expenses. The bounty for killing a wolf was 10s 6, ($1 75.) This appears to have been claimed but once after 1700, viz. by Samuel Lotrop.

No better haunts for rattlesnakes could be found than among the rocks and glens of Norwich. Imagination still associates the idea of these formidable reptiles with many a dark ravine and sunny ledge. There are certain rocks and declivities that even yet are known by such names as Rattlesnake-den and Rattlesnake-ridge. They grew here to the size of a man's wrist, and to the length of three and four feet.

There is a tradition that an adventurous lover, returning home late one evening from a visit to the lady of his heart, was both snapped at by a wolf and hissed at by a rattlesnake, just as he passed through a turnstile, near the place now known as Strong's corner. There was then no road through the wood on the river side of the square, but only a footpath. The road this way is still called by aged people of the vicinity "The Grove." This young man, whose name was Waterman, lived above the meeting-house, and the lady he visited, below the Little Plain. To walk two miles at that period, through thicket and swamp, to make an evening visit, and back again at midnight, was an undertaking almost equal in heroism to that of swimming over the Hellespont.

In the spring of 1721, the bounty was claimed for killing one hundred and sixty snakes. In the hope of eradicating them by an extra effort, in 1730, the bounty was raised for that year to two shillings a piece : three hundred were killed in fifteen days, and the law was successively renewed for four years.

In 1735, twenty pounds were paid out of the treasury for killing snakes. The bounty was then reduced to four pence. A large number were killed that year also, if we may judge from the memorandum of one of the selectmen, of those that were exhibited to him :

" May, 1736—An account of rattlesnakes tails brought in to me, Joseph Perkins.

| | | | |
|---|---|---|---|
| Jacob Perkins | brought | 7 | tails. |
| Thomas Pettis, | " | 5 | " |
| Samuel Lawrence brought | | 3 | rattles. |
| Abijah Fitch, | " | 1 | " |
| John Bingham, | " | 3 | " |
| Robert Kinsman, | " | 4 | " |
| Joshua Hutchins, | " | 23 | " |
| Ezra Lothrup, | " | 2 | " |

In 1739 the bounty was again raised to ten shillings a head for all killed, except in the months of June, July and August; provided that the killer took oath that he went out for no other purpose than to destroy them. Among those who claimed the bounty, we frequently find the names of females. The Widow Woodworth was one year paid for twenty-three and the widow Smith for nine. At another time the bounty was claimed for killing one, by *David Hartshorn* 4th, whom we may suppose to have been a child of very tender age. One can almost fancy, that like the infant Hercules, he strangled the serpent in his cradle. Simon Huntington, a grandson of the first settler of that name, while engaged in haying, at the Great Plains, was bitten by a rattlesnake, and died in consequence. This was in July, 1707; the young man was twenty-one years of age.

Waweekus Hill was famous for these reptiles. It is said that a cunning player on the violin, once went on to that hill with his instrument, and enticed a large one to follow him into the town street, fascinated by his music.

We find no legislation on the subject of rattlesnakes, after the year 1764, at which time the bounty of twenty shillings, old tenor, was commuted into six shillings lawful money. It is believed that the last rattlesnake of Norwich was destroyed in 1786. His traces had been often observed, and his haunt sought, but without success. He dwelt under a large rock, and his hole had an outlet on both sides, with a branch in another direction to which he could retreat, so that it was a work of some difficulty to outwit him. But he was at last both "scotch'd" and killed.

The Red Snake, vulgarly called the Rattlesnake's mate, also abounded in Norwich, and is still occasionally found. It is very beautiful in color, being of a chocolate or deep purple, mottled with the richest red. It draws up, leaps, and bites, in the space of two seconds, and it is said, will reach the flesh through a thin boot. The wound is followed by immediate pain, swelling, and great inflammation. Instances have occurred in which it has become serious, by neglect, improper treatment, and exposure to cold and wet, breaking forth afresh every year in the snake season, and causing lameness or other infirmities.

The Black snake is now rare and comparatively harmless ; but stories are current of these reptiles having attacked children in the whortleberry fields, or haymakers in the meadows, and wound themselves about the body and throat, so as to produce suffocation. When Waweekus Hill was first cleared, the workmen were greatly annoyed by them. There is a tradition to the
12*

following effect :—A party of laborers were out on the
hill at work, and one of them being employed at some
distance from the other, his companions were suddenly
alarmed by his cries and shrieks for help.  They ran
to his assistance, and found him rolling on the ground
with several black snakes on his body.  He stated
after his rescue, that these reptiles came upon him out
of a thicket, with such fury as to put it out of his power
to defend himself.  They wound about his legs, lashed
them together, bound up his arms, and were near his
throat when his friends came to his assistance.  No
attempt will be made to prove the truth of this story,
but doubtless it is as well founded as that of Laocoon.
Supposing the man to have been asleep, when the
reptiles swathed his limbs, it is not impossible.

One species of black snake, which formerly infested
this region, was called Ring-snake, or *racer*, and was
known by a white or yellow ring around the neck.
They would erect the head seven or eight inches from
the ground, and in this attitude, with tongue out, and
eyes glaring, run with the swiftness of a horse.  They
were bold, fierce, and dangerous.  It was this species
which was remarkable for winding about the limbs.  -

# CHAPTER XIV.

Bell. Meeting-House. Ecclesiastical Dissensions. Councils. Ministers Woodward and Lord. Deacons.

In 1708 the town was presented with a bell by Capt. René Grignon, a French Protestant, who had come up the river for the purposes of trade, and who resided awhile at the landing-place, being accepted as an inhabitant in 1710. A vote of thanks was tendered to the generous Captain, and the bell being conveyed to the meeting-house plain, was ordered "*to be hung in the hill between the ends of the town*," and to be rung on the Sabbath, and on all public days, and at nine o'clock every evening. The phrase *in the hill* is a rather doubtful one; but probably the bell was suspended from a scaffolding, on the rocks that overlook the plain, that it might be heard in all parts of the town. Salary of the bellman, who was also to sweep the meeting-house, £5, 10*s*. per annum.

In 1710 a vote was passed to build a new meeting-house, but a long and vehement dispute arose with respect to its location. One party was for having it stand on the site of the old one upon the hill; the other on the plain. Both sides were exceedingly violent and obstinate, and for two or three years the whole town was absorbed by the question. At length they agreed to submit it to three impartial gentlemen of Lebañon. Capt. Wm. Claık, Mr. Wm. Halsey, and Mr. Samuel Huntington were designated as umpires. These persons came to Norwich, examined the premises with care, heard all that either party had to allege, and after due deliberation recommended that it should be built on the plain. But the town refused to concur, and after two or three alternate votes, and much bitter contention, decided that they would have it on the hill, and the building was there commenced. Nothing further respecting it appears upon the records of the town or society, but there is reason to infer from other testimony that the plan was soon abandoned, and the house finally built upon the plain.

John Elderkin, 2nd, was the architect of this church, as his father was of the former. After its completion he presented his petition, stating that he had suffered considerable loss by his agreement, and praying "the worthy gentlemen of the town to make some retaliation." He was accordingly relieved by a grant of fifty acres of land.

The expense of this edifice was mainly defrayed by sales of land. A meeting-house committee was in the first place appointed, who offered land in lieu of money to be advanced for the work. Capt. Grignon, among others, advanced small sums at several different times, and received in return four portions of land at the landing, viz: ten acres on both sides of Stony brook; five and a half acres on Waweekus hill; a quarter of an acre near the water; and four acres on the little plain at the N. W. corner of Waweekus hill.

Ensign Thomas Waterman, in consideration 1718.  of his labor and cost in providing stones for steps at the meeting-house doors, [this edifice had an entrance on three sides,] obtained a grant of twenty-two acres at the Landing Place. His price for said stones was 14s. It will further show the value of land at this period, to state Mr. Leffingwell's 1713.  agreement with the Committee. He advanced in money £6, 10s., for which he was to have "forty-three acres of rough land on the west side of the brook that runs into Shetucket river above Wequonuk island, at the Rattlesnake's house"; thirty-three acres at the north end of Plain hills, value £5; and six and a half acres of rough land near the Isinglass rock, value £1.

One of the fixtures of this meeting-house was an Hour-Glass, placed in a frame and made fast to the pulpit; [cost 2s. 8d.] This hour-glass, in 1729, was placed under the particular charge of Capt. Joseph Tracy, who was requested to see that it was duly turned when it ran out in service time, and that the time was kept between meetings; the bellman being charged to attend his orders herein.

Among those who were active in the business of the meeting-house, was Capt. Robert Denison. This gentleman's farm, which was very large, lay at the N. W. corner of Norwich, extending considerably over the line. His dwelling-house was at first supposed to lie within the bounds of the town, and the freemen chose him for their representative to the General Court. When the line was more accurately stated, he was cast into New London. This farm now lies partly in Bozrah and partly in Montville.

The old meeting-house was sold to Nathaniel Rudd, for £12 5s. 6d.; but the purchaser, afterwards representing to the town that he was "sick of his bargain," relief was granted.

In the new meeting-house, among the persons seated, we find mention made of Mrs. Sarah Knight, who has been noticed before. Aug. 12, 1717, the town by their vote, gave "liberty to Mrs. Sarah Knight, to sit in the pew where she used to sit."

Ecclesiastical dissensions about this time began to

rage in the society. In town meeting, 1714, a vote
was passed, declaratory of dissent from the new Platform of Church Discipline, and complaints presented
against Mr. Woodward's " management in the ministry." Mr. Woodward was one of the delegates that
assisted in the formation of this Platform at Saybrook,
in 1708, and secretary to the Synod. Of course, he was
strenuous for its adoption by the church of which he
was pastor. But it was then very unpopular in Norwich ; and a warm contest between him and his flock
ensued. It is said that when he received the act of
the legislature, accepting and establishing the Platform as the ecclesiastical constitution of the colony, he
read off the first clause of it to his congregation, but
suppressed that part of it which allowed dissenters to
regulate their worship in their own way. Whereupon
the representatives of the town, Richard Bushnell and
Joseph Backus, rose in their seats and laid the whole
act before the people. A vote of the church was however obtained for the adoption of the Platform, upon
which the two gentlemen mentioned above and many
others withdrew from the church and held meetings on
the Sabbath by themselves. They had, moreover, the
influence and address to obtain the following vote, le-
galizing their meetings :

> " This town grants liberty to those that are dis-
> Dec. 16, satisfied with the Rev. Mr. Woodward's manage-
> 1714. ment in the ministry to call another minister to
> preach to them at their own charge until the dif-
> ficulties they labor under are removed."

A protest against the vote was signed by eighteen
persons. The minister and major part of the church
considered these measures highly reprehensible, and
made such representations to the Assembly at its next

session, that Messrs. Bushnell and Backus were formally expelled from that body.

A council was soon afterwards called to settle these difficulties ; and they had council after council for the space of six years. Mr. Saltonstall, then Governor of the Colony, visited them and used all his influence to bring about a reconciliation of parties and harmony of opinion ; but no compromise could be effected. Mr. Backus went to Boston, Ipswich and various other places to consult with the learned and pious upon this affair.

In 1715, a town vote was obtained to dismiss Mr. Woodward, forty-four to twenty-five ; but the contention then grew more violent than ever, and the inhabitants petitioned the General Court that they might be separated into two societies. This was not granted, but the Governor wrote them a letter of advice, recommending them to try the effect of another council. A body of the most respectable ministers in the country was accordingly convened : Mr. Stoddard, of Northampton, was appointed moderator. After long deliberation, the council recommended a dissolution of the connection with Mr. Woodward, and he was accordingly dismissed, Sept. 13, 1716.

Mr. Woodward was a native of Dedham, Mass. After settling in Norwich, he married in 1703, Mrs. Sarah Rosewell ; on which occasion "houseing and lands" were liberally provided for him by the 1711. town. He afterwards, requested an increase of salary, but it was refused. After his dismission, he ceased to preach, and retired to a farm which he owned in East Haven, where the Woodwards, his descendants, are still found. Before he left Norwich, however, the town sued him for damages on the parsonage lands, and for one quarter of a year's salary which had been overpaid him; a fact sufficiently indicative of the exasperated feeling that had been produced by these ecclesiastical dissensions.

A few weeks after the removal of Mr. Woodward, Mr. Benjamin Lord, a native of Saybrook, and a graduate of Yale college, then about twenty-four 1716. years of age, began to preach in Norwich. In June, the town appointed a day of fasting and prayer, to seek divine direction, in respect to giving him a call; the Rev. Messrs. Whiting of Windham, and Williams, of Lebanon, being invited to assist in the exercises of that occasion. Soon after this, by *a unanimous vote*, Mr. Lord was invited to become their minister, with the offer of £100 per annum for salary, with the use of the parsonage lands, and wood sufficient for his use, to be dropped at his door,—" provided he settle himself without charge to the town."

He was ordained Nov. 20, 1717; both parties uniting in their esteem for him, so that he was accustomed to say he could never tell which was most friendly to him. At his ordination, the Church explicitly renounced the Saybrook Platform, or code of faith.

The following members of Mr. Fitch's church were still alive:

| | |
|---|---|
| William Backus, | Joseph Lothrop, |
| Stephen Gifford, | John Elderkin, |
| Th. Leffingwell, | Caleb Abell, |
| Joseph Bushnell, | Joseph Reynolds, |
| Richard Bushnell, Esq., | Chr. Huntington, |
| Josiah Reed, | Simon Huntington, |
| Solomon Tracy, | Samuel Griswold, |
| Samuel Lothrop, | Nathaniel Backus. |

These, and fifteen others, received into the church

by Mr. Woodward, composed at this time the male members of the church.

The two deacons of Mr. Fitch's church, chosen before they removed from Saybrook, were Thomas Adgate and Hugh Calkins. With these was afterwards associated Simon Huntington, the elder. Towards the close of the century, Simon and Christopher Huntington, brothers, of the second generation of settlers, one born in 1659, and the other in 1660, were appointed to office; deacons Huntington and Adgate, being still alive, though aged and infirm. Soon after the ordination of Mr. Lord, the two Huntingtons having acted as deacons more than twenty years, two others were set apart to assist them, viz: Thomas Adgate and Thomas Leffingwell, both of the second generation. Mr. Leffingwell dying in 1724, his three venerable coadjutors requested that an entire new set of deacons might be designated to office. This was not done until after the death of the two Huntingtons, [Christopher in 1735, and Simon in 1736,] when their sons, Ebenezer, son to Simon, and Hezekiah, son to Christopher, were chosen to succeed them in conjunction with Mr. Adgate.

The venerable deacon Adgate born in the eighth year of the settlement, lived to be ninety-two years of age. His existence nearly covers the whole space from the settlement to the revolution.

No other deacons were appointed until 1764, when Simon Huntington, son of deacon Ebenezer, and Simon Tracy, Esq., were chosen and introduced into office, with great solemnity. Hands were imposed, and Dr. Lord preached on the occasion from 2 Tim. iii. 8, 9, 10. [Aug. 31.]

13

# CHAPTER XV.

Chelsea, or the Landing.  Bridges over the Shetucket.

CAPTS. James and Daniel Fitch appear to have been the first persons who began improvements at the Landing-place.  The former obtained from the town " a privilege four rods in breadth by the salt water," in 1668, when he was but nineteen years of age.  Little importance was then attached to this station, the chief trading points being at Trading Cove Point, on the river below the Landing, where, both before and after the settlement, a small trade had been carried on with the Indians, and on the Yantic Cove, both at Elderkin's mill, and farther down, just above the present Wharf Bridge.  These, for a number of years after the settlement, were the principal places of landing and deposite.  They were the old landing places that had been used by the Indians.

In 1685, Capt. James Fitch obtained a second grant at the Landing of a piece of ground to build upon, and the next year an additional spot for the conveniency of his ware-house.

In October, 1694, Mr. Mallat, a French gentleman, desired liberty to establish a ship yard, and build vessels upon the river, which was freely granted, with permission also to cut what wood he wanted from the Town's Commons east of Shetucket river.  There is no record of any farther improvements at the Landing previous to the year 1700.  The only road thither, led

Fisher.

E. B. & E.C. Kellogg.

PORT OF NORWICH.

through Mason's Swamp, thence across the Little Plain, and over Wawecos Hill, whence it came by a long, steep and dangerous descent to the water, with a branch leading to the Shetucket, where a ferry had been kept up ever since the year 1671, at first by Hugh Amos, and afterwards by Stephen Roath.

The greater part of the tract from the Little Plain to the Shetucket was a wilderness of rocks, woods, and swamps, with only here and there a cow path, or a sheep track around the hills; where the trunk of a fallen tree thrown over a brook or chasm served in lieu of bridge. Not only in the spring floods, but in common heavy rains, a great part of East Chelseâ, the Point where the Shetucket comes into the river, and all the lower, or Water street, up to the ledge of rocks on which the buildings upon the north side of that street are based, were overflowed; and even in the dry season these parts of the town were little better than swamps. What are now only moist places, and slender rills, were then ponds and broad, impetuous brooks. The Mill Pond, in the rear of Allen street, was a considerable sheet of water, and in the time of a freshet, all the land below the hills presented the appearance of a lake.

There is a close connection between extensive woods and the moisture of the earth, so that ponds and streamlets often diminish and disappear as a country is cleared of its forests. Trees condense moisture and exhale it again, and moreover prevent the profuse evaporation of the earth, so that an uncultivated country is usually wet and spongy. These facts account for the shrinking of many of our pools and brooks.

1714. Caleb Bushnell obtained a grant of "a convenient place for building vessels," on the west side of the river, opposite the old Landing-place.

1616. Joseph Kelley, shipwright obtained permission to build vessels on the Point, the town to have the free use of his wharf.

1722. Other applications of the same nature having been made, the proprietors directed Lieut. Solomon Tracy and Ensign James Huntington, " to go down to the Landing-place and lay out what may be needful for the town's use." The next year, Lieut. Simon Lathrop, Joshua and James Huntington, and Daniel Tracy, all spirited and enterprising men, then in the prime of life, each obtained *a conveniency*, as it was expressed, and began improvements at the Landing-place.

Joshua Huntington's grant is thus defined : " twenty feet square upon the water, on the west side of Rocky Point, on the north side of Lieut. Lothrop's grant, if it be there to be had ; not prejudicing the conveniency to be laid out by James Huntington and Daniel Tracy."

1725. Permission granted to Lieut. Lothrop to build a wharf at his own expense, "provided it be free to all mortals." The town also built a wharf the same year.

This was in fact the era of the commencement of Chelsea; but as yet there were no dwelling houses. The land, with the exception of these footholds upon the water's edge, all lay in common. At that time, the young people from the farms around Norwich, after haying was over, came in parties to the Landing, to wander over the hills, eat oysters, drink flip, and have a frolic. The Point was but a confused heap of rocks, and might have been bought, it is said, for £5. Kelley's shipyard stood near the spot where afterwards was the store of old Capt. Bill, which in its turn has given place, together with a part of its rocky foundations to the spacious building of the Norwich and Worcester Railroad Company. Every thing on this side

of the river has changed its appearance, but the opposite bank, in Preston, has been very little altered.
The rocks, the barren hills, the cedars, remain unvaried;
the projecting points, with their stunted trees, are still
the same. With the exception of the recent railway
cut through the hill, the last hundred years has made
no change in those rocky declivities around which the
Shetucket sweeps into the Thames. In 1726 and 1727,
the East Sheep-walk was surveyed and distributed into
shares, each share into tenths, and each tenth into
eight parts. Israel Lothrop and James Huntington
were the town agents to execute this task. The lots
varied in shape and size, and extended along the
water from the Shetucket ferry to the mouth of the
cove, reserving a highway through them two rods
wide. A second tier was laid out in the rear of these.

After this division into small lots both buildings and
inhabitants increased rapidly. In 1730 the town built
another wharf; and in 1734 Lieut. Lothrop obtained
leave to build a second ware-house on the undivided
land upon "the side hill, opposite his dwelling-
house, thirty feet by twenty, and to hold it during the
town's pleasure." Daniel Tracy, Capt. Benajah
Bushnell, Nathaniel Backus, and others, about this
period built dwelling-houses near the water. A flourishing village was soon formed, and called *New Chelsy.*

A very sad accident happened in the year 1728.
The inhabitants were engaged in raising a cart bridge,
twenty feet high and two hundred and fifty feet long,
"over Showtucket river, near three miles from town,"
and had nearly completed the frame, when, on the
28th of June, just as they were putting together the
upper work, a principal piece of timber which lay in
the foundation of this upper work, being spliced, gave
way at the joint, and falling, tripped up the dependent

13*

frame, which with its own weight careened and over-
set.   One hundred feet of the bridge fell, with forty
men on it.   The water was very low, and the people
were precipitated upon the rocks in all directions.   No
one escaped without bruises and contusions; twenty
were severely wounded and two killed.   These two
were Jonathan Gale, of Canterbury, nineteen years of
age, the only son of a widowed mother, who was killed
instantly—"a very hopeful youth, the darling of the
family"—and Mr. Daniel Tracy, son of Lieut. Thomas
Tracy, and one of the last survivors of the old stock
that came from Saybrook, who died the next day of
his mortal wounds.   Mr. Justice Backus published an
account of this accident in a small pamphlet.  "When
the men were extricated, and carried up the banks,"
says he, "it formed the nearest resemblance to a field
where a hot battle had been fought, that mine eyes
ever saw."

Mr. Tracy "was not," says Mr. Backus, "a person
concerned in the affair, only as he was a benefactor to
it, and went out that day to carry the people some provision, and happened to be on the bridge, at that junc-
ture of danger: a man that had been always noted for
an uncommon care to keep himself and others out of
probable danger, and yet now himself insensibly falls
into a fatal one.   And very remarkable is it, that to
keep his son at home this day, and so out of danger by
that occasion, he chooseth to go himself on the fore-
named errand, and is taken in the snare which he
thought more probable to his son."

Many hair-breadth escapes occurred.   Solomon
Lathrop fell forty feet from the top of a needle post,
and was pitched head foremost between two rocks, into
a hole of deeper water than ordinary, and yet not
killed.   This Mr. Lathrop was father to the Rev. Jo-

seph Lathrop of West Springfield, who was born about three years after this narrow escape of his parent.

1737. A bridge was erected over the Shetucket connecting the Landing with Preston. To defray the expense, a public subscription was taken up which amounted to £85 15*s.* The number of contributors was eighty-three, and the sums varied from five shillings to five pounds. The highest on the list were Joshua Huntington, John Williams, Samuel and John Story, Isaac-Clarke and Samuel Backus, who were probably the men doing the most business at that time. The bridge lasted only seven years ; it then sagged so much that it was pronounced unsafe, and blocked up.

The contract for the building of the Shetucket Bridge was made with Capt. William Whiting, whose name first appears on the list of inhabitants in 1732. He was the second son of Col. William Whiting, a man of courage, talents and address, who is often named in the early history of the country, for the part he took in various engagements with the French and Indians, in Maine and Canada. He was also Colonial Agent at the court of St. James, and on leaving England was constituted by royal commission Colonel of a regiment of foot, to be raised in Connecticut for the Queen's service. The original of this commission, upon parchment, dated April 1, 1710, and signed *Sunderland*, is still in possession of the family.

# CHAPTER XVI.

ABOUT the year 1720, the followers of John Rogers, a kind of Quaker, began to raise disturbances in New London County. This sect sprung up in the vicinity of New London, and has since been known as *Rogerenes*. The special object of their leader's mission, was to destroy priestcraft, and the *idolatry of Sunday*. They saw no more feasible project of effecting this, than by breaking up the worshipping assemblies of the Sabbath. For this purpose they were accustomed, on that day, to separate into small bands, and go through the country, entering the meeting-houses, in time of divine service, and by various noises and other provocations, interrupting the worship. They would carry their knitting, sewing, hatchelling, joinering, &c. into the house, and by hammering, singing and shouting, endeavor to drown the voice of the speaker. They made several visits to Dr. Lord's meeting-house, but that excellent man always treated them with great lenity. John Rogers himself, the founder of the sect, beset Dr. Lord, one Sunday morning, as he came out of the house, to go to meeting, and followed him thither, inveighing and shouting against priestcraft, as was his usual custom. Just as the venerable minister reached the porch of the meeting-house, and taking off his hat displayed an august and graceful white wig, Rogers exclaimed in a loud voice, Benjamin! Benjamin! dost thou think that they wear white wigs in heaven? No answer was returned, but the good man might have retorted, that a white wig would gain entrance there much more readily than a railing tongue.

In July, 1726, six of the followers of Rogers were taken up at Norwich, for travelling on the Sabbath, and committed to prison. They were tried the next day. One of them was a woman, Sarah Culver by name, called by them a *singing sister*. They stated that they were on their way from Groton to Lebanon, to baptize a person, or see him baptized by others, as circumstances should be. One of their party, named Davis, they declared vested with apostolic commission and authority to preach and baptize. Some of this sect, had previously been taken up in other parts of the county, and fined five shillings per head for breaking the Sabbath, and they now travelled in defiance of the law and its penalty, boasting that they could buy the idolators' Sabbaths for five shillings a piece. But on arriving at Norwich, they found, as Mr. Justice Backus observed, that they had *risen in price*, for being taken before the said Justice, they were sentenced to pay a fine of twenty shillings per head, or to be whipped ten or fifteen lashes each. Not being able to pay the fine, they were obliged to submit to the latter punishment. The next day they were carried out upon the plain, and there whipped with lashes of *prim*. It is said, also, that one of them, probably Davis, had warm tar poured upon his head, and his hat put on, while in that state, as a punishment for his contumacy, in refusing to pull off his hat in court. They were then dismissed, and proceeded on their way to Lebanon, where, the next Sabbath, they were again arrested, on the same plea, but their fines were paid for them by some compassionate citizens. They then challenged the ministers of

Lebanon, Messrs. Platt and Williams, to a public debate, at which, says Mr. Backus, they were completely
foiled.

The Hon. Joseph Jenks, deputy governor of Rhode
Island, took the part of the despised Rogerenes, and
issued a proclamation, respecting the proceedings at
Norwich, which he caused to be posted up in various
parts of his own state, in order, as it stated, that the
people might see what was to be expected from a Presbyterian government, in case Connecticut should succeed in the efforts she was then making, to get the
rule over the Rhode Island and Providence Plantations.
In reply to this proclamation, a small pamphlet was
published by Joseph Backus Esq. (who appears to
have succeeded Mr. Bushnell as the *factotum* of the
town,) explanatory of this affair of the Quakers. He
considers their conduct as sufficiently odious, to justify
the severest castigation of the law, and declares, that
as they acted in defiance of the law, " they may be
said to have whipped their own backs."

# CHAPTER XVII.

Currency.

IT has been observed that Mr. Lord's salary was fixed at £100 per annum. In 1726, a present was made him of £25, and the next year twelve contributions were granted him, to be taken up on the first Sabbath of every month. These gratuities were to compensate for the depreciation of the currency.

Bills of Credit began to be emitted in Connecticut in 1709, and the emissions were repeated in small parcels at intervals, afterwards. For many years, however, there was little or no redundancy of the circulating medium, and of course the depreciation was trifling. The bills were not counterfeited until 1735; but at that time, so large a quantity of the false impression was put in circulation, that the Assembly ordered the issue of bills with an entire new stamp, to the value of £25,000, to be exchanged for the old ones then in use. These and subsequent emissions were called Bills of the New Tenor. In 1740, on account of the war with Spain, £45,000 more were emitted, and some smaller sums afterwards.

Until the emission of the New Tenor, the credit of the old bills was tolerably supported. The depreciation now ran on with rapid strides, and confusion in accounts, perplexity and want of confidence in the dealings of man with man, suspension of activity and pecuniary distress was the consequence. The clashing of old and new tenor rendered the currency mazy and uncertain. Prices were greatly enhanced, but fluctuating; impositions frequent, and speculation triumphed over honest industry. It was a difficult thing to graduate price to value, with a currency so vague and fluctuating.

In 1736, the town expenses were £84, of which one item was a charge of Dr. Perkins—

For keeping and salivating Christian Boyle and
    expenses to Hannah Rood       £24 1s 0d.

Yet the next year, the whole amount of the town expenditure, including the doctor's bill, did not amount to £14.

In 1740, wheat was 13s. per bushel; rye, 9 and 10s.; Indian corn, 7s.; oats and turnips, 3s. 6; pork, 8d. or 10d. per lb.; butter, from 18d. to 2s.; sugar, the same; molasses, 7 and 8s. per gall.; rum, 10s. 6; men's shoes, from 15 to 18s. per pair; candles, 2s. 6 per lb.; a bushel of salt, 14s.; a quire of paper, 5s. 6 or 6s.; a quart of mustard seed 2s. 6; sheep's wool and *cotton wool*, about the same price, viz. 4s. per lb.

This uncertain currency was by no means confined to Connecticut. The other New England Colonies suffered in the same way. In Boston, they had little else in circulation than "Land Bank Money" and old Tenor. The following memorandum from the day-book of a Boston huckster of the same date as the above, will show that prices were very much enhanced in that capital also:

Molasses, 8s. 6 per gall.; "a bushel of Ingin meel," 18s.; a beaver hat, £3 15s.; side of sole leather, £1 19s. 6; "half a pees of Rusha Duck," £8; a sheepskin, 10s.; a bushel of onions, 18s.; a pair of buckles, £4 10s.; a pair of yarn stockings, 12s.; "13½ yards of Osimbrogs," £3 11s. 6; a grate of Diamond glass, £10.

Let it be observed, that at this time, the depreciation had but just commenced. In 1741, the rate levied for the payment of Mr. Lord's salary had risen from 2d. and 3d. on the pound to 10d., and £200 was allowed him in addition to his nominal salary.

In 1751, the current expenses of the town was £751. The currency continued its downward course until 1753, when Mr. Lord received £850 as an equivalent for £100, lawful money. The bellman's salary was £40 per annum. Schooling per month from £15 to £22.

In 1757, the currency was flowing once more in its old channel. Mr. Lord's salary was reduced to £66 13s. 4d. lawful money, and twelve contributions; the bellman's to £3 10s.

14

# CHAPTER XVIII.

In 1718, there was a division of proprietary lands, called the forty acre division. In 1726, the undivided lands that remained, were mainly comprised in two Sheep-walks. A public meeting was called, in which the names of the proprietors of each, were distinctly declared and recorded in order to prevent, if possible, all future " strifts and law-suits." The East Sheep-walk of 900 acres, more or less, was divided into shares of twenty acres each, and ratified and confirmed to forty-two proprietors, mentioned by name, or to those who claimed under them. The West Sheep-walk, by estimation 700 acres, was in like manner divided and confirmed to thirty-seven proprietors. Each share was then divided into tenths, and the tenths into eighths, and distributed apparently by lot. It is expressed in the records by the phrase, " making a pitch," as thus—" Capt. Bushnell made his pitch for his portion of the sheep-walk," at such a place. The last general division of proprietary lands, was in 1740, after which the accounts were closed, and the company dissolved.

The three plains were from the first settlement, reserved for public use. As early as 1670, the Little Plain was enclosed, and a fine of 5s. imposed on any one who should with horse or cattle, pass over the fence in going to, or from the town. It is pleasing to notice the care taken from time to time, to free the plains from all obstructions, and render hem orna- mental as well as useful to the town. Repeated ap- plications to build upon them by individuals, were re- fused, and all encroachments reprehended. " There shall be no shop, house or barn, or any other private building erected on any part of said plain," was the language of these resolutions.

The proprietors agree, vote, and grant, " that 1729. the Plain in the Town Platt, called the meeting house plain, with all the contents of it, as it now lyeth, shall be and remain, to be, and lye com- mon for public use for the whole town forever, without alteration."

A similar vote was passed at the same time with respect to " the Plain at the westerly end of the Town Platt, lying between Richard Egerton's and John Waterman's, Abial Marshall's and the widow Hide's houses."

Many of the local names by which the Indians and early settlers distinguished various parts of the nine miles square have become obsolete. The following list, taken from the descriptions of land in old deeds and grants, some of which have quite gone by, and others are but partially and locally known, are offered for the curious to identify and locate.

1661.   Little Fort,—this was between the Landing and trading Cove.
Woquanuk Little River.
Sunamansuck,—Wesquacksaug river.
Middle Hill,—Pauquoh-hog brook.
1679.   Puppie Hill,—on the road to Peagscomtok.
The Major's Pond,—over the river, on land granted by the town to Capt. John Mason.
Stonie Brooke.
The Kimicall Spring.

Little Lebanon,—at the end of Yantick.

Little Lebanon Hill and Valley.

　　'Scotch Cap Hill.

1700.　White Hills on Showtucket.

　　　Butternut Brook,—Great Cranberry Pond.

Cheeapschaddok,—near Robert Roath's and Owen William's.

Dragon's Hole,—Kewoutaquck river, east of Shetucket.

Huckleberry Plains.

The Great Darke Swampe.

The Goat's Hill.

The Rocky Hill,—called Wenaniasoug.

Bundy Hill,—Newent.

Little Faith Plain,—south of Wawecos Hill.

Connecticut Plains,—first, second and third Plains towards Connecticut.

　　　Wequonuk,—Pequonuk.

1662.　Pabaquamsquee,—on Quinnebaug.

　　　Peagskumsuk,—a tract in a turn of the Quinnebaug.

　　　Pottapauge.

1690.　Nipsquanoug,—Nipsconoag.

　　　Wolf-pit Hill.

Clay Banks of the Great River.

Skunkhungannok Hill,—in the Quinnibaug lands.

Conaytuck Brook.

Wheel-timber Hill,—at Plain Hills.

Great Beaver Brook and Little Beaver Brook.

Harthstone Hill.

Great Ox Pasture.

Rowland's Brook,—near Peagscomsuk.

Pine Swamp,—at Yantick.

Isinglass Rock. Anchamaunnackkaunock Pond, east of Shetucket.

Saw-pit Hills.

Sukskotumskot or Saw-mill Brook,—Great Hill east side of it.

Stonie Hollow,—in East Sheep-walk.

Ayers Mountain.

Wanungatuck,—towards Canterbury.

New Roxbury,—on Quinnibaug.

Momogegwetuk Brook,—falling into Peagscomtok.

In connection with the subject of names, some of

those borne by the worthy ancestors of the town may be mentioned.

### MALES.

Jepthah Elderkin.
Cordile Fitch.
Merit Rockwell.
Friend Weeks.
Aquilla Giffords.
Shadrach Lampheer.

Zorobabel Wightman.
Retrieve Moore.
Rezen Geer.
Hopestill Armstrong.
Yet-once Barstow.

### FEMALES.

Experience Porter.
Submit Peck.
Thankful Willoughby.
Zipporah Haskill.
Theodia Wallbridge.
Leah Armstrong.
Zinah Hide.
Ruby Tracy.
Zillah Grist.
Millescent Scott.
Remembrance Carrier.
Deliverance Squire.

Charity Perkins.
Obedience Copp.
Temperance Edgerton.
Patience Larrabee.
Love Kingsbury.
Civil Tracy.
Silence Leffingwell.
Hepzibah Ladd.
Diadema Hide.
Mercy Polley.
Tirzah Morgan.

In a family of five sons and one daughter, the following were the names, Absalom, Zebulon, Obadiah, Ichabod, Elam and Tabitha.

In another, with four daughters and two sons, are these ; Lebbeus, Ozias, Love, Batthiah, Beulah, and Miriam. Another family consists of Barnabas, Enoch, Elkanah and Dorcas. Another of only Aaron and Zipporah. The daughters of Mr. Samuel Bliss 2nd, were Desire, Thankful, Freelove and Mindwell.

14*

# CHAPTER XIX.

Mason Controversy.

THE history of the Mohegan Indians is so closely connected with that of Norwich, that it is necessary frequently to revert to them. It seems to have been generally conceded by the English, that the ulterior right to dispose of land in this region, belonged to Uncas. The Governor and Company, however, claimed that he transferred this right to them by a deed of September 28, 1640. This deed, the Indians said, was never executed by Uncas, or if executed it was a mere form, intended to deceive the Dutch, who were then endeavoring to get a footing in these parts. Indeed, the transactions and declarations of the Colony long after this period, prove incontestably, that they considered the property, as distinguished from the jurisdiction, still to continue in the Mohegans. August 15, 1659, the year before the settlement of Norwich, as has already been stated, Capt. Mason obtained of Uncas and his brother, a general deed of all the lands belonging to them, not then actually occupied by the tribe. In this business, it was generally understood that he acted as the agent of the colony, and it was proved by the State Records, that he formally surrendered his claim to the Gen. Court, March 14, 1660; they granting him, in compensation for his services, a farm of five hundred acres. This farm he chose at a place called Pomacook, and it was confirmed to him as his personal property, by the Indian Sachem, about two months afterwards.

The descendants of Mason claimed, not this farm at Pomacook only, but the whole tract, conveyed in the deed of 1659, alleging that it had never been alienated by him. The records of the colony contain a minute of the surrender, as having been performed in open court, but nevertheless, as no specific instrument to that effect could be found, under the signature of their ancestor, they either questioned the intent of the transaction, or denied its authority. They asserted that the conveyance made to Mason, by Uncas, was with the intent to secure those lands to the Indians, by putting it out of their own power to convey them to others, that Mason received them as their trustee, and had passed over to the colony merely the right of jurisdiction, not the ownership of the lands.

Oweneco confirmed the grant of his father and uncle to the two sons of Mason—Samuel and Daniel, Feb. 12, 1683-4, fearing, as he said, that he might be ensnared by strong drink, and in that state be induced to dispose of his lands injudiciously. From this time the Masons acted as trustees to the Indian Sachem, in conjunction with Capt. James Fitch, whom Oweneco had empowered to act for him, in 1680. The government allowed of this guardianship, if they did not in the first place originate and recommend the measure. The main object of all the parties appears to have been to benefit the Indians, by taking care of their interests. An act of 1692 thus confirms the right of the Masons to be considered as the trustee of the tribe.

" The General Court, on the request of Oweneco, son of Uncas, approve of his giving his land to Josiah, since deceased, and also approve of his now giving them to Mowhamet, son of Oweneco, he being the rightful Sachem of Mowheag after Oweneco; but these lands are not to pass to any other person, without the consent of Capt. Samuel Mason."

The business, however, did not long run on in this smooth and harmonious manner. Out of these premises a long and troublesome dispute arose; the case every year becoming more complicated and important. The Masons and Mohegans became closely linked in a claim against the colony for the possession of large tracts of land, occupied by numerous settlers, and comprising the major portion of Colchester, Windham, Mansfield, Hebron, and considerable tracts in some other towns. A vigorous and persevering effort, extending over a period of seventy years, was made by Mason and his descendants to recover the possession of this territory for the Indians.

The citizens of Norwich entered into this controversy with great warmth and zeal, most of them espousing the cause of the Indians, from an honest opinion that they had been injured and defrauded, and a benevolent desire to have some restitution made. The case was often tried without being brought to an issue. Many persons put themselves to great inconvenience and expense in entertaining and clothing the Indians, and forwarding their cause, expecting to be remunerated when they should recover their rights. On the Indians themselves it had a very unhappy effect, puffing them up with hopes never to be realized, and leading them into courses of idleness, itineracy and extravagance. Norwich suffered severely for her indiscretion, her streets and houses being often filled with these exacting and troublesome guests.

The case was first submitted to Commissioners chosen out of all the New England Colonies, and acting under the immediate authority of Queen Anne. This

court was held at Stonington, in 1705. Thomas Leffingwell, of Norwich, a tried friend of the Indian Sachems, was one of the Commissioners, and from his
intimate acquaintance with the case, and with all the
affairs of the tribe, had great influence with the other
members. The colony protested against the authority
of this Court, and, refusing to appear before it, no defence was made. The decision, as might be expected,
was against her, but no attempt was made by the English Government to enforce the decree.

A subsequent investigation of this case, under the
authority of the General Court, was made at Norwich,
in the winter of 1717–18, and was pending at the time
of the great snow storm, famous over all New England,
February 17. The proceedings of the Commissioners,
who met in the house of Richard Bushnell, Esq., were
much impeded by the snow. For several days the
members were scarcely able to get together.

The next October a further Committee was appointed by the Assembly, and directed to repair to
Mohegan, to hear the grievances of the Indians, and
to endeavor to settle all differences between them and
their neighbors. This Committee, consisting of James
Wadsworth, Esq. and Capt. John Hall, met at the
house of Mr. Joseph Bradford, in Mohegan, February,
1720–21, and were apparently very successful in settling the various claims, and reconciling all parties.
In conclusion they laid out and sequestered to the use
of the Indians between 4 and 5000 acres of good land,
which was never to be alienated until the tribe became
extinct. These proceedings were ratified by act of
Assembly, May 11, 1721.

Nevertheless, the old controversy soon revived, and
a Commission of Review was appointed by George II.
to examine the proceedings of the Court held at Ston-

ington, in 1705. This Court, consisting of the Lieut.
Governor and Council of New York, and the Governor
and Assistants of Rhode Island, convened at Norwich,
May 24, 1738. The Commissioners not agreeing as
to the course to be pursued, the members from New
York, at the outset, entered a protest and withdrew.
The remainder, after an examination of witnesses, reversed the decision of the Court, and gave judgment
in favor of the Colony.

John and Samuel Mason, however, would not suffer
the matter to rest here; they presented a memorial to
the King, alleging that the proceedings of the Court
were irregular, and in behalf of the Indians, praying
for a redress of grievances. Orders were therefore issued for a new Commission of Review.

This second Court of Commissioners convened at
Norwich, June 28, 1743, and the trial lasted seven
weeks. The sessions commenced at the house of Simon Lathrop, Esq., but on the third day, was adjourned to the meeting-house, where the remainder of the
sitting was held. Of course, this Court did not, as that
at Stonington had done, continue its sessions on the
Sabbath. The town at this time literally overflowed
with strangers, and no business of any kind was done,
except what was connected with the pending controversy, and the necessary purposes of life. All the officers of government and distinguished men in the colony were present; the whole tribe of Mohegans was
quartered upon the inhabitants, and hundreds of persons in the neighboring towns who had lands at stake,
came in from day to day, to hear the proceedings.
The Lathrops, Huntingtons, Leffingwells, Tracys and
all the principal men in Norwich were of the Indian
party, and kept open house for John Uncas and his
people. Ben Uncas was upheld by the state, and his

party was rendered respectable by the notice of all the officers of governm nt. The rival sachems maintained considerable pomp and state while the trial continued, which was until the 17th of August.

The decision was again in favor of the colony ; but the Masons appealed from the judgment to the King in council, and henceforth all legal action upon the case, was transferred to England. The final decision was not until 1767. Sir Fletcher Norton, then prime minister, advised that the English should be conciliated by a decision against the Indians.

It was the prevalent opinion in England, that the Mohegans had right on their side, but that it was not expedient to do them justice, and indeed not equitable, as the English had long possessed and improved the lands in question, and the Indians had dwindled away and did not need them. One of the Masons, however, remained long in England, prosecuting his claim : obtained money upon it, sold out rights in it, ran in debt upon it, was at one time a prisoner in the Fleet, and never returned to his native country. The Revolutionary war, soon afterwards broke out, the Mohegans found themselves at the mercy of the State, and never afterwards showed any disposition to renew their claims. Occom, the eloquent advocate and preacher of this tribe, on hearing of the termination of this affair, writes thus to a friend : " The grand controversy which has subsisted between the colony of Conn. and the Mohegan Indians, above seventy years, is finally decided in favor of the colony. I am afraid the poor Indians will never stand a good chance with the English in their land controversies, because they are very poor, they have no money. Money is almighty now-a-days, and the Indians have no learning, no wit, no

cunning : the English have all." [MS. Letter of Occom.]

In this controversy, our sympathies are very naturally enlisted in favor of the Indians; nevertheless, it
does not appear that they were treated with any un-
due severity or injustice by the colony. Most of the
settlers on the debatable lands, fairly purchased them,
and had obtained deeds, though not, perhaps, always
of the lawful owners. And there is reason to believe
that the Indians themselves would not have complained had they not been instigated by others. This case
may fairly be merged in the great question still pending and unsettled, whether a civilized race has a right,
under any circumstances, to take possession of a country inhabited by savages, and gradually dispossess the
original proprietors.

# CHAPTER XX.

Indian Deeds.  Sachems.

I**T** is a singular fact, that while the Indian Sachems were conveying away such large tracts of land, that they and their subjects should be in want of room for their own accommodation. So early as 1669, Oweneco requested of the town of Norwich "a yerll of land lying near Showtucket river;" and the town accordingly granted him out of their Commons, three hundred acres on Shetucket river, abutting southerly on Quinebaug, and secured it to his successors, not allowing them the privilege of alienating it. At the same time they bound the Indians to forbear all trespass upon the lands or cattle of the town, upon penalty of forfeiting the grant. The act concludes in this manner.

"It is further engaged by Oweneco, that whereas as he hath received these lands by gift from the town of Norwich, the town does order that he shall forbear on the Sabbath day from working, hunting, fishing, or any servile labor, and if any of his subjects be found guilty of this violation, they shall be liable to be punished, and to these said, and above specified particulars, the said Oweneco doth bind and engage himself, his heirs and lawful successors."

The reason assigned for this grant was, "that he was in hazard of the loss of his Sachemdom, for want of lands to accommodate his subjects." A number of Indians then resided upon this grant, and others removed to it, and were called the Showtucket, or Shotuck

15

Indians.  In 1695, we find Capt. Samuel Mason, the Indian trustee, calling upon the town to fix the bounds of this grant upon which the English were fast intruding.

The aged Uncas was also in his last days a petitioner to the town for land ; yet at the same time these Sachems were in the habit of assigning over to others, tracts large enough for townships.   In 1687, Oweneco conveyed to James Fitch jun., a tract by estimation six or seven miles in length, and one in breadth, lying west of Quinebaug river, and extending " to the new plantation given by Joshua;"—another portion west of the same river, beginning north of the Norwich line and running up the river to the clay pits, a mile and a half in breadth ;—two other parcels east and north of the town line, and a large meadow east of the Quinebaug, extending from the town line to Peagscomscot, [now Canterbury.]   For these grants the Sachem acknowledges the receipt of £60.   Major Fitch became ultimately one of the greatest land owners in the state.  The above lands comprise but a very small portion of the various tracts recorded to him in the Norwich books.

A part of the above described grants lay in the crotch of the Shetucket and Quinebaug rivers; and here also was the three hundred acre grant, secured by the town to the Indians.   The title to this tract afterwards caused much perplexity and some litigation.   In 1696, Capt. Fitch being then the proprietary clerk, recorded nearly the whole tract to himself; but as his claim covered the Indian reservation, the town entered a formal protest against the record, objecting especially to his claim at the Quinebaug falls.

In 1723, the Indian title to the reserved lands in the crotch of the rivers, was considered entirely extinct;

the Shetucket indians having dwindled away or removed elsewhere. Joseph and Jacob Perkins, Samuel Bishop, and others, claimed it as purchasers and improvers, and the town confirmed their title.    This tract now forms the greater part of the town of Lisbon.

More than thirty deeds are recorded in the Norwich books, bearing the signatures of Uncas, Oweneco, or Joshua, conveying to various individuals tracts of land, most of them comprising hundreds of acres.    The condition expressed is frequently of this nature : " To my very good friend John Post, for the love and friendship received from him," 200 acres, in 1685 : to Israel Lothrop " for kindnesses received and three coats in hand paid," 150 acres in 1695 : " to Richard Bushnell, for kind and free entertainment for many years," 400 acres, in 1699.    A large number of deeds of similar import may be found recorded in New London and other neighboring towns.

Wawecquaw, the brother of Uncas, claimed considerable tracts in and around Norwich.    Two hills in the town have borne his name : one of considerable extent in the Northwest part, and the other in Chelsea, around the base of which the city lies.    The name is now usually spelt Waweekus.    Uncas, (as well as the English,) was much troubled, at various times, with the intrigues of Wawecquaw, who is represented as being mischievous and quarrelsome.

Joshua, the brother of Oweneco, in 1676, conveyed to Capt. John Mason, a tract claimed by him, N. W. of Norwich, and now forming a part of the town of Lebanon.    In 1716, Cesar, who is styled " the prince and Sachem of Mohegan," made several conveyances of land to individuals.    One was to Capt. Robert Denison ; another to Lieut. Benajah Bushnell, of two parcels, lying between Trading Cove brook, and the south line of Norwich.

These are but a few specimens, out of a great number that might be mentioned, of Indian grants in this vicinity. Some of them covered others, three or four times over, and led to those many disputes as to titles, and perplexities as to bounds, which entangled the rights and claims of the settlers in an inextricable maze. One is almost inclined to join in the declaration of Sir Edmund Andros, that he did not value an Indian deed, any more than *the scratch of a cat's paw.*

The following record shows that an amicable settlement of all differences with respect to land claims and boundaries, took place between the town and the aged chieftain of the Mohegans. It is the last notice that has been any where found of Uncas.

" Whereas Uncas, Sachem of Mohegan, hath of late made application to the Town of Norwich for some Releife with Reference to a small Tract of Land which fell out to be within the bounds of the Town, on the south Bounds, over the Traiding Cove Brook. This Town, Considering of his Request and of him as an OLD FRIEND, *see Cause to Gratify him* with the said Land as a Gift to him & his heirs forever, and Whereas the s$^d$ Uncas doth also Recon upon three pounds yet due to him as arrears of the payment of the purchas of Norwich Township, though there is nothing appearing how the said money is due, neither by written nor any other Evidenee—Yet notwithstanding the Town have Granted his desire as not willing to dissatiefie an OLD FRIEND in such a small matter, and the said Uncas Also Declaring himself to be in some fears Respecting his Posterity, whether they may not be infringed of their Liberty of Fishing and making use of the Rivers and other Royalties by some English : that being the Reason why he Gave place at the first that we should run the Line of the Two miles on the East side of the Great River, Beginning at the River : We also satisfie him in this writing about it, that he and his successors shall from Time to Time, and at all times have full and free Liberty to make use of the Rivers and ponds, with other Royalties as abovesaid, not debaring Ourselves, and having thus done, we whose names are subscribed being appointed by the town of Norwich to treat with him the said Uncas upon the premises, or any thing Elce that might Conduce to mutual satisfaction, we asked him whether now he was fully satisfied as to the former, so Concerning any thing Elce depending between him and us, and he hath declared himself: as witness by his hand that he is FULLY SATISFIED with us as concerning the premises, so Respecting all our Bounds and boundaries, and particularly Concerning the Running of the Line on the East side of the River, and Concerning the beginning of the said Line at the River, and the end of said Line to a Tree marked near the Dwellinghouse of Robert Allen : Dated in Norwich, September 1st, 1682 :

the mark of UNCAS.

Thomas Leffingwell.
William Backus.
John Birchard.
John Tracy.

Entered in Libr the second folio 1st, October 18th, 1682.

By me, CHRISTOPHER HUNTINGTON, Recorder.

Uncas is supposed to have died in 1683. Oweneco lived till 1710. Notwithstanding the title of Sachem and the lordly idea attached to the disposing of such extensive regions as they were accustomed to convey to their friends, these chieftains were but little elevated, either in their habits or morals, above the common level of savages. Oweneco was in his youth a bold warrior, and an enterprizing partizan. His exploits at the Narragansett Fort fight, and through the whole of Philip's war, obtained for him considerable renown.

But in maturer years, destitute of the stimulus of war, and the chase, he used to wander about with his blanket, metomp and sandals, his gun and his squaw, to beg in the neighboring towns, quartering himself in the kitchens and out-houses of his white acquaintances,

15*

and presenting to strangers, or those who could not well understand his imperfect English, a *brief* which had been written for him by Mr. Richard Bushnell. It was as follows :—

> Oneco king, his queen doth bring,
>    To beg a little food ;
> As they go along, their friends among,
>    To try how kind, how good.
>
> Some pork, some beef, for their relief,
>    And if you can't spare bread ;
> She'll thank you for pudding, as they go a gooding,
>    And carry it on her head.

The last line alludes to the Indian custom of bearing burdens in a sack upon the shoulders, supported by a back strap called a *metomp*, passing across the forehead.

# CHAPTER XXI.

APRIL 28, 1730, all the freemen were enrolled. They amounted to 158; thirteen more were added in September, making 171. The first on the list, and probably so placed in respect to age and dignity, were Joseph Backus Esq., the three reverend ministers, Lord, Willes and Kirtland, and the two deacons, Simon and Christopher Huntington. After these come Samuel and Israel Lothrop, William Hide Esq., Mr. Thomas Adgate, Capt. Jabez Perkins, Capt. Benajah Bushnell, and Capt. John Leffingwell.

It is worthy of note, that at this time and for many years afterwards, there was but one or two citizens at a time, who bore the title of Esq., denoting a Justice of the Peace. Mr. Birchard was the first civil magistrate mentioned; Lt. Thomas Tracy was in the Commission of the Peace from 1678 to 1685.

Richard Bushnell Esq. was the next magistrate, and some years later, Capt. Jabez Hide. As these became aged, Joseph Backus Esq. appears upon the stage, and a little later, Wm. Hide Esq. Next to these gentlemen, we find their two sons advancing as the fathers recede, viz., Ebenezer Backus Esq. and Richard Hide Esq.; and these appear to have been all who bore the office and title before 1760.

The most conspicuous points at this time in town,

and those where all notifications were ordered to be set up, were, the sign-post on the meeting-house plain —Joseph Backus' shop door—Benajah Leffingwell's gate post, and at the parting of the paths at the corner of Ebenezer Backus' garden. This last position is still a conspicuous one. The house stands alone, embraced by highways, which run together above and below. It was the homestead of Joseph Backus Esq., familiarly known for many years as Mr. Justice Backus, and afterwards of his son Ebenezer, who built the present house, and set out with his own hand the two fine elms before the door. One of the daughters of Ebenezer Backus married the second Gov. Trumbull.

In 1720, the first project for the erection of a Town house was started. Subscriptions were taken and liberty granted to set the building on the corner of the plain, but the measure not being generally popular, the house was not erected.

Fifteen years afterwards, the plan was resumed, and a penny rate granted towards defraying the expense. This vote, however, did not pass without vehement opposition, and a protest of thirteen citizens entered against it. The building was erected on the south corner of the parsonage, lot which is precisely the spot now occupied by the old Court-House. The same year, (1735) the inhabitants petitioned the General Assembly that the Supreme Court in March, and the Superior Court in November, for New London Co. might be held in Norwich. The agents for the town in this business, were Capt. John Williams, Capt. Joseph Tracy, and Mr. Hezekiah Huntington. The petition was granted, and Norwich became a half-shire town. A building had been previously erected for a town jail, but a "new prison" was now built on the area of the plain, which with land near it, for a "prison-house," was made over to the county. A whipping-post and pillory were also erected in the vicinity.

The road between New London and Norwich passing through the *Mohegan fields*, was also considerably improved about this time. This road was first laid out by order of the General Assembly, previous to the year 1700. It was surveyed and stated by Joshua Raymond, who was remunerated with the gift of a fine farm upon the route.

1737. The key of the town-house was formally delivered into the custody of Capt. Joseph Tracy, and a room ordered to be finished under his direction, in the garret, for the town's stock of ammunition. The following vote was then passed : "It is now ordered and enacted, that if any man shall smoke it, in the time of sessions of any town meeting, within this house, he shall forfeit the sum of 5 shillings."

Capt. Joseph Tracy was son to John Tracy, one of the thirty-five proprietors. He was a very respectable and dignified man, and for a long course of years was uniformly chosen moderator of all public meetings in alternation with Capt. Jabez Hide. He died in 1765, aged eighty-three. In 1745 we find the care of the town-house and arms committed to Capt. Philip Turner, and this is the first time that gentleman's name appears on the records. He afterwards performed the duties of constable and selectman, and was captain of the troop of horse ;—a spirited band of young men whom he took much pride in parading and exercising. He died in 1755, aged thirty-nine. His son, Dr. Philip Turner, became a very eminent surgeon, being applied to in difficult cases from various parts of the country. His grandson, Dr. John Turner, was also distinguished for surgical skill.

In 1743 Messrs. Richard Hide and Ebenezer Harts-

horn were appointed to survey the town, and draw a
plan of it, embracing the course of the rivers and
larger rivulets. The town now comprised eight ecclesiastical societies, viz : First, West, Newent, East, New-
Concord, Chelsy, Hanovei and Eighth ; but the First
or Town Plot society still maintained its preeminence,
possessing twice the number of inhabitants, and three
times the amount of influence of any other. No census of the town appears till 1756, when the population
stood—

> Whites, 5,317
> Blacks,    223—Total, 5,540.

Schools were maintained by what was called a
*country rate* of forty shillings upon the thousand
pounds, and all deficiences made up by parents and
guardians. The schools were distributed over the town,
and kept a longer or shorter period, according to the
list of each society. In 1745 the appointment was as
follows—

School at the landing place
> to be kept,    .    . 3 months and 17 days.
> "    two in the Town-plot,
> one at each end, .    5½ months each.
> "    at Plain Hills, .    . 2 months 19 days.
> "    Waweekus Hill, .    1    "    16    "
> "    Great Plain,    .    . 2    "    18    "
> "    Wequanuk, .    .    2    "    15    "
> "    on Windham road, .    2    "    11    "

If any of these schools should be kept by a woman,
the time was to be doubled, as the pay to the mistress
was but half of that to the master.

Law books and other publications for which the town
were subscribers, were also generally distributed among
the several societies according to their respective lists.
Election sermons, and "the sermon books," were fre-

quently made the subject of a town order. These last mentioned publications were probably "Russell's Seven Sermons," a book of considerable note in that day. The last record respecting books appears a little before the Revolutionary war, as follows,—

"Whereas, there are a number of books called the Saybrook Platform, now in the town treasury to be disposed of for the town's use, and also a number of Election Sermons, this town do now order the selectmen to distribute said books to, and among the several societies in this town, in proportion to the list of said societies."

In 1751 the selectmen were empowered to prosecute with vigor, all who should sell or convey land to strangers, and all sales of this kind were declared null and void. Orders were given likewise that no strangers should remain in the town without the public consent, and this consent seems to have been very cautiously dispensed. Applications were frequently made for permission to stay in town for a limited time, but this was seldom granted without some condition annexed ; such as, if he then remove—if he behave himself—if he do not become chargeable. These votes stretch down to 1769.

The inhabitants were but little given to change ; they may rather be selected as conspicuous examples of what has been called Connecticut Steady Habits. Offices, even of an annual tenure, were frequently held for a long course of years, by the same incumbent. The case of the Huntingtons, the time immemorial Town Clerks, has been already mentioned. The office of Town Treasurer is another instance, held by Daniel Tracy from the year 1735, and perhaps before, until after 1760, and probably till his death, in 1771. He was then eighty-three years of age. In later times, the two De Witts, of Chelsea, father and son, officiated

as Society Clerks for a period of sixty years. Many
similar instances of perpetuity of service faithfully
rendered, without any respect to the emolument, which
was very trifling, might doubtless be gathered.

The office of Constable and Collector is one which
we might expect to find less fixed, and more upon the
plan of rotation than most others, yet Joseph Tracy
Jun. held this office nearly thirty years in succession.
In 1769 this faithful public servant, falling greatly into
arrears in his accounts, presented a touching petition
to the town, praying to be discharged from his obligations, and stating that he was then a prisoner in his
own house, " through fear of being confined in a worse
place."

"I have spent (said he) almost all my time in the business of my office, so that I have not had time to do any other
for the support of my family ; and I have not ever crowded
any poor man into prison for payment of his rate, but have
shown favor to poor men to my own disadvantage, and turned
every way to ease them. My long, unhappy and expensive
law suits with Capt. Abel, in the year 1751 and 52, put me
behind hand, so that I could not ever recover, and when I
found that I should fall in rears, I refused to be collector any
longer ; and for many years past the townsmen have granted
execution to the sheriff against me before I had collected the
rate, and by that means all my funds went to the sheriff."

" In the space of twenty-seven or twenty-eight years that
I have been collector, I have collected about thirty or forty
thousand pounds, and I am informed that there is scarce one
collector in the government that hath been collector half that
time, but what hath been reduced to low circumstances
thereby. What little I had of my own when I began I have
lost entirely, which I suppose was not less than £300 lawful
money."

Mr. Constable Tracy died 1787, aged eighty-one.

# CHAPTER XXII.

Civil Affairs. Cases of Trespass. Chaises. Biographical Sketches. Africans.

In 1759 a new Court House was commenced, fifty feet by forty. It stood on the south-west part of the Plain, just in front of its present situation. It was completed in a couple of years and placed under the care of Samuel Huntington, Esq. This gentleman, afterwards Governor of the State, was just then beginning to practice as an attorney. The Court House was removed, in 1798, from the area of the plain, to its present position, which is the site of the old Town House, that was standing when this was first built. It is still a respectable building, occupied by an accademical school.

A house for ammunition was built at the same time with the Court House, on the declivity of the hill near the Meeting-house. Some arms, a quantity of shot, and about 3000 lbs. of powder were deposited in it.

This Powder House was blown up in the year 1784. The train was laid by some unknown incendiary, but being discovered half an hour before the explosion, it might have been easily extinguished, if any one could have been found sufficiently daring to attempt it. The timely discovery, however, prevented any injury to life or limb, as all in the neighborhood were advertised of the danger and kept out of the way. The concussion was violent; windows were broken, timbers loosened, roofs started, plastering cracked, and furniture thrown

16

down.  Where the building stood, the ground was left entirely free of rubbish ; not even a stone of the foundation remained on the site, and only one of them could be identified afterwards, and that descended upon a roof at some distance, and passing through two floors, lodged in the cellar.  A bag of cannister shot flew into the chamber window of the parsonage.  The meeting-house was much shattered by this explosion.

To show that the rigid supervision of the public morals established by the first settlers, continued until a late period, a few minutes of cases of trespass will be given from MS. papers of Richard Hide, Esq., Justice of the Peace, between the years 1760 and 1780.

"A man presented for profane swearing having been heard to say at the public house—*damn me.*  Sentenced to pay the fine of 6*s.* and the costs, 6*s.* 3*d.*

Another for a similar offence, the culprit using the words *Go to the devil.*  Fine 6*s.*, costs 8*s.* 10*d.*

A breach of peace by tumultuous behavior,—fine 10*s.*, costs 18*s.* 8*d.*

Case of assault,—offence, knocking a man down with a chair,—fine 15*s.* and to pay costs, as follows,—warrant 1*s.*, summons 4*d.*, court fees 2*s.*, constable's travel five miles 1*s.* 3*d.*, arresting 6*d.*

1771.  A young woman presented for laughing, in a meeting for public worship, at Mr. Grover's, Sabbath evening—two females for witnesses—culprit dismissed with a reprimand.

1774.  Eben[r] Waterman Jr. presented by a grand juror, for profaning the Sabbath, in the gallery of the meeting-house in West Society, by talking in the time of divine service in a merry manner, to make sport.  Plead guilty—fine 10*s.*

"To Richard Hide, Esq., of Norwich, one of his majesty's Justices of the Peace for the county of New London, comes Ezra Huntington of said Norwich, one of the grand jurors of said county, and on oath informs and presents, that Asa Fuller, apprentice to said Ezra Huntington, and Ede Trap, son to Thomas Trap, and Lemuel Wentworth, son to James Wentworth, and Hannah Forsey, and Elizabeth Winship, a minor, and daughter of the widow Winship, all of Norwich

aforesaid, did, in Norwich aforesaid, on the evening following the 27th day of May last, it being Sabbath or Lord's Day
evening, meet and convene together, and walk in the street
in company, upon no religious occasion, all which is contrary to the statute of this colony in such case made and
provided.

For evidence take Peter Latham and Unice Manning.

Dated in Norwich, this 11th day of June, 1770."

Five endorsements are made on the back of this
presentment—one for each of the offenders—of the
following import.

" June 13, 1770. Then personally appeared Hannah Forsey,
and confessed guilty of the matter within, and sentenced to
pay 3s. to the Treasury of the Town and 1s. cost.—Before
Richard Hide, Justice of Peace.—Judgment satisfied."

The first person who set up a *chaise* in Norwich, was
one Samuel Brown; he was fined for riding in it to
meeting. In those simple and severe days, the rolling
of wheels through the streets was considered a breach
of the Sabbath. It would undoubtedly have a tendency to attract attention, and cause the thoughts to
wander from the peculiar duties of the day. If a man
at the present day, should arrive in town on Saturday
night, in a balloon, and go to meeting in it on Sunday,
it would be a similar case. Brown died about 1804,
aged 90. Col. Simon Lathrop, also rode in a chaise at
a very early period, but his effeminacy in this respect
was excused on account of the feeble health of his wife.
At the period of the revolution, only six *chaises*, or as
they are now called, *gigs*, were owned in the place.
Probably the number was not increased, until some
time after the peace. The owners of these six, were,
1st, Gen. Jabez Huntington: [this gig was large, low,
square-bodied, and studded with brass nails that had
square and flat heads—it was the first in town that had

a top which could be thrown back.]   2d, Col. Hezekiah
Huntington.   3d, Dr. Daniel Lathrop : [this was long
distinguished by its yellow body with a very large window in the side.]   4th, Dr. Theophilus Rogers.   5th,
Elijah Backus Esq.   6th, Nathaniel Backus Esq. of
Chelsea : [This afterwards belonged to Capt. Seth Harding.]   Within the same limits, since that period, between three and four hundred gigs have been owned
at one time; but recently this species of vehicle has
given place, in a great degree, to waggons and other
four wheeled carriages.

The first Druggist in Norwich, and the first in the
state, was Dr. Daniel Lathrop.   He resided three
years in England, to perfect himself in his business,
and afterwards made several voyages thither to select
and purchase his stores.   He imported £8000 worth
of drugs at one time, and made a large fortune by the
business.   His was the only apothecary's establishment
on the route from New York to Boston, and had a great
run of custom, supplying all the country for nearly
one hundred miles in every direction.   Dr. Lathrop
often received orders from New York.   His drugs were
always of the best kind, well prepared, packed and
forwarded in the neatest manner.

Benedict Arnold and Solomon Smith were apprentices in this shop at the same time.   The latter, when
of age, removed to Hartford, and there established the
second Druggist's shop in the state.   Dr. Lathrop furnished a part of the surgical stores to the northern
army in the French war.   His wife was a daughter of
Gov. Talcott, a lady of strong mind, considerable cultivation, and extensive benevolence.   Dr. Lathrop
died in 1782.   Madam Lathrop long survived him, and
was regarded with universal esteem and veneration.
Her death took place in 1806.   The early childhood

of a gifted daughter of Norwich, Mrs. L. H. Sigourney, was passed under the roof of this excellent lady. Having lost her own children, in their infancy, she lavished all her maternal affection and fostering care on this child of her heart, who repaid her tenderness with filial veneration, and has embalmed her memory in hallowed verse.

Dr. Lathrop left a legacy of £500 sterling to Yale College, and the same sum to the town of Norwich, towards the support of a free grammar school. This legacy, though subject to some restrictions, was accepted, and the school went into operation in 1787. Under the preceptorship of Mr. William Baldwin, it was for many years a large and flourishing school. It has since declined, and the restrictions in the will, rendering the fund in a great degree valueless to the town, it was relinquished in 1843, with the consent of the Legislature, to the heirs at law.

Dr. Joshua Lathrop, the brother of the preceding, succeeded to the business, the property, the benevolence and the public esteem of his relative. He died in 1807, at the age of eighty-four. He was the last in Norwich of the ancient race of gentlemen, that wore a white wig.

The two gentlemen mentioned above descended from Samuel Lathrop, one of the early settlers, through his second son, Samuel Lathrop 2d. Israel, the third son, was the head of a numerous collateral line. He had seven sons and six daughters. One of the former was the Rev. John Lathrop, a distinguished minister of Boston. He was born at Norwich in 1740. After completing his education at Princeton, he became for a time, an assistant to Mr. Wheelock, in his Indian School at Lebanon, but in 1768, was ordained to the pastoral charge of the old North Church in Boston.

16*

This church having been demolished by the British while they had possession of Boston, the society united with the new Brick Church, and Mr. Lathrop became the pastor of the United Society.  He published a variety of sermons, and died in 1816, aged seventy-five.

The celebrated Dr. Joseph Lathrop, of West Springfield, Mass., whose theological works are so numerous, and have been so widely disseminated, was a descendant of Samuel Lathrop, through his fourth son Joseph, and was born at Norwich in October, 1731.  The farm house in which his father lived, and where he was born, was not far from the Shetucket.  A half-filled cellar in a farm now owned by G. B. Ripley Esq., still designates the spot.  Dr. Lathrop was the pastor of one church sixty-three years, and for a long period was regarded with unusual veneration, as the Patriarch of the Congregational Churches of New England.  He died in 1820, aged eighty-nine.  His works comprise eight or ten volumes.

Col. Simon Lathrop was another distinguished scion of this stock.  He was the third son of Samuel Lathrop 2d, and born in 1689.  He was long a Captain of foot, and noted for his military bearing.  He afterwards commanded a regiment, and was in the expeditions against Annapolis and Lewisburg.  This regiment was not made up of the lowest grades of society, as is often the case in an army, but its members were mostly active, useful and respectable men.  After the troops had obtained possession of Louisburg, one of the British naval officers was walking in the street with a French lady of distinction, who had on a robe that trailed far behind, and under the train a lap dog was running. A young soldier belonging to Lathrop's regiment, out of mere roguery, threw something under the train at the dog.  It yelled, the lady resented the insult, the

officer ordered the offender to be bound and receive a
certain number of lashes, but the regiment turned out
of their quarters to a man, at a minute's warning, and
rescued their comrade. Their Colonel, though not
with them at the time, approved the deed, and the
commanding officer allowed it to pass without repre-
hension. Col. Lathrop was an exellent officer, and a
great favorite with his men, but prudent, thrifty, and
fond of adding land to land, and house to house.
There was a doggerel song that the soldiers used to
sing after their return from *Capertoon*, that alludes to
this propensity.*

> Col. Lotrop he came on
>   As bold as Alexander :
> He want afraid, nor yet asham'd,
>   To be the chief commander.
>
> Col. Lotrop was the man,
>   His soldiers lov'd him dearly ;
> And with his sword and cannon great,
>   He help'd them late and early.
>
> Col. Lotrop, staunch and true,
>   Was never known to baulk it ;
> And when he was engag'd in trade,
>   He always fill'd his pocket.

Col. Lathrop died Jan. 25, 1775. He was an upright man, zealous in religion, faithful in training up
his family, and much respected and esteemed for his

---

* In connexion with this trait of character, the following anecdote
is told, though perhaps an apology ought to be made for perpetuating
such a trifle. Some laborers were one evening sitting under a tree,
and conversing about the moon. One said there was land there, as
well as upon earth; others doubted it. At length Col. Lathrop's negro
man, who was near, exclaimed—"Poh! poh! no such thing—no land
there, I'm sure. If there was, Massa have a farm there before now."

abilities and social virtues.   His wife was a Separatist,
and he carefully abstained from any interference with
her predilections, but was accustomed every Sunday to
carry her in his chaise up to her meeting, half a mile
beyond his own—then return to his own place of worship, and after the service was over, go up town again
after his wife.

Other descendants of the Rev. John Lathrop, besides
the Norwich branch, are numerous in New England;
but most of them adhere to the orthography of their
ancestor, and spell the name Lothrop.   Dr. Daniel
Lathrop, who had seen the name of his ancestors in
the register offices in London, introduced the more
correct form into the Norwich family.

The Lathrops, Huntingtons, and other principal
families of Norwich, owned slaves, whom they employed for house-servants.   The colored population
was therefore numerous for a northern town, and it was
not until near the era of the revolution, that the reasona-
bleness and equity of holding their fellow creatures in
durance, began to be questioned by the citizens.   At
length it was whispered about that it was inconsistent
to complain of political oppression, and yet withhold
from others the privileges to which they were entitled :—to fight for liberty, and yet refuse it to a portion of their fellow creatures.   Several persons voluntarily emancipated their slaves.  The following instance
is from a newspaper of the day :

"Dec. 1774.   Mr. Samuel Gager, of Norwich, from
a conscientious regard to justice, has lately liberated
three faithful slaves, and as a compensation for their
services, leased them a valuable farm on very moderate
terms.   Mr. Jonathan Avery also emancipated an
able industrious negro man, from the same noble
principle."

But whether slaves or freemen, the Africans of Norwich have always been treated with forbearance and lenity. They have been particularly indulged in their annual elections and trainings. In former times, the ceremony of a mock election, of a negro governor, created no little excitement in their ranks. This was a great festival to them, but so demoralizing in its effects, that it is strange it should have been tolerated by the magistrates, in a town so rigid in its code of morals. A very decent grave stone in the public burial ground, bears this inscription—"In memory of Boston Trowtrow, Governor of the African tribe in this town, who died 1772, aged 66." After the death of this person, *Sam Hun'ton* was annually elected to this mock dignity for a much greater number of years, than his honorable namesake and master,—Samuel Huntington Esq., filled the gubernatorial chair. It was amusing to see this sham dignitary after his election, riding through the town on one of his master's horses, adorned with plaited gear, his aids on each side, a la militaire, himself puffing and swelling with pomposity, sitting bolt upright, and moving with a slow, majestic pace, as if the universe was looking on. When he mounted or dismounted, his aids flew to his assistance, holding his bridle, putting his feet into the stirrup, and bowing to the ground before him. The Great Mogul, in a triumphal procession, never assumed an air of more perfect self-importance than the negro Governor at such a time.

# CHAPTER XXIII.

In the year 1748 two highways to the landing were
opened, east and west of the Little Plain and Wawecos Hill. These coincided with what are now called
Crescent and Washington streets. The road across
the Hill from the Little Plain to the Landing was
henceforth but little used, and permission was given
to Benajah Bushnell to enclose it, he maintaining convenient bars for the people to pass. This hill, a prominent feature in the scenery of the place, was called
by the first planters Fort Hill. The conjecture may
be allowed, that the rude Indian fortress which crowned
its summit, stood near where Mr. Rockwell has erected
an observatory. It might there keep a look-out both
ways from the Shetucket to the Yantic. This hill was
afterwards called Wawecos, from Waweequaw, the
brother of Uncas, who claimed it as his personal
property.

1750. A highway was opened " by the water, from
Nathaniel Backus' dwelling-house, to Capt. Bushnell's ware-house." At these points it met the east
and west highways, and formed a continuous road
round the base of the hill. This is now Water street.
There was also a highway laid out leading down to
Sandy Beach. The boundary between Chelsea and
the Town Plot, was " at the parting of the paths on
the Little Plain, at Oliver Arnold's corner."

Chelsea was now an important section of the town, and it was voted "that all future warnings for town meetings be set up at the Landing-place, on some post to be provided by the inhabitants there." A sign-post was accordingly set up "at Mr. Peter Landman's corner," as the most conspicuous place, and remained there many years. Another noted station where public notifications were soon after this directed to be posted up, was "the Little Elm before Capt. Lothrop's door." This was at the Lathrop farm, on the Shetucket, where a public ferry or bridge had been kept up ever since the settlement. Upon these posts, and those before mentioned in the town plot, all warnings and announcements which any way affected the interests of the people were affixed; with the exception of intended marriages, which always appeared on the meeting-house doors.

Mr. Peter Lanman's corner mentioned above, by the opening of Main street, and other changes, has long ceased to be a corner. It was on the spot afterwards occupied for a long term of years as a druggist's store, by Dr. Dwight Ripley. The sign of "Lee & Osgood" now indicates the location.

The common lands and flats upon the *Cove*, extending as far up as "Elijah Lathrop's Grist Mills," were laid out in 1760, or near that period. The shares were divided into tenths, and each tenth into eight several parcels or lots, as the sheep-walks had been.

Mr. Elijah Lathrop, whose name was thus early connected with the *mills* of Norwich, was for a long period almost the sole resident at the Falls. Elderkin and Lathrop are the only names popularly connected with that quarter of the town previous to the year 1800.

In 1794 Mr. Lathrop had a valuable oil mill destroyed by fire. The canal around the Falls was con-

structed by him at a great expense.   For a considerable
distance it was blasted through solid rock, and, at the
period when it was done, was considered a great work.
Mr. Lathrop was the second son of the brave Col.
Simon Lathrop, of Cape Breton memory.   He died in
1814, aged ninety-four.

Mr. Andrew Huntington and Mr. Ebenezer Bushnell, were also early proprietors at the Falls.   They
established a paper manufactory in 1794.

From the General List of 1757, it appears that there
were then eighty-seven resident proprietors of rateable
estate in " the society of New Chelsy," and twenty-
five non-residents.

The year 1760 may be taken as the era when the
commerce of Norwich, which at two distinct periods,
before and after the war, became important, received
its first great impulse.   A foresight of this prosperity
was obtained by the fathers of the town, in 1751, when
they made the following declaration.

" Whereas, the town did formerly grant to Mr. Joseph
Kelley, shipwright, to build vessels at the Landing-place,
where he is now building, during the town's pleasure, and
would give him twelve months notice, do now declare that
their will and pleasure, as to his building in said place, is at
an end, the place being much wanted for public improvement, and do now give him notice thereof accordingly, and
order the selectmen to notify him, by sending him a copy of
this act."

The coasting trade was now carried on to some extent, and many sloops and schooners were owned and
fitted out.   In the " New London Summary," then the
only newspaper in this part of the colony, the adver-
tisements of the merchants and packet masters of
" New Chelsy," are frequently inserted.   Very soon

also, the place began to take its proper name and orthography, Chelsea.

By the peace of 1763 a large territory was acquired by the English in Nova Scotia. A part of this was laid out into towns and sections by the provincial government, and associations of individuals were formed in the colonies to purchase and settle these lands, which were offered them on very easy terms. The inhabitants of the eastern part of Connecticut, and several citizens of Norwich in particular, entered largely into these purchases, as they did also into the purchases, made at the same period, of land on the Delaware river. The proprietors held their meetings at the Town-house, in Norwich, and many persons of even small means were induced to become subscribers, in the expectation of bettering their fortunes. On the Delaware they purchased of the natives, Coshaiton. In Nova Scotia, Dublin, Horton, Falmouth, Amherst, &c., which were laid out and settled by New England emigrants—a considerable number of whom were from the eastern part of Connecticut. Sloops were continually plying back and forth, from Norwich and New London to Menis and Chignecto, with emigrants and provisions; one hundred and thirty-seven settlers sailed at one time from these two places.

Norwich, as well as many other towns was inundated with the French Neutrals, a harmless and much abused people, who, in the year 1755, had been driven from their peaceful seats in the Northern Provinces, by their English conquerors, and forced to take refuge in New England. They met with sympathy and charity in Connecticut: New London, in particular was overrun with them, but most of them afterwards returned to Canada. Capt. Richard Leffingwell, of Norwich,

17

in the brig Pitt, carried 240 of them, with their priest, to Quebec, in the year 1767.

The West India trade also began to thrive in Chelsea, about the year 1760. A back country of some extent made its deposites in Norwich, and its citizens were induced to enter largely into commercial affairs. Chelsea was their Port, and instead of exhibiting, as heretofore, nothing but ship-yards and warehouses, fishermen's cabins and sailors' cottages, it now began to show some respectable buildings. Let us suppose ourselves walking through its streets about this period. We might see lying at the wharves, perhaps departing or entering, the coasting sloops, Defiance and Ann, the *London* Packet, Ebenezer Fitch, master ; the Norwich Packet, Capt. Fanning ; the brig Two Brothers, Capt. Waterman ; sloop Betsey, Capt. Billings ; the Nancy, Capt. Rogers ; the Charming Sally, Capt. Matthew Perkins, &c., &c. Here is the new establishment of Jacob De Witt, just settled in town, and opening an assortment of merchandize : that of Gershom Breed, for all sorts of shipping materials and groceries : that of John Baker Brimmer, who keeps a little of every thing, and gives " cash for ox-horns, old pewter and hopps :" that of Ebenezer Colburn, iron-monger and cutler, at the sign of the Black Horse : that of Isaiah Tiffany, who keeps " ribbons, fans, calicoes, lawns and china-ware, just imported from London :" and that of Nathaniel Backus, Jr. This last store was the corner building, long occupied by Messrs. Charles and George Coit. The door, which by the gradual filling up of the street, was in later years, on a level with the ground, was then entered by three steps ; the broad one at the top serving for a horse-block, where females from the country, who came into town for shopping, mounted and dismounted from their horses. Main street was not then opened, and the position was not as conspicuous as afterwards. If we enquire the prices of articles, we shall find some of them as follows:— best London pewter, 1s. 6 per lb. : Bristol do. 1s. 5 ; brass kettles, 2s. 2 ; German serge, 5s. per yard ; black Taffety, 8s. ; blue and red Duffles, 4s. 3 ; Barbadoes rum, 3s. 4 per gall.; molasses, 1s. 8 ; Bohea tea, 4s. 8 per lb. ; Muscovado sugar, 6d.

The goods in the retail stores of that day were somewhat oddly assorted. For instance, one man advertised sheep's-wool, codfish, West India products and an assortment of European dry goods. "N. B. As the subscriber has an interest in a still-house at Chelsea, he expects to have New England rum constantly to sell."

At this period, the best assortments were all up town, and the ladies of Chelsea were as much accustomed to go thither to do their shopping, that is, if dry goods or fancy articles were wanted, as the ladies of the town now are to go to Chelsea. Social intercourse was at this time, on the most easy and delightful footing, in both divisions of the town. Visits were frequent, long and familiar. The customs, in some respects, were the reverse of the present. The visit was made, and the visiters returned home by *day-light.* Instead of the lady giving out invitations to her guests, the guests sent word to the lady, (all the neighborhood joining together on such occasions,) that they would come and spend the afternoon with her.

At the period of which we are speaking, West Chelsea consisted of some two or three small buildings and a ship yard. There was no bridge over the river, and no road from that side, except a cart track to the Great Plain. The Ferry extended from the rear of Mr. Clark Kinney's house, to the opposite bank, and here for many years, old Capt. Adams used to ply his boat, for the accomodation of passengers. In 1764, a highway was opened from the Landing to the Great Plain.

Water Street, in the time of the spring floods, was usually impassable. Every high tide brought water into it, and people now living can remember the scow, bottom upwards, that served as a causeway for foot-passengers over the worst place. To show how much the streets have been gradually raised, we may mention that the King house in Union street, which is now entered by a descent from the streets, was when built, so far elevated above the street, as to have an ascent of one or two steps to the front door.

# CHAPTER XXIV.

Ecclesiastical Affairs.

THE ministry of Dr. Lord was eminently useful and successful. When he settled in 1717, there were about thirty male members in his church, and as many females. In the first fifty years of his ministry, three hundred and thirty were admitted. In 1721, there was a revival in his church. In 1735, he took a journey to Northampton, in order to see with his own eyes, and hear from Mr. Edwards himself, the particulars of the great revival there. His report, and his labors on his return, were the means of another revival in his church, and again in 1740 there was another. It is remarkable, that at each of these periods, there was also a powerful revival in Windham, a town ten miles from Norwich, a place which after that period, was, for a long time said to be, in a spiritual sense, like Egypt, without rain.

Dr. Lord's public services were always impressive. One of his contemporaries said, that "he seemed to have an inexhaustible fund of proper words, pointed sense, and devout affections." The revival in his church in 1721, was at a time of very general religious declension throughout New England. The great revival period in America commenced in 1735, but was most extraordinary in 1740 and 1741. Whitefield was at this time laboring in America, and his great success led many others into a course of itinerant and often

17*

erratic preaching. Irregularities, and sensible demonstrations of the effects of the Spirit, were too often coun-
tenanced, but the clergy, as a body, opposed them,
and in some instances carried their zeal so far, as to
condemn the revival itself. The work however was
generally considered a great and glorious work, and
several associations of ministers gave testimony in its
favor. June 23, 1743, twelve ministers convened at
Norwich, for the purpose of acknowledging the good-
ness of God in this revival. The churches in this quarter, however, had for some time been in a state of
internal commotion with respect to doctrinal points,
and this was aggravated by the difference of opinion in
regard to revival measures.

At Mr. Lord's ordination, the Church had renounced
the Saybrook Platform; but in 1744, the pastor and a
majority of the members were in favor of it, and a vote
was passed to receive it as their rule of discipline.
This led to an important schism in the church. Thirty
male members, including one of their deacons, drew
off, and forming a separate church, were known by
the name of Separatists. They had among them several of the most wealthy and respectable men in the
Society. They built a house for public worship, just
at the foot of Bean Hill, and for a number of years had
the Rev. Mr. Fuller for their minister.

Another church of this description was organized at
Norwich Farms at the same period, and ministers provided for both. Thomas Denison being ordained at
the Farms, Oct. 29, 1746, and Jedediah Hide at Norwich Town the next day, Oct. 30. Similar disputes
also agitated the Rev. Mr. Kirtland's church, in the
third or Newent Society, and a seceding church of seven
members was formed there in 1750—Jeremiah Tracy,
one of the seven, becoming their minister, and preach-

ing to them—a work which the Newent Church, in their records, solemnly declare that they believe the Lord had not called him to do.

The reasons given by the seceders in this society, for withdrawing, were various. One said it was because he found no edification in the church : another, because "the church in words profess Christ, but in works deny him." Mr. Joseph Safford, one of the most zealous of the Separates, gave his reasons as follows :—1st, because the church was not organized with sufficient church officers ; 2d, they admitted members who could not say that Christ was formed in them, or that they had acted faith in him ; 3d, they admitted members into covenant, who were not in full communion.

The Newent church was greatly harrassed by these divisions ; that at the *Farms* still more so, as it led to the dismission of Mr. Wills in 1749. Indeed there was scarcely a church in the whole state, which was not at this time troubled and torn by conflicting opinions, respecting church government and the terms of communion. In the course of ten years, as many as twenty churches of Congregational Separates were formed in different parts of Connecticut ; but they have since, one after another, become extinct, or been merged in other denominations, particularly the Baptist.

As these churches were not recognized by the Legislature, the members were still taxed to support their former ministers, and this led to various instances of petty persecution and private suffering, imprisonment and distraining of goods, the memory of which is still hoarded and perhaps aggravated by tradition. At Norwich the number of Separates was considerable, and their influence still greater, so that at one period, they out-voted the standing regular church, and de-

clared that they would not support a minister by a tax.
The other party appealed to the Legislature, and obtained an order to enforce the rates.   Violent commo-
tions were the consequence, and it is said that no less
than forty persons were imprisoned on this account in
one season.   One of the most aggravated cases of this
kind, was that of a respectable widow lady, of the
name of Backus.   Her son had previously suffered an
imprisonment of twenty days, and herself, on a dark
night in October, 1752, about nine o'clock, was seized
by the collector, carried to jail, and kept there thirteen
days.   Her tax was then paid, but without her consent,
by her son-in-law, Gen. Jabez Huntington.   At a subsequent period, her grandson, Gen. Jedidiah Huntington, pledged himself to pay her rates annually, that
the venerable lady might not be disturbed by any soli-
citations for that purpose.   This lady was mother of
the Rev. Isaac Backus, of Middleborough, Mass., who,
in his Church History, has preserved a letter from her,
giving an account of her imprisonment, and the abundant measure of divine support that she received under
it.   She states, that Mr. Griswold, formerly a deacon
of Mr. Lord's church, and then officiating as deacon of
the Separate Church, and Messrs. Hill, Sabin and
Grover, were imprisoned at the same time.   Mr. Backus
adds—"They went on in such ways for about eight
years, until the spiritual weapons of truth and love,
vanquished those carnal weapons, which have not been
so used in Norwich since."

The last instance of distrainment that is remembered
to have taken place, was in the case of Mr. Ezekiel
Barrett, who died recently, at a very advanced age.
He had refused to pay the usual rates, and was arrested at the Court House, just at the close of a town meeting.   He made an obstinate resistance, and it took the

constable and six other men to convey him to jail. He was considerably bruised in the scuffle, and by being dragged upon the frozen ground. After a week's imprisonment, he gave his note for the sum demanded, and was released. Subsequently he refused to pay the note, alleging that it was forced from him by oppression. It was sued at law, and his cow taken and sold at the post to pay the rate and costs.

It is undoubtedly this instance which has given rise to the reports that these taxes were always rigorously exacted, even to the seizure of the poor man's cow and his last bushel of grain. The cases above mentioned are believed to be the only ones that occurred in which any severity was exercised. Dr. Lord always treated the Separatists with kindness and respect, and this led the way to the restoration of a considerable number of them to his church. But the mode of raising the minister's salary, by rates, soon became excessively odious to the society. In 1783 a liberal subscription was made and a fund established, in order to do away with the necessity of rates. Dr. Daniel Lathrop, by his will, left £500 towards this fund, his successor, Dr. Joshua Lathrop, added £150 more; it was raised by other gentlemen of the society to £2000. Another step was to induce the pew-holders to relinquish their rights, so that the pews might be sold annually, and the avails applied to the same object. This was happily accomplished except in the case of three individuals, who obstinately refused to give up their pews, averring that if they could not sit in the same place where they had hitherto sat, they would not go to meeting. This matter was, however, at length accommodated, the pews sold, and the fund advantageously employed; so that a sum was annually raised

sufficient to discharge all ecclesiastical expenses, and
the minister's rate tax happily abolished.

The first annual sale of pews was in 1791. This
was in the fourth Meeting-house of the society, which
seemed to have been destined to misfortune from its
first origin. Its erection was vehemently opposed by
a strong party. A vote to build was, however, obtained, in 1748, seventy-two to thirty-two, and again,
in a second meeting, seventy-six to thirty-eight. Ebenezer Backus, Esq., was directed to lay the matter
before the General Assembly, to ask leave to build, to
request that the site should be fixed, and that the Separates should be exempted from paying any thing
towards it. The next year it was determined not to
build a new house, but to repair the old one. In 1750
they rescinded this vote, and ordered the building committee to renew their operations. £7000, old tenor,
was subscribed towards it, and the shell was soon completed. But the sum was insufficient to go any farther,
and it long remained in this unfinished state. The
bell was, however, hung, the clock fixed in its place,*
and divine worship performed in the half-built house.
Mr. Whitfield, in one of his tours through the country, preached in it while in this rough and incomplete
state; fourteen years afterward he came round again,
and it was still in the same condition. He publicly re-
proved the people for their negligence, and in consequence measures were taken for its completion. They
did not proceed with much spirit, but a little was done
every year. Spaces for pews were bought by individuals, and enclosed at a common expense. Four slips
in front of the pulpit were reserved for old men and

---

* This was the first Town Clock, and cost £8; the fixtures something more. It was purchased in 1745.

women, and low benches were placed in the aisles for children. The galleries were built, stone steps set up, bannisters placed around the bell, and finally, in 1769, a vote was passed to *colour* the meeting-house.

This house, like others of that day, had doors on three sides. Watt's version of the Psalms was introduced in 1772. In 1801 this church was destroyed by fire, together with a store and dwelling-house near it. The fire was supposed to have been kindled by an incendiary, but the culprit was never discovered. The present Church was built the succeeding year, and the expense defrayed partly by subscription, and partly by a lottery.

The Church of the Separates flourished for some years; Mr. Fuller was an excellent man and a good preacher, but eventually he re-united with the Congregationalists, and was settled at Plainfield. After his removal the Church dwindled away; most of the females, and some of the males, returned to their ancient home, and were received with cordiality. Among these was the venerable Deacon Griswold. It created considerable emotion in the meeting-house when, for the first time after his secession, his gray locks were seen in the old man's seat. As he was somewhat deaf, he soon afterward asked permission of the young pastor to go up the pulpit stairs and lean over the door while he was preaching, that he might hear more distinctly. Mr. Strong immediately invited him to take a seat in the pulpit, which he ever afterwards did, when able to attend meeting.

Before the final extinction of the Separate Church, a small party seceded from these Seceders, and embraced the doctrine of the universal salvation of all mankind, or the final restoration of all to a state of happiness. These proved to be a soil ready prepared, into

which Murray and Winchester afterwards cast their
seed, and reaped something of a harvest in Norwich.
They held their meetings in the large front kitchen of
the house then occupied by Mr. Ebenezer Grover, and
still known as the old Grover house—the Grovers,
father and son, mother and daughter, down to the venerable spinster and school-mistress, Miss Molly Grover,
the last of the family in Norwich, sympathizing heart-
ily with all seceders from the prevailing order.   Here
Mr. Hide used occasionally to hold meetings, and after
him Mr. Gamaliel Reynolds.   The latter was a stone
mason by trade, a man of no education, but of considerable native talent.   He was one of that original class
of men,—keen, witty and observing; famed for hu-
morous sallies, and those apt remarks that are treasured
up, and retailed as sayings, of which the present day
seems to exhibit fewer specimens than of yore.   Norwich, in former days, possessed many of these original
characters, both of the whimsical and shrewd species.

The meeting-house built by the Separatists after the
extinction of the sect, was used for a female academy,
which, under some of its teachers, was sufficiently distinguished to call in a considerable number of pupils
from the neighboring towns.   Dr. Morse, so well
known for his Geographies and Gazetteers, was for a
short time its preceptor.   The building was always in
use for the joint purposes of education and religion.
The upper part was occupied for many years as a place
of worship by the Methodists.   They relinquished it
in 1834, on the completion of their present Chapel on
Bean Hill.   It was taken down in 1843.

# CHAPTER XXV.

Ministers. Rev. Dr. Lord. Rev. Dr. Strong.

DR. LORD preached his half-century sermon, Nov. 29, 1767, from II Peter, 1 : 12–15. He was then seventy-four years of age, and in firm health and strength. He preached another interesting retrospective discourse eleven years afterwards, on the sixty-first anniversary of his ordination. This was printed, and is entitled " The aged minister's solemn appeal to God, and serious address to his people." He preached also a sixty-fourth anniversary sermon in 1781, but it was not published. After this period infirmity came fast upon him. In his eighty-seventh year his eye-sight failed him, and he preached ever afterwards extemporaneously. He however continued to write his discourses, keeping his place upon the paper with his left hand, and though the lines could not be very straight, and the words frequently ran over each other, his grand daughter Caroline used to study it out, and then read it over slowly and repeatedly to him, until it was sufficiently imprinted on his memory to enable him to deliver it with fluency from the pulpit. It was observed by his people that the sermons thus preached, were some of his best; for generally Mr. Lord's style was diffuse and somewhat reduplicative, but the difficulty of writing when he had become blind, led him to think longer and to condense his thoughts into as few words as possible. His rea-

18

soning powers were even at this age very little impaired, and to use the language of one of his most intimate friends, " his meekness, humility, philanthropy, and heavenly-mindedness, were apparently increased, and he seemed to

> ' Stand with his starry pinions on,
> Drest for the flight, and ready to be gone.' "

He resumed his pastoral labors, at intervals, and being assisted up the pulpit stairs, graced the public worship, with his venerable presence, by the side of his young associate, almost without interruption, until his death, which took place March 31, 1784, almost sixty-seven years after his ordination. He preached the last time, about six weeks before his death. His funeral sermon was delivered April 2d, by the Rev. James Cogswell, of Windham.

Dr. Lord was a small man, and in his latter days stooped much, yet his appearance was pleasing and interesting. Though he lived to old age, his constitution was far from robust, and in his early years he was subject to pain and disease. Age, therefore, personified in him, looked still more aged, and no one could approach him without being struck with the reverend antiquity of his appearance. His intercourse with his people was like that of an affectionate father in his family. " I have lived, (said he,) in their hearts, and they in mine." In addition to a sickly frame, Dr. Lord had great trials in his family. His first wife, Ann Taylor, of Westfield, to whom he was married in 1720, was confined to the bed sixteen years, and eight years of that time was incapable of feeding herself, but these dispensations were all sanctified to this good man. He found time to perform well, all the regular duties of his office, and in the course of his life published twelve sermons, which were preached on special occasions. A part of his Diary, written in his old age, was preserved by his colleague and successor, who to the day of his death, cherished a most affectionate veneration for his predecessor. On his eighty-first birth-day, Dr. Lord wrote in his Diary thus:

"It is a wonder to many and especially to myself, that there are any remains of the man and the minister at this advanced age, and that I am still able to preach with acceptance to my numerous assembly. It is much that I have survived two former climacterics, in which many have died, and ministers not a few, and still more that I have lived to this greater climacteric, nine times nine. But the climax is at hand — the certain crisis. Death has not gone by me, not to come upon me."

On his eighty-third birth-day he makes similar reflections, praying that his sensible failure in vigor and usefulness may be balanced by larger portions of the Divine presence. He alludes to his being the oldest preaching minister in the State, yet considers himself but a babe and dwarf in religion, in proportion to its high demands, and is confounded to think how low he is under such means of rising high. On a subsequent anniversary he writes thus:

"This day completes the eighty-fifth year of my age, from which to look back into early life, through all the stages and various scenes thereof, makes the affecting retrospect swell with the idea of a very long term. But what is this to the more affecting prospect of an eternity before me, infinitely larger than the largest circumference to the smallest point of time. Oh my soul, hast thou on the garment of salvation, both inherent and imputed righteousness, the one to qualify for heaven, the other to give the title! art thou the subject of that effectual calling which is both the fruit and proof or evidence of election?"

In 1778, March 18th, the Rev. Joseph Strong was

settled as a colleague with Dr. Lord, who was then
eighty-four years of age. Mr. Strong was the son of
the Rev. Nathan Strong of Coventry. By his mother's
side, he was descended from the Williams' family, who
were taken captives by the Indians at Deerfield, in the
night of Feb. 28, 1704. The general circumstances
of this tragedy are well known. The two little
daughters of Mr. Williams who went into captivity
with their father, were named Eunice and Esther.
The former was never redeemed, but being adopted
into the family of a chief, she became attached to the
Indian manners and customs, refused to return to her
relatives, embraced the Roman Catholic religion, and
married a chief, named Roger Toroso, who resided at
St. Johns, twenty miles from Montreal. Esther was
ransomed and returned home with her father. She
married the Rev. Mr. Meachum of Coventry, and one
of her daughters became the wife of the Rev. Nathan
Strong, who was ordained Pastor of a Second Congregational Church in Coventry, in 1745, and was the
father of the Rev. Nathan Strong, D. D. of Hartford,
and the Rev. Joseph Strong, D. D. of Norwich. At
the ordination of the latter, the sermon was preached
by his brother, and the charge given by his father.—
The text was from Isaiah 52, 7. " How beautiful,"
&c. The scene was deeply affecting and impressive,
particularly when the speaker turned to the young
candidate and said :

" My dear brother,—I may now address you by that en-
dearing epithet in all its senses. We received our being under God, from the same parents, were educated by the same
nurturing kindness, have professed obedience to the same
glorious Father in heaven, and this day introduces you a
brother laborer in the Lord's vineyard. Very pleasant hast
thou been unto me, my brother, and never was my pleasure
greater in beholding thee, than on this day's solemnities.

Long may your feet be beautiful on these mountains of Zion. The God of heaven bless and preserve thee."

Nor was the emotion of the audience less intense, when the father of the candidate, in solemn and affecting terms, where deep feeling contended with ministerial gravity, invested him with the priest's office, and addressing him as a dearly beloved son, charged him to take heed to the ministry which he had received, and to serve with his venerable colleague, " as a son with a father, as a Timothy with Paul the aged."

Mr. Strong married soon after his ordination, Mary, daughter of the Hon. Jabez Huntington.

At the time of his settlement, there were two seceding congregations in the society, considerably numerous, but they soon became extinct, and an uncommon degree of peace and unanimity existed in the society, during the whole of his prolonged ministry. He was distinguished for the benevolence of his disposition, and the fervency and solemnity of his prayers. In social intercourse, he exhibited the manners of the gentleman and the character of the christian. Many of the facts in these sketches owe their perpetuation to his retentive memory and rich flow of conversation.

Dr. Strong's pecuniary dealings with his people were uniformly marked by great generosity on his part. His salary was never raised above the stipulated sum of $444, except for a very few years, when an annual gratuity was added to it, on account of the high price of provisions. The financial arrangements at his settlement, throw some light on the currency of the day. The society agreed to give him £300 as a settlement, in three annual payments, of £100 each; a salary of £100 per annum for the first three years, and

18*

after that term, £133 6s. 8 per annum.  This was to
be proportioned to wheat at 6s. per bushel; rye at
3s. 6; Indian corn at 3s.; pork at 3½d. per lb., and
the best grass fed beef at 40s. per cwt.  To this salary
was added twenty-five cords of wood annually, to be
delivered at his door.  The regulation of prices in
these times of fluctuating currency, was a matter of no
small perplexity.  For the first payment of Mr. Strong's
settlement, he received £1200 in bills of credit, as an
equivalent for £100.  In 1779, £2500 in bills was
equal to 100, and in 1780, he received for his salary,
£7200—72 to 1; being then the proportion between
continental paper and silver money.

In 1829, Dr. Strong applied to the society to settle
a colleague, wishing, as he said, to have the same satisfaction that his venerable predecessor had enjoyed
towards the close of his life, in beholding the society
harmoniously unite in settling a successor.  That this
object might be accomplished with less inconvenience
to his people, he voluntarily proposed to relinquish his
salary after the first year.  The society acceded to his
request. and the Rev. Cornelius B. Everest was installed as his colleague the same year.  Dr. Strong died
Dec. 18, 1834, aged eighty-one—in the fifty-seventh
year of his ministry.  The Rev. Dr. Nott, of Franklin,
his senior in age, and nearly his coeval in office, assisted at his interment, and since that event, seems to
stand alone, the patriarch of the county.  The minis-
tries of Drs. Lord and Strong comprise one hundred
and seventeen years, besides six years of joint service.
This case is more extraordinary than even that of the
Mayhews of Martha's Vineyard.

Mr. Everest was dismissed in April, 1836.

Rev. Hiram P. Arms installed as his successor, Aug.
3, 1836.

# CHAPTER XXVI.

### The Revolutionary Period.

THE first public act from which we gain any idea of the spirit of the citizens of Norwich, with regard to the great subjects pending between England and the colonies, was on April 7, 1765. The Stamp Act had become a law, and it remained to be seen whether its operation could be enforced. The freemen were convened by the Town-clerk, and the question submitted by him, whether he should proceed in the duties of his office as heretofore, without using the stamps :— " Whereupon it was agreed unanimously, and voted in full town meeting, that the clerk shall proceed in his office as usual, and the town will save him harmless from all damage that he may sustain thereby." Soon after this, the citizens scornfully refused to receive the stamps, and burned Ingersoll, the stamp distributor, in effigy, upon the high hill overlooking the plain. No bolder spirit was manifested in Boston than in Norwich.

March 18, 1767, the anniversary of the repeal of the Stamp Act was celebrated by a number of gentlemen under Liberty Tree, with great festivity. This tree was erected in the centre of the open plain; was very lofty, decked with standards and appropriate devices,

and crowned with a cap.   A tent, or booth, was erected under it, called the Pavilion.   Here, almost daily,
people assembled to hear the news, make speeches
and encourage each other in the determination to resist
all oppression.

Early in December of that year, the town received
the famous Boston Circular from the selectmen, recommending the disuse of certain enumerated articles of
British production.   A town meeting was immediately
convened to consider the subject, and a committee
appointed to bring in a report, which was presented in
less than half an hour, and an agreement entered into
substantially the same as that of Boston, viz.—To dis-
courage the use of tea, wines and spirituous liquors,
china ware, superfluities of every kind, mourning apparel, and in general, all foreign manufactures.   They
recommended also the raising of sheep's wool, flax
and hemp, and the establishing of domestic manufactures; and that the citizens should especially promote
those new manufactures that had been set up among
them of paper, stone and earthen ware.   The report
closes in this manner:—

" And it is strongly recommended to the worthy ladies of
this town that for the future they would omit tea-drinking
in the afternoon ; and to commission officers, to be moderate
and frugal in their acknowledgments to their companies for
making choice of them as their officers, which at this dis-
tressing time will be more honorable than the usual lavish
and extravagant entertainments heretofore given."—Voted
unanimously Dec. 14, 1767, and ordered to be printed in the
New London Gazette.

The names of the Committee bringing in this report,
will show who were the leading patriots of the town at
that time.

| | |
|---|---|
| Hon. Hezekiah Huntington, | Mr. Gershom Breed, |
| Hon. Jabez Huntington, | Mr. Jeremiah Kinsman, |
| Simon Tracy Esq. | Elisha Fitch Esq. |
| Capt. Richard Hide, | Col. Wm. Whiting, |
| Capt. Hugh Ledlie, | Eben'r. Hartshorn Esq. |
| Major John Durkie, | Capt. Jabez Perkins, |
| Mr. Isaac Tracy, | Dr. Daniel Lathrop. |

It will be observed, that in this agreement there is an allusion to the infant manufactures of Norwich. It was the first town in the colony, and one of the first in New England, that commenced any regular manufacturing establishments. Col. Christopher Leffingwell erected a Paper Mill in 1765, near Noman's acre. The Connecticut Gazette was first printed on paper from this factory, Dec. 12, 1766. If this was not the first paper manufactory established in the Colonies, it was certainly not far behind the first. Col. Leffingwell was one of the most enterprising citizens of that period. He encouraged and aided several artizans and mechanics to commence new kinds of business. Through his exertions a pottery for the making of stone and earthen ware was established, and the manufacture of pot and pearl ashes undertaken.

Extensive iron works were soon after established in the upper part of the town, by Elijah Backus Esq.; and a second forge was erected on the Yantic, three miles above that of Mr. Backus, by Mr. Nehemiah Huntington. Mechanics, such as carpenters, joiners, black-smiths, silver-smiths, shoe-makers, tailors, &c. were distributed in tolerably fair proportions, all over the town. There was one " Distiller of Geneva," and one " manufacturer of flower of mustar." Two taverns were kept upon the plain, by Joseph Peck and Azariah Lathrop, and between Bean Hill and the Landing, there were six retail shops, containing assortments

of dry goods and groceries. Lawyers were more numerous than at present, the bounduries of land being
less strictly defined, and the customs of society, as
well as the dispositions of men, leaning more towards
litigation. Three of the physicians and surgeons were
eminent in their line, viz. Drs. Turner, Tracy and
Perkins. In addition to these, there was in the Town
Plot, " Dr. Jonathan Marsh, surgeon and bone-setter."

This man was one of the self-installed members of
the faculty. He died soon afterwards, but his widow
took another doctor into immediate partnership, and
advertised that the business would be carried on as
before, adding,—"she herself understands bone-set-
ting."

In the summer of 1768 a stage coach was established
between Norwich and Providence; leaving Lathrop's
tavern every Wednesday morning, and forming a
weekly line. This was the first public conveyance upon
this route.

June 7, 1768, an entertainment was given at Peck's
tavern,* adjoining Liberty Tree, to celebrate the election of Wilkes to Parliament. The principal citizens,
both of town and landing assembled on this festive
occasion. All the furniture of the table, such as plates,
bowls, tureens, tumblers and napkins, were marked
"No. 45." This was the famous number of the
"North Briton," edited by Wilkes, which rendered
him so obnoxious to the ministry. The Tree of Liberty
was decked with new emblems, among which, and
conspicuously surmounting the whole, was a flag emblazoned with "No. 45, WILKES & LIBERTY."

In September of that year another festival was held
at the same place, in mockery of the pompous proceed-

* This was in the long house on the Plain, owned by Bela Peck Esq.,
not occupied for a tavern since the revolution.

ings of the Commissioners of Customs, appointed for
the colonies by the British Ministry. These Commissioners had published a list of holidays to be observed
by all persons in their employ, and among them was
" *September 8th*," the anniversary of the date of their
commission. The citizens of Norwich were resolved
to make it a holiday also. At the conclusion of the
banquet, toasts were drank, and at the end of every
one was added,

" AND THE 8TH OF SEPTEMBER."

Thus : " The King and the 8th of September."

" Wilkes and Liberty and the 8th of September."

" The famous 92 and the 8th of September."

Songs were also sung with this chorus; nor did the
assembly disperse without indignant speeches made
against " British mis-government," and the disgrace
of wearing a foreign yoke.

October 4. A town meeting was called to consider
" the critical and alarming conjuncture of affairs." This
was a full assembly, and all hearts were warm and unanimous. There was no need of discussion or debate.
The record of the meeting in the Town Book is inscribed upon the margin with the word

" Liberty ! Liberty ! Liberty !"

three times repeated. This word alone shows the
spirit that pervaded the assembly. They passed a vote
of cordial approbation of the measures of the Bostonians, saying—

" We consider the noble cause they are engaged in
as the common cause of our country, and will unite
both heart and hand in support thereof, against all enemies whatsoever." They also instructed their representatives, Joseph Tracy and Elisha Fitch, to use their
influence at the approaching session of the legislature,
to carry the following points :

1. That the Colony Treasury accounts be settled.
2. That the true state of the Treasury be made known.
3. That the colonels have a special muster and review of their respective regiments.
4. That encouragement be given to manufactures.
5. That union with the neighboring colonies be promoted.
6. That the debates be open.
          January 29, 1770.

The margin of the public record is again emblazoned with **LIBERTY! LIBERTY!** The following is an extract from the resolutions then passed.

" We give this public testimony of our hearty and unanimous approbation of the agreement the merchants have entered into, to stop the importation of British goods ; we will frown upon all who endeavour to frustrate these good designs, and avoid all correspondence and dealings with those merchants who shall dare to violate these obligations."

They proceeded to choose two diligent and discreet persons from each society, in addition to the Merchant's Committee, to make critical inspection into the conduct of all buyers and sellers of goods, who were to publish the names of those that should counteract the intent and meaning of the non-importation agreement, to the intent that such persons might be exposed to the odium and resentment of the people. They also recommend to the wealthy persons in town to enter into subscriptions for setting up and carrying on the making of nails, stocking-weaving, and other useful branches of manufacture, and every one in his respective sphere of action to encourage and promote industry and frugality.

In August, repeated meetings were convened for the same purpose; that is, to devise methods to support the non-importation agreement, which was the leading measure of the day. They declare their fixed opinion of the wisdom and importance of this measure ;—"that

they will " spare no pains to give it a fixed and solid
form, by following every breach thereof with the full
weight of their indignation, and withholding all commerce from any who dare to violate it ;" and that they
are " both grieved and incensed at the alarming conduct
or New York in violating the same."

Elijah Backus, Esq., and Capt. Jedediah Huntington were selected to represent the mercantile and
landed interest, at a meeting proposed to be held in
New Haven, the day after the college commencement,
to resolve on measures to support this agreement.

Let it not be supposed that all this spirit evaporated
in votes and public speeches; there is abundant evidence that the action was suited to the word, and not
a threat returned void.    The committees of inspection
were exceedingly vigilant; the lady who continued to
indulge in her cup of tea, or the gentleman in his glass
of brandy, were obliged to do it by stealth.    Any person who was found to have violated the agreement,
had his name posted in hand-bills through the town,
and published in the New London Gazette, a proceeding usually followed by insults, at least from the boys
and populace.    As the citizens were so strenuous upon
this subject, it may be gratifying to curiosity to see a
list of the articles specifically enumerated in the pledge
not to " import, purchase, or use, if produced or manufactured out of North America."

| | |
|---|---|
| Loaf sugar, | Wrought plate, |
| Snuff, | Gloves, |
| Mustard, | Shoes, |
| Starch, | Women's hats, |
| Malt Liquors, | Men's hats, except felts, |
| Linseed oil, | Muffs, tippets, and ermine, |
| Cheese, | Lawns and gauze, |
| Tea, | Sewing silk, |
| Wine, | Women's and children's stays, |

19

| | |
|---|---|
| Spiritous liquors, | Broadcloths above 9s. 6d. per |
| Cordage, | yard, |
| Anchors, | Cambrics above 5s. |
| Sole leather, | Linens above 2s. 6d. |
| Deck nails, | Silks of all kinds except taffety, |
| Clocks, | Silk handkerchiefs, |
| Jeweller's ware, | Silk and cotton velvets, |
| Gold and silver buttons, | All sorts of head-dress for wo- |
| Gold and silver lace, | men, as caps, ribbons, flow- |
| Thread lace, | ers, feathers, and turbans. |

As an example of the proceedings of the Committee, the case of Mr. Ebenezer Punderson may be cited. This person was a man of good manners and education, who kept a school upon the plain; but whose name was posted through the town with the charge of having repeatedly drank tea, and being questioned about it, declared that he would continue to do so. He said, moreover, that Congress was an unlawful combination, and their petition to his majesty haughty, violent, and impertinent, and uttered other words indicating disregard of the Continental association. The Committee thereupon ordered "That no trade, commerce, dealings, or intercourse whatever be carried on with him, but that he ought to be held as unworthy the rights of freeman, and inimical to the liberties of his country." This had the desired effect. A public recantation was made by Punderson, who averred that he was *sorry* for what he had done, and would drink no more tea until the use should be fully approved in North America; moreover, that he would no more vilify Congress, nor do any thing against the liberties and privileges of America.

Great exertions were made about this time to establish regular posts, and safe transportation lines through the colonies. Norwich was not behindhand in this business. In addition to the regular stage route to

Providence, individuals were engaged to ride weekly to all the larger cities in the vicinity, conveying letters, papers, memorandums, and small bundles. No effective system, however, was established in concert with other parts of the country, till May, 1774. At that time Mr. William Goddard, a distinguished printer, of Baltimore, arrived in town, being on a tour through the northern colonies to engage the friends of liberty to abolish "the illegal and oppressive parliamentary post office, and establish a provincial subscription post." Mr. Goddard held a conference with some of the citizens, who entered readily into his plans, and a regular weekly communication was forthwith established between Norwich and Boston. Mr. Moses Cleveland, a trusty and active person, was engaged as the post, to leave Norwich on Thursday, reach Boston on Saturday, and start the next Monday for Norwich again. This was the first regular post between the two places.

The manufactures of the place were now becoming important. Stocking weaving, which had been introduced in 1771, under the patronage of Col. Leffingwell, was a considerable business. The first operator was William Russell; afterward it was carried on by William Cox. At a later period it passed into other hands, and was continued in the town until 1825.

In 1773, Mr. Thomas Harland, from London, commenced the business of clock and watch making. He taught a number of apprentices, who established themselves in other places, and thus, through his means, the business became extensively spread in the surrounding country. This very ingenious artisan also constructed, in 1778, without any model, the first fire engine used in Norwich. [Mr. Harland died in 1807, aged seventy-one.]

The comb-making business was established in 1773

by Noah Hidden, near the meeting-house.  Mr. Alvan
Fosdick about the same period undertook the manufacture of *Cards,* for the breaking of wool and forming it into rolls, but the enterprize was not very successful.   More extensive and cheaper factories elsewhere soon put a stop to it in Norwich.   The manufacture of cut shingle nails from old iron hoops was
also commenced and continued during the war.   It
was a small business, but merits notice from its being
one of the first attempts in this country to make nails
in a way less slow and tedious than the old operation
of hammering them out of solid iron.

At the Landing, a tape weaver, from Manchester,
(England,) by the name of Zurishaddai Key, set up a
tape factory ; Messrs. Hubbard and Greene, of Boston,
opened an insurance office, and Samuel Loudon, from
New York, established a bookseller's shop ; the first in
that society.   In the town there were already two
booksellers' shops, one kept by Nathaniel Patten, and
the other by John Trumbull, but the assortments were
limited.

In 1773, the first newspaper was established in Norwich.  This was an important measure, as it respected
the business of the town, and it gave the Sons of Liberty an organ of their own, through which they could
breathe the spirit of patriotism into other minds.   The
first numbers contained a series of well-written patriotic essays, entitled "The Alarm," and signed Hamp-
den.   They were written by a distinguished patriot of
New York, and were directed against East India mo-
nopolies, the importation and use of Tea, and the Declaratory and Revenue Acts of Parliament.   Many
other spirited addresses appeared from time to time in
this paper, calculated to cherish and inflame the growing desire for political freedom.

This paper was called " The Norwich Packet, and Connecticut, Massachusetts, Rhode Island and New Hampshire Weekly Advertiser," — an imposing title and making pretensions to a wide circulation. It was printed by " Alexander Robertson, James Robertson, and John Trumbull, at their Printing Office, near the Court House, at 6s. 8d. per annum." The printers were also the editors and conducted the paper with considerable shrewdness and ability. The Robertsons, after the war, withdrew from the concern, but the junior editor Trumbull, continued the paper for many years alone, and on his death left it to his sons. Mr. Trumbull died in 1802, and was the first person buried with masonic honors in Norwich.

In some of the first numbers of this paper, we find proposals issued for publishing " An American Magazine;" also, " Watts' Psalms and Hymns," neatly bound and gilt on the back for 1s. 8. The New England Almanac, calculated for the meridian of Norwich, by Lemuel Warren, Philom: The New England Grammer, by Jacob Avery, school-master at Poquetannoc : " The History of Louisiana, or the western parts of Virginia and Carolina : " The Conquest of Canada or siege of Quebec, &c. &c. Marriages were notified in such terms as these :

" Last Thursday evening, Mr. Mundator Tracy an accomplished young gentleman, was married to the agreeable Caroline Bushnell, a young lady endowed with every qualification to make the connubial state happy."
" John Chester, Esq. of Wethersfield, to the amiable Miss Elizabeth Huntington, dau^r of Col. Jabez Huntington."

Deaths in this way :

" On Friday last, departed this life at Pomechoag, her saffron colored majesty, Ann Queen Dowager, of the Mohe-

19*

gan Indians, and yesterday her remains were interred in a manner suitable to her high rank, in the Indian burying ground at Chelsea."

As the older files of this paper are very scarce, a few more items from them may not be uninteresting.— *They* will serve to illustrate the times :

May 2, 1774.   A great military parade took place at Woodstock, accompanied by a mock fight, under the direction of Capt. Samuel M'Clellan.   A party dressed as Indians, seized upon some children who were looking on, and ran off with them, but were pursued by the troop and the children rescued.

Oct. 28.   The season has been so very mild, that a mess of green peas was picked the last week in this town, spontaneously grown from seed produced this year.

Dec. 13.   The officers and soldiers who belonged to Gen. Lyman's regiment of Provincials, and were at the taking of Havannah, are notified to meet at the house of Mr. John Durgie Innholder, in Norwich, to enquire why the last dividend of their prize money has not been paid, &c.

Feb. 10.   Yesterday, Mr. James Burnam, of this town, brought to market a sled load of wood which completes the number of 2,500 loads, which he has drove in himself, 4 miles, and sold since 1754.   A great part he cut himself— all but 50 loads on his own land—all which he has done without upsetting a cart, breaking a wheel or sled, bruising a finger, or injuring an ox or horse by any wound.   He sold his wood for £820 :—has about 5 times as much more on his land, which he intends leaving for some other person to cart and draw, he having done his full share that way.   He has also expended 500 days of labour on 2 acres of land, in subduing and fencing it.

April ——   Dr. Turner has recently extracted the bone of an alewife from the throat of Mr. Ebenezer Lord, where it had been lodged for 25 years, and at various times had given him exquisite pain.   It was about the size of a brown thread needle and was barbed from end to end.

July 7, 1774. To all those who call themselves Sons of Liberty in America, Greeting :—

My Friends. We know in some good measure the inestimable value of liberty. But were we once deprived of her, she would then appear much more valuable than she now appears. We also see her, standing as it were tiptoe on the highest bough ready for flight. Why is she departing? What is it that disturbs her repose? Surely some foul monster of hideous shape, and hateful kind, opposite in its nature to hers, with all its frightful appearances and properties, iron hands and leaden feet, formed to gripe and crush, hath intruded itself into her peaceful habitation and ejected her. Surely this must be the case, for we know oppositions cannot dwell together. Is it not time, high time to search for this Achan? this disturber of Israel? High time, I say, to examine for the cause of those dark and gloomy appearances that cast a shade over our glory. And is not this it? Are we not guilty of the same crime we impute to others? Of the same facts that we say are unjust, cruel, arbitrary, despotic, and without law, in others? Paul argued in this manner : — " Thou therefore that teachest another, teachest thou not thyself? Thou that preachest a man should not steal, dost thou steal? Thou that makest thy boast of the law, through breaking the law, dishonorest thou God?" And may we not use the same mode of argument and say— We that declare (and that with much warmth and zeal) it is unjust, cruel, barbarous, unconstitutional and without law, to enslave, *do we enslave?*—Yes, verily we do. *A black cloud witnesseth against us and our own mouths condemn us.* How preposterous our conduct! How vain and hypocritical our pretences! Can we expect to be free, so long as we are determined to enslave? HONESTY.

Boston, Jan. 17, 1775. Tuesday last the Princess Caroline Matilda, alias Princess of Cronenburgh, alias Marchiness of Waldegrave, who has travelled through all the Southern Provinces, set out, from hence for Portsmouth, N. H. She is the most surprising genius of the female sex that was ever *obliged* to visit America.

June 6, 1774, a town-meeting was convened on that oft-repeated plea, " to take into consideration the melancholy situation of our civil, constitutional liberties, rights and privileges, which are threatened with de-

struction." The citizens at first assembled in the
court-house, but were obliged to adjourn to the meeting-house in order to accommodate the large concourse
of people who came together. The Hon. Jabez Huntington was chosen moderator, and a series of patriotic
resolutions drawn up by Capt. Joseph Trumbull, and
Samuel Huntington, Esq., were passed, almost by
acclamation, and a standing committee of correspondence appointed, consisting of

| | |
|---|---|
| Capt. Jedidiah Huntington, | Capt. Wm. Hubbard, |
| Chr. Leffingwell Esq., | Capt. Joseph Trumbull. |
| Dr. Theophilus Rogers, | |

These were some of the leading patriots of the day,
whose images still linger, beloved and honored in the
memories of the aged. Samuel Huntington was afterwards President of Congress, and Governor of Connecticut; Jedidiah, aid-de-camp to Washington, and Brigadier General in the U. S. service: William Hubbard
was a gentleman greatly revered for his benevolence
and philanthropy. He neither commenced nor ended
his life in Norwich, but during his long residence there,
promoted in various ways the honor and prosperity of
the town. His charities to the poor, and his liberal
subscriptions to all works of public utility, were such
as frequently to call forth votes of thanks from the
town. He was a gentleman of the old school of politeness, bringing with him and preserving while here,
the best style of Boston manners.

Capt. Joseph Trumbull was a very amiable and
promising young man, who had settled in Norwich as
an attorney. He was a native of Lebanon, the youngest son of Gov. Trumbull, and entered with characteristic ardor and singleness of heart into all the measures
of the Sons of Liberty. He was a member of the
Conn. Council of Safety, and afterwards Commissary

in the colonial army. The hopes of his friends, who expected much from his talents and integrity, and whose affections were fondly fixed upon his person, were blasted by his untimely death. In the eulogy pronounced at his funeral, great praise is awarded to his abilities, his patriotism and his moral worth, and it is added, " In all the winning and agreeable arts of life, he had no superior." These qualities account for the tender attachment of his friends, and the lamentations that were uttered on his death.

July 4, 1774. Mr. Francis Green, an eminent merchant of Boston, being on a journey into Connecticut, in order, as he stated, to collect debts and transact some private business, put up at a tavern in Windham. This gentleman was a loyalist, and of course obnoxious to the sons of liberty, who affected to believe that he had some sinister designs in this journey. He had been stigmatized in the patriotic papers as " one of that insidious crew who fabricated and signed the adulatory address to strengthen the hands of that parricidal tool of despotism, Thomas Hutchinson." The patriots of Windham were no sooner aware of his presence, than they proceeded to show their displeasure. Assembling early in the morning, they surrounded the tavern, uttering shouts of insult and threats of *exalting him upon a cart*, unless he instantly left their precincts. This he did without delay, being followed with hoots and execrations. An express had been previously despatched to Norwich, with information that he was bound thither. The whole town was moved with this intelligence, and the sexton was ordered to give notice of his arrival by ringing the bell. Mr. Green's carriage, therefore, no sooner stopped at Lathrop's tavern, than the bell rang an alarm, and the citizens were in an uproar.

The plain was soon alive with the concourse, and a message was transmitted to Mr. Green, giving him his choice, to depart in fifteen minutes, or to be driven out *on a cart.* He was very reluctant to go ; pleaded business ; that he had debts in town to collect, and stepping out upon the green, attempted to address the people : whereupon Capt. Simeon Huntington, a very stout man, collared him and called him *rascal.* By this time a horse and cart, with a high scaffolding in it for a seat, made its appearance, and demonstrations of lifting him to this conspicuous station being made, Mr. Green took the most prudent course, entered his carriage, and amid shouts and hissings drove off ; a part of the populace following him with drums beating and horns blowing, till he was fairly out of their precincts. On his return to Boston, Mr. Green offered one hundred dollars reward, for the apprehension " of any of the ruffians who had forced him to leave Windham and Norwich, particularly for Capt. Simeon Huntington." This advertisement was a subject of merriment to the good people of Norwich, who republished it in hand-bills, and hawked it about town with a running commentary.

About this time subscriptions were made in various towns in Connecticut, for the poor of Boston. Norwich sent on a noble donation, consisting of cash, wheat, corn, and a flock of *three hundred and ninety sheep.* This liberality was greatly applauded in the public prints.

The sympathy felt for the Bostonians was yet further displayed by the spirit manifested in September of this year, on the reception of a piece of intelligence which proved to be false, of a rupture between them and the royal troops. On Saturday, Sept. 3, at four; P. M. an express arrived from Col. Israel Putnam, that

Boston had been attacked the night before, and six of the citizens killed. This was but a rumor, yet it caused the greatest consternation ; the citizens assembled around Liberty Tree, then adjourned to the Court-house, and resolved to despatch an express to Providence. Mr. David Nevins volunteered on this service, as he had on many similar occasions, and departed at eight, P. M. On Sunday morning, four hundred and sixty-four men, well armed, and the greater part mounted on good horses, started for Boston, under the command of Maj. John Durkee, and rendezvoued at Capt. Burnham's inn, seven miles from town. Here at eleven o'clock, A. M., they were met by Mr. Nevins, on his return from Providence, with intelligence that the report was without foundation. Upon which they dispersed. That same morning, two hundred men, well armed and mounted, left Windham at sunrise, and had proceeded twenty or thirty miles, before they learned the falsity of the rumor. The people of Colchester were attending divine service, when a messenger entered and announced the report that Boston had been attacked by the troops. The minister immediately suspended the service, and all the men able to bear arms, equipped themselves and marched. It was supposed that upwards of 20,000 men, from this colony alone, were on the march to Boston that day.

September 8. A convention of delegates from the counties of New London and Windham, met at Norwich to consider the necessity of revising the militia laws. Of this meeting the Hon. Gurdon Saltonstall was chairman, and Col. William Williams, of Lebanon, clerk.*

---

* For the resolutions passed at this convention, see Hinman's "Historical Collection of the part sustained by Connecticut in the War of the Revolution." Hartford, 1842.

In October, the General Court of the Colony ordered, that all the militia should be called out for drill twelve half days before the next May. No regiment of militia had at this time ever been reviewed east of Connecticut river; the trainings had all been by companies. In the town were three companies, that were mustered together upon the plain, under Captains Jedidiah Huntington, Samuel Wheat, and Isaac Tracy. One at Chelsea, under Capt. Gershom Breed. In the autumn of 1774, the General Court ordered that Norwich should comprise the 20th regiment of infantry, and appointed Jedidiah Huntington, Lt. Colonel of the same; who gave notice that a regimental training would be held at Norwich on the first Monday of the next May. But before that time arrived, a great part of the men were in actual service near Boston, and the review was relinquished.

There was no regular uniform for the militia of the state at that period, nor for many years afterwards. Rifle frocks and trowsers were much worn, mostly white with colored fringes. One of the words of command in training was "Blow off the loose corns;" and before and after the command to "Poise arms," came "Put your right hand to the firelock" — "Put your left hand to the firelock." An odd kind of aspirate was sometimes used after a command; thus "Shoulder! hoo!" The great object in the exercises then was to make the soldier familiar with his gun; that he might charge quick and aim sure. Now the trainings consist much more in maneuvering, wheeling, marching, &c. Instead of firelock, *arms* is used.

During the winter the town passed a vote approving and adopting the measures proposed by the Continental Congress at Philadelphia, and at the same time they ordered a quantity of military stores to be purchased.

Such was the unanimity of the citizens, that through the whole revolutionary struggle, their proceedings were principally town-wise. They were not obliged to have such continual recourse to the committees of Correspondence and Safety, nor to invest them with such arbitrary powers as was done in most parts of the country. The public acts were all municipal, the dissenting voices few and weak, and very little change took place in laws or officers. The town was an independent community, actuated by a single impulse, swayed only by a Governor whom they loved, and a Congress which they revered.

_ March 28, 1775. In full town-meeting the following resolution was passed :

"Whereas numbers of persons are removing from the town of Boston to this place and others may remove :— Voted, that this town request the select-men and committee of inspection to take effectual care that none of the addresses to Gov. Hutchinson or any others who have evidenced themselves to be inimical to the common cause of America, be admitted or suffered to reside in this town, unless they shall produce a proper certificate from the Provincial Congress that they have altered their conduct in such a manner as to give full satisfaction."

Among the persons alluded to in the above preamble, that at this time removed their families to Norwich, where they remained during the greater part of the succeeding contest, were some of the Hubbards Greenes and Philipses of Boston, the Malbones of Newport, and Col. Moore, afterwards a Commissary in the Colonial army.

The attention of the whole country was at this time turned towards Boston; the Norwich Packet was rife with such remarks as these :

20

"Boston is now reduced to an alarming crisis, big with important events. Like a new piece of ordnance, deeply charged for the trial of its strength; we listen with attention to hear its convulsed explosion, suspending ourselves in mysterious doubt, whether it will burst with dreadful havock, or recoil upon the engineers to their great confusion." "The blocking up of Boston is like turning the tide of a murmuring river upon the whole land, and thereby spreading a dangerous inundation through the continent, for resentment already flows high at New York, Philadelphia, and the southern towns, and if it join with the flux at Boston, it may occasion a sea of troubles."

The explosion waited for in such dread suspense at length broke upon the land. The battle of Lexington commenced early on Wednesday morning, April 19. The news arrived in Norwich by an express from Woodstock in the afternoon of the next day. The facts were greatly exaggerated and the public sympathy highly excited. Mr. Nevins, with his usual promptness, again mounted and proceeded to Providence after correct information, returning on Saturday evening. Handbills were immediately struck off and dispersed through the town before day break the next morning.

At this time volunteers were almost daily departing for the army at Cambridge, in squads of two, three and four ; and in May, a company of one hundred choice men, raised under the superintendance of Col. John Durkee, a bold Bean-hill man, marched in charge of Lieut. Joshua Huntington to the scene of action, and were annexed to Gen. Putnam's regiment. This company under the command of Col. Durkee [field officers in these enlistments frequently performed the duties of Captains,] was in the battle of Bunker Hill, in camp during the succeeding winter on Prospect and Cobb's Hills, accompanied the army to New

York in March, endured all the hardships of the retreat through the Jersies, fought at Germantown, &c. &c. Mr. David Nevins, one of the veterans of this band, to whom we have already repeatedly alluded, was perhaps its last survivor. He lived to enjoy *a green old age*, and having surpassed his ninetieth year, died among his children in New York in 1838.

Col. John Durkee died in 1782, aged 54.

Lieut. Andrew Griswold, another of this band, was a grandson of Deacon Joseph Griswold, and a very brave and spirited soldier. He fought at Bunker Hill and in several other severe engagements, until a ball in the knee, received at the battle of Germantown, disabled him from further service. He died in 1827, aged 72.

# CHAPTER XXVII.

Bird's-eye View of a scene in Norwich. 1775.

Suppose it to be that Sunday in June which succeeded the battle of Bunker Hill. It is 10 o'clock, and the second bell has just commenced ringing. The inhabitants are gathering slowly and solemnly to the house of worship. From Bean Hill come a throng of Backuses, Hydes, Rogerses, Wheats, Tracys, Thomases, Griswolds. Here and there is a one horse chaise, almost large enough for a bed-room, square-bottomed, and studded with brass nails, looking something like a chest of drawers or an antique book-case on wheels. Those stout-looking men on horseback with women and children upon pillions behind, are reputable farmers from Waweekus and Plain Hills. That young man with such erect form and attractive countenance, is Dr. Elihu Marvin, unconscious that he alone of all this population is to be the victim of a future pestilence, that will nearly desolate a neighboring city. That one with the staid demeanor and grave aspect, whose hair is already silvered with age, is deacon Griswold, destined to live nearly to the confines of another century.

Farther down, the stream is increased by the families of the philanthropic Dr. Elisha Tracy and Dr. Philip Turner, the surgeon, and Elisha Hyde, an enthusiastic young attorney, and Mr. Billy Waterman and Mr. Jo. Waterman. Many of the foot people have turned off

by the willow tree, and ascending the rocks, proceed
by a rude pathway, once the beaten road that led to
the ancient meeting-house upon the hill; others pursue their way through the town street, winding under
the eaves of precipitous rocks till they reach the church.

But see, from opposite quarters are advancing the
Lathrops, Huntingtons, Leffingwells, Tracys, Adgates,
Blisses, Reynoldses, Baldwins, Pecks, Trumbulls, &c.
*There* is a very aged man in a white wig, creeping
slowly along, supported by a staff in either hand; it
is the venerable Deacon Simon Tracy. The respectable group that accompany him are his descendants.
Samuel Tracy Esq., his son, he also a man of mature
age, and his wife Sybil, are among them. You may
see other men in white wigs; some five or six in all.
Dr. Daniel Lathrop wears one; he has just rode up to
the church with his dignified companion, the daughter
of old Gov. Talcott.

There comes the Hon. Samuel Huntington, Judge of
the Superior Court and recently elected member of the
Continental Congress, with his wife and their adopted
children : there too is the patriotic Gen. Jabez Huntington and his five sons, two of them attended by their
children, and the family of the late Hon. Hezekiah
Huntington, and other Huntingtons and Lathrops and
Tracys innumerable.

Around the Plain, every threshhold seems to be
simultaneously crossed; the two taverns kept by Azariah Lathrop and Joseph Peck pour forth a goodly
number. Mr. Ben. Butler and his family and Mr.
Joseph Carew are coming up on one side, and Mr.
Elly Lord and his two daughters are just passing the
Court-house. And see, the Parsonage door opens, and
the venerable pastor comes forth, and slowly walks to
the church and up the broad aisle, tottering as he as-

20*

cends the pulpit stairs.  How reverend are the curls
of that white wig!  The very wig which he wore some
twenty years previous, when the old Rogerene so
abusively followed him into meeting, exclaiming :—
"Benjamin! Benjamin! dost thou think that they wear
white wigs in heaven!"  And again: "Benjamin!
thou art a sinner! thou wearest a white wig!"

Old Deacon Tracy, too, is assisted up those stairs
and takes his seat by his minister, that his deaf ears
may receive some few of the words of salvation.

Below the pulpit, in the broad aisle, are chairs and
cushioned benches, where a few old people sit; the
gallery is filled with the young, and with a choir of
singers, which though mainly made up of young people, have several grave men and women for their
leaders.

The services commence ; the sermon contains many
pointed allusions to the critical state of affairs, and eyes
sparkle and hearts throb, as the pastor sanctifies the
cause of liberty by mingling it with the exercises of
religion, and justifies resistance to oppression by arguments from scripture.  Just as the sermon is finished,
a loud shout is heard upon the plain, the trampling of
a hurried horse, an outcry of alarm, which brings the
audience upon their feet: uproar enters the porch, the
bell is violently rung, several persons rush into the body
of the church, and amid the confusion nothing can be
heard; but "a battle! a battle has taken place on
Bunker Hill: the British are beat; hurrah! hurrah!"
The meeting is broken up amid noisy shouts of "Huz-
zah for Boston!  Huzza for liberty!"  The audience
rush out upon the plain, and gather round the panting
courier: his despatches are read aloud,—rejoicing and
indignation, patriotism and military fire, hatred of
British tyranny and defiance of British power take

the place of those quiet devotional feelings, with which they assembled together.

That night, bells were rung, cannons were fired, bonfires blazed far and wide, and the Tree of Liberty was decked with triumphant devices. Enlistments too were begun, arms were burnished, addresses made, and tories insulted ; nor even by these and a hundred other exuberant demonstrations of excited feeling, could the agitated minds of the people be scarcely appeased.

Among the audience that day, was a poor German basket-maker, named John Malotte, a deserter from the English army that took Canada, some few years before, who, wandering through the wilderness, had come down into the northern part of Norwich, and there pursued the humble occupation which he followed in his native land, before he had been impressed as a soldier, and sent away to fight the battles of a foreign power. He was at this time but a spectator of the enthusiasm of others, but he too loved liberty ; he treasured up the scene, and more than forty years afterwards, described it for the amusement of a child, in such vivid colors, that the above picture is but a remembered transcript of his recollections.

Among the audience that day, were doubtless *two*, if not more, who did not sympathize in these patriotic proceedings, and were therefore stigmatized as *tories and grumbletonians*, viz : Mr. Thomas Leffingwell and Mr. Benjamin Butler, both men of talent and respectability, who remained loyal to the king during the whole contest. They were of course exposed to many insults, public and private, prosecuted, imprisoned, threatened with the skimmerton, and their goods impressed. Mr. Leffingwell was the fourth, in a right line, from the first settler of that name. Mr. Butler emigrated from

Hampton. He was arrested and imprisoned in 1776, on a charge of "defaming the Honorable Continental Congress." His trial came on before the Superior Court at New London, and the fact being proved, he was prohibited from wearing arms, and declared incapable of holding office.

Mr. Butler regarded this sentence with indifference. He was a man of strong sense and original humor, and his company was much sought after on that account. He died of a lingering disease in the year 1787. A few years before, while in good health, he had selected a sapling, to have his coffin made of it when it should grow large enough; but finding that it increased too slowly, he had the coffin constructed of other wood, and kept for a long time this affecting memento of his end constantly in his chamber. As he pined away, he would frequently put his hands upon his knees and say, "See how the mallets grow!" He lies interred in the Norwich grave yard; his wife Diadema, and his two daughters, Rosamond and Minerva, repose by his side. "Alas, poor human nature!" is the expressive motto engraved by his own direction, upon his headstone. His family removed from Norwich, to Oxford, N. Y. The accomplished lady of Commodore John Rogers, was one of his grand-children.

In April, 1776, the army from Boston, on their route to New York, passed through Norwich. Here General Washington, by appointment, met Gov. Trumbull. They dined together at Col. Jedidiah Huntington's, and Washington proceeded that evening to New London.

# CHAPTER XXVIII.

Continuation of Revolutionary Events.

THOUGH not on the sea-board, nor particularly exposed to invasion, the bustling scenes of war were exhibited in various parts of Norwich.

Dr. Church, a prisoner of the Continental Congress, having been delivered by Gen. Washington into the hands of Gov. Trumbull for safe keeping, the latter directed him to be confined in the gaol at Norwich. He was accordingly conveyed thither and given into custody of Prosper Wetmore, Esq. Sheriff of New London county. The orders respecting him were strict and minute. He was to be debarred the use of pen, paper and ink; no person was allowed to converse with him except in the English language, and in presence and hearing of a Magistrate or the Sheriff; and he was not to go out of a close prison but once a week, and then only with the Sheriff in person. Subsequently for his further security, a high fence with pickets was built around the gaol. He was kept in Norwich from Nov. 1775, to the 27th of May 1776, and then by order of Congress was transported under charge of the Sheriff to Watertown, Massachusetts.

Other prisoners of war, occasionally in large bands, were brought hither for confinement.

A battery and redoubt was built below the Landing on Waterman's point, for the defence of the place against invasion by way of the river : four six-pound-ers from New London were planted here, and a regular guard and watch kept. For further defence of the place two wrought iron field pieces, and several other pieces of ordnance were mounted, manned and placed in the charge of Capt. Jacob De Witt.

William Lax established a manufactory of gun-carriages in town, and succeeded so well as to be employed by the state to furnish apparatus for much of the cannon used by them. Elijah Backus, Esq. at his forges upon the Yantic, manufactured the ship anchors used for the State's armed vessels, two of which weighed 1200 pounds each. He afterwards engaged in the casting of cannon.

In the summer of 1776 a row galley was built at Chelsea for the State, by Capt. Jonathan Lester. Her dimensions were " sixty feet keel, eighteen feet beam, five feet hold, and seven inches dead rising." The whole expense was £861, 16s, 6d. She was named " The Shark," and the command given to Capt. Theophilus Stanton, of Stonington. Capt. Harding, of the armed brig " Defence," and Capt. Robert Niles, of the armed schooner " Spy," both belonged in Norwich. After the completion of the Shark, Capt. Lester with twenty-five carpenters under him, was sent by the Governor to Crown Point to build batteaux for the Lake, in compliance with a request of Gen. Schuyler. The Shark, in July 1776, at the urgent request of Gen. Washington, was sent to New York and left subject to his orders.

In 1777, Congress ordered two frigates to be built in Connecticut, under the direction of the Governor and Council of Safety, one of 36 guns, the other of twenty-eight. The former was built at Gale Town, between Norwich and New London, under the superintendence of Capt. Joshua Huntington.

The Oliver Cromwell, owned by the State, was built at Saybrook, 1776, by Capt. Uriah Hayden, assisted by Capt. Harding. Its first commander was Capt. William Coit; but he having resigned, Capt. Timothy Parker, of Norwich, was appointed to the command in September, 1777.

Capt. Ephraim Bill, of Norwich, was in the service of the State as a marine agent, and Capt. Jabez Perkins, as contractor and dispenser of the public stores. The Governor and Council of Safety sometimes held their sessions in town. From these details it will be evident that the earlier years of the war, were seasons of very general stir and enterprize in Norwich.

In 1777, Connecticut raised eleven regiments; nine for Continental service, and two for the defence of the State. Col. Jedidiah Huntington and Col. John Durkee of Norwich, commanded two of the Continental Regiments. On the decease of Gen. Wooster in that year, Jabez Huntington, Esq., (previously the second Major General,) was promoted to the office of Major General over the whole militia of the State. The five sons of Gen. Huntington, were all in the service of the country during the greater part of the war, either as commissaries, purchasers, or soldiers in actual service. Col. Jedidiah Huntington raised some battalions for continental service, to serve during the war or for three years; these were distinguished by a *British* uniform; the State having appropriated to them a quantity of English red coats, taken in a prize vessel.

In the earlier periods of the contest, the town's quota of soldiers was always quickly raised, and the necessary supplies furnished with promptness and liberality. The requisitions of the Governor were responded to from no quarter with more cheerfulness and alacrity. In September 1777, when extraordinary exertions were made in many parts of New England, to procure tents, canteens, and clothing for the army ; many householders in Norwich voluntarily gave up to the committee of the town, all that they could spare from their own family stock, either as donations, or where that could not be afforded, at a very low rate. The ministers of all the churches on thanksgiving day, exhorted the people *to remember the poor soldiers and their families.*

In January 1778, a general contribution was made through the town for the army. The ladies, with great industry, assembled to make garments, and bring in their gifts. The whole value of the collection was placed at a low estimate at £1400—[Continental money, probably ; real value, uncertain.]

" Cash, £258 ; pork, cheese, wheat, rye, sugar, corn, rice, flax, and wood in considerable quantities; 386 pair of stockings, 227 do. of shoes, 118 shirts, 78 jackets, 48 pair overalls, 15 do. breeches, 208 do. mittens, 11 buff-caps, 9 coats, 12 rifle frocks, and 19 handkerchiefs."

Every year while the war continued, persons were appointed by the town to provide for the soldiers and their families at the town expense ; but much also was raised by voluntary contributions.

Those who remained at home as well as those who went into actual service, were often called on to perform military duty. When most of the able bodied men were drawn off, a *Reformado corps* was established; consisting of those whose age, infirmities, or other circumstances, would not allow them to become regular soldiers, and endure the fatigue of the camp, but who were willing to go forth on a sudden emergency. The situation of New London was one of constant alarm, in which all the surrounding towns participa-

ted.   It was first menaced in December 1776, when
the hostile fleet found a rendezvous among the small
Islands in the Sound, previous to taking possession of
Newport.   All the militia in the eastern part of the
State turned out to oppose the expected descent.   It
was observed, as band after band marched into New
London, that no company, in order and equipments,
equalled the Light Infantry of Norwich, under the
command of Col. Chr. Leffingwell.   The veteran
guards also turned out at this time under Capt. John
McKall; they were soon after ordered to New York.
Many times during the war, the militia were summoned to New London or Stonington, on the appearance of
an armed force, or the rumor of one.   If a hostile
vessel entered the Sound, no one knew its commission, and the alarm was quickly spread from the
seaboard into the country.   The dreaded foe perhaps
hovered near the coast a few hours, made some start-
ling feints, and then passed away.   Orders were given
and countermanded, and the wearied militia, hastily
drawn from their homes, returned again without having had the satisfaction of seeing the enemy, or of
arriving on the spot before the danger was over.

Detachments from the Continental army frequently
passed through Norwich.   In 1778, a body of French
troops on the route from Providence to the south, halted
there for ten or fifteen days, on account of sickness
among them.   They had their tents spread upon the
plain, while the sick were quartered in the court
house.   About twenty died and were buried each side
of the lane that led into the old burying yard.   No
stones were set up, and the ground was soon smoothed
over so as to leave no trace of the narrow tenements
below.

Gen. Washington several times passed through, but never stopped longer than three or four hours at a time.  The inhabitants also had an opportunity of seeing La Fayette, Stuben, Pulaski, and other distinguished foreigners then in our service.  There were some who long remembered the appearance of the noble La Fayette, as he passed through the place on his way to Newport.  He had been there before and needed no guide ; his aids and a small body guard were with him, and he rode up to the door of his friend, Gen. Jedidiah Huntington, in a quick gallop.  He wore a blue military coat, but no vest and no *stockings ;* his boots being short, his leg was consequently left bare for a considerable space below the knee.  The speed with which he was travelling, and the great heat of the weather, were sufficient excuses for this negligence.  He took some refreshment and hastened forward.

At another period, he passed through with a detachment of 2000 men under his command, and encamped them for one night upon the plain.  In the morning, before their departure, he invited Mr. Strong, the pastor of the place, to pray with them, which he did, the troops being arranged in three sides of a hollow square.

Nearly fifty years afterwards, August 21, 1824, the venerable La Fayette again passed through Norwich. Some old people who remembered him embraced him and wept ;—the General wept also.

At one time during the war, the Duke de Lauzun's regiment was quartered for a few weeks in Lebanon, ten miles from Norwich.  Col. Jedidiah Huntington invited the officers to visit him, and prepared a handsome entertainment for them.  They made a superb appearance as they drove into town, being young, tall, vivacious men, with handsome faces and a noble air, mounted upon horses bravely caparisoned.  The two

Dillons, brothers, one a major and the other a captain
in the regiment, were particularly distinguished for
their fine forms and expressive features.  One, or both,
of these Dillons, suffered death from the guillotine
during the French Revolution.

Lauzun was one of the most accomplished but unprincipled noblemen of his time.  He was celebrated for
his handsome person, his liberality, wit, bravery ; but
more than all for his profligacy.  He was born in 1747,
inherited great wealth, and high titles, and spent all
his early years in alternate scenes of dissipation and
traveling.  He engaged in no public enterprise till he
came to America, and took part in the Revolutionary
contest.  The motives which actuated this voluptuous
nobleman to this undertaking are not understood ; very
probably the thirst for adventure, and personal friendship for La Fayette.  He had ran the career of pleasure to such an extent that he was perhaps willing to
pause awhile and restore the energy of his satiated
taste.  Certain it is, that he embarked in the cause of
the Americans with ardor, bore privations with good
temper, and made himself very popular by his hilarity
and generous expenditure.

After Lauzun returned to Europe he became intimate
with Talleyrand, and accompanied him on a mission
to England, in 1792, where one of his familiar associates was the Prince of Wales, afterwards George IV.
On the death of his uncle, the Duke de Biron, he succeeded to the title, quarreled with the court, and became a partizan of the Duke of Orleans.  Afterwards
he served against the Vendeans, but was accused of
secretly favoring them, condemned, and executed the
last day of the year 1793.  Such was the future stormy
career of this celebrated nobleman, who, as already
mentioned, in the midst of friends and subordinates,

enjoyed the banquet made for him by Col. Huntington.
After dinner the whole party went out into the yard
in front of the house, and made the air ring with Huz-
zas for Liberty! Numerous loungers had gathered
around the fence to get a sight of these interesting foreigners, with whom they conversed in very good English, and exhorted *to live free, or die for liberty.*

A very great evil experienced during the war, was
the high price of salt, and the difficulty of procuring it
at any price. It was almost impossible to get a suffi-
ciency to put up provisions for winter's use.*. The
State government was obliged to send abroad for supplies of this necessary article, and distribute it to the
various towns. It was then apportioned by the selectmen to the districts in proportion to their population,
and again dealt out by a committee to individuals.

Another scarce article was molasses. But in 1776,
the people of Norwich, hearing that a vessel laden
with molasses had arrived at Stonington, which belonged to a family unfriendly to the cause of freedom,
they immediately collected a spirited company of men,
and proceeded forthwith to Stonington, where they
took possession of the vessel, and brought her, with
the cargo, round to Norwich. They then made report
of the affair to the Governor and Council, who approved
of their proceedings, and sequestered the prize for the
use of the State. The molasses was doled out to hospitals, and used for various public purposes. Forty
hogsheads were distilled for the use of the soldiers;
thirty were sent to Portipaug, West Farms and New
Concord, for safe keeping. The *tory molasses*, as it

---

* Mr. Butler, willing to have a little sport with his neighbors, put up
a sign over his shop door one day, "Hard money to let, and old pork
to sell." This of course brought every passer-by to a stand, these being the two articles not to be found in the place.

was called, was at that time considered a valuable acquisition.

The scarcity of wheat was a still greater evil. The authorities were obliged to enforce a strict scrutiny into every man's means of subsistence, to see that none of the necessaries of life were withheld from a famishing community by monopolizers and avaricious engrossers. Each family was visited, and an account of the grain in their possession, computed in wheat, was taken. The surplusage, down to the quantity of four quarts, was estimated. One hundred and twenty-six families were at one time reported deficient, viz :

"42 up town, 26 down town, 12 West Farms and Portipaug, 2 Newent and Hanover, 9 East Society, 27 Chelsea, 8 Bozrah."

The following certificate is also upon record.

"This may certify, that the whole number of inhabitants in the town of Norwich is hungry ; for the quantity of grain computed in wheat is scanty ; the deficiency amounts to a great many bushels, as pr return of the selectmen unto my office, agreeable to the act of assembly.

Certified by GALETTIA SIMPSON.

It is well known that during the Revolutionary war attempts were made to regulate the prices of articles by public statutes, in order to reduce the quantity of the circulating medium. In Connecticut prices were fixed by the civil authorities of each town, in all cases not determined by acts of Assembly. The list of articles to which the selectmen affixed prices, in the year 1778, will furnish data to show the various kinds of business then pursued in the town, as well as the current expenses of living. The following is an abstract.

"Farming Labour varied according to the season of the year, from 3s. 6d. pr day to 5s. 3d.

21*

Women's labor: nursing 9s. pr week; house work 5s. 3d.; tailoring 2s. 4d. pr day; spinning 1s. 2d. pr run.

House carpenters, joiners and painters, 7s. pr day.

Ship-carpenters, master-builders, 10s. 6d., finding themselves.

Masons 8s. 9d.; master-riggers 7s.

Tailors, for making a full trimmed coat 21s., vest and breeches each 10s. 6d.

Paper-makers, finding themselves, if foreman 31s. 6d. pr week; under workmen 26s. 6d.

Comb-makers; Horn combs 1s. 9d.; crooked do. the same; ivory small tooth combs from 1s. to 5s.

Tape-makers; broad tape pr piece 6s.; narrow 4s.

Block-making; blocks for vessels 3½s. pr inch, &c.

Coopering: Heart-white-oak hhds. 21s.; common white oak 17s. 6d.; common black oak 14s.; flax-seed tierces 5s. 3d.; barrels from 6s. to 7s.

Button-making: best silver plaited coat buttons 6s. pr doz., &c.

Weaving: shirting width 2s. 4d. pr yd.; yard wide linen 1s. 5d., &c.

Clothiers: Fulling, shearing, and dying with Am. dies, 2s. pr yd.

Currying and Tanning Leather: calf-skin 3s 6d.; currying side 5s. 3d.

White oak bark per cord 32s.; black oak 28s.

Pewterers: Pewter quart pots 6s. 5d.; pint pots 4s. 4d.

Weaving stockings: men's pr pair 6s. 4d.; women's 5s. 6d.; breeches patterns 10s. 10d.

Black-smith's work: plow irons 1s. 6d. pr lb.; anchors 10d. 2qr. do., &c.

Wool cards pr pair 10s.

Saddlers: Good hunting saddle, leather housing, 105s. Women's saddles, common sort £8, 15s. Plain bridles 8s. 9d.

Good beaver hats £3. 3s. Felt hats 12s.

Foot wheel complete 31s. 6d. Woolen wheel and spindle 17s. 6d.

Post writing paper pr quire 2s. 8d. Foolscap 3s.

Fire wood: In Town Plot, walnut pr cord 22s.; oak 18s. 6d.; at the Landing, at people's doors, pr cord 24s.; oak 20s.; in Newent, fire wood pr cord 10s. 6d.; West Farms wood pr load 6s. 8d.; 8th society 5s. 3d., &c.

Hay per ton in Town Plot and Landing, (English herd

grass,) £3. 18s.   Flanders pr ton £3.   25 pr cent. added in winter.

Good sheeps wool 3s. per lb.   Well dressed flax 1s. 6d.

Good mutton and veal 5d. per lb.; turkeys and fowls 6d.; geese and ducks 5d.; store swine 3½d.

Checked flannel, yd wide, 5s.; checked linen do. 5s.

Men's yarn stockings pr pair 7s.

Potatoes, in the fall, 1s. 9d. pr bu.; winter and spring, 2s. 7d.

Cider pr bbl, 9s.; drawn off in the spring 15s.

Chocolate pr lb. 10s.; Hard soap 1s. 2d.: Rice 8d.

Allspice and ginger 3s.

River oysters 3s. per bu., 1s. 2d. pr qt.

Fresh bass and perch, at the Landing, 3½d. pr lb.

Boat fare between Norwich and N. London, single person, 2s. 6d.; freight for hhd 6s.; barrel 1s. 6d.

Pressed hay, at the Landing, pr ton, £5, 5s. 0d.

Horse hire pr mile, for journey, at Landing 7d.

Goldsmiths : making gold necklace 35s.; wrought gold pr dwt. 7s.; Buckles, best open work, 21s.; Table spoons, plain, 5s. 3d.; Tea spoons 2s. 8d.; reversed and carved in proportion.

Best stock buckles 14s.; Knee buckles 14s.; silver pr oz. wrought 9s.; Cleaning watches 5s. 3d.

Taverners: gill of Rum 1s., N. England do. 8d.; mug of flip or toddy made with W. India rum 2s. 6d., N. Eng. do. 1s. 8d.; meal of victuals 1s. 9d.; pottle oats 6d.; bowl sour punch 3s.; best Madeira wine pr bottle 18s.; French brandy and foreign Geneva 2s. pr gill.    Signed per order,

SIMON TRACY, Chairman.

SAMUEL TRACY, Clerk.

" April 7, 1777. Voted, strictly to adhere to the law of the State regulating the prices of the necessaries of life ; and we do resolve with cheerfulness to exert our best endeavours within our sphere, to support the honor of that good and salutary law.

Dec. 29. Voted, that the town consider the articles of confederation and perpetual union proposed by the Continental Congress wise and salutary."

1778. Abstract of instructions to the representatives of the town.—

" 1. To use their influence to have taxes more equitable.

2. To have bills of credit called in.

3. Forfeited estates confiscated.

4. The yeas and nays on all important questions published.

5. Profane swearing punished by disability to sustain offices.

Oct. 1. Voted, to present a memorial to the General Assembly, praying for a just and equitable system of taxation and representation."

Extract from the memorial :—

" The Poll-tax your memorialists consider at the present day, an insupportable burden on the poor, while a great part of the growing estate of the rich is by law exempt from taxation. The present mode of representation is also objected to by your memorialists. They believe all who pay taxes and are of sober life and conversation, ought to have a voice in all public communities, where their monies and properties are disposed of for public uses."

It is not surprising that the subject of taxation should be one of exciting interest in a community who were annually paying 6*d.*, 9*d.* and 12*d.* on the pound for the use of the army. At one time in Connecticut, when the currency was at par, a rate of even 14*d.* was necessary to meet the exigencies of the treasury.

The town afterwards presented another petition to the Assembly, the substance of which was, that every kind of property, and that only, should be the object of taxation. This general principle, they say, is in their view, the only equitable one. Committees were sent to several neighboring towns, to get their minds on the subject, and they at length resolved to publish at the expense of the town, the prevalent views of the citizens on taxation, in the form of a letter to the freemen of the state, a copy of it to be sent to every town. In this letter, the deficiencies of the existing system were ably pointed out. The objections against the poll-tax were these :

" That it is a personal tax, and ought to be paid in personal service, that is, in defending the community ; that it is a double tax, the poor man paying for his poll, which is the substitute for his labor, and for the avails of his labor also ; that it is impolitic, as tending to prevent early marriages, which promote industry, frugality, and every social virtue."

Again, three years later, the town made another effort through their representatives, to obtain their favorite measures ; that polls should either be struck out of the list of taxation, or set at a very low rate ; and that all who pay taxes should vote as freemen.

" June 30, 1779. Voted, that a committee of fifty able, judicious men be appointed to engage fifty able-bodied, effective men, required of this town to fill up our complement of the Continental Army for three years, or during the war ; each member of the committee to procure one soldier, and pay him twenty silver dollars bounty, over and above the bounty given by the state, and pay him the same annually, as long as he continues in the service ; also 40s. per month in silver money, or Indian corn at 3s. per bushel, fresh pork at 3d. per pound, and wheat at 6s. per bushel."

The Committee were not able to carry this vote into effect : the term of enlistment was too long ; nor were the men raised until by a subsequent vote the term of service was restricted to six months. In July of the same year, upon a requisition of the Governor, twenty-seven more men were enlisted for six months, to whom the same bounty and pay were given.

In 1781, the General Assembly passed an act to arrange all the inhabitants of the State into classes, each class to raise so many recruits and furnish such and such clothing and other supplies. Norwich at first refused to enter upon this system, and remonstrated.   With great reluctance, the measure was at last adopted by the inhabitants, and being found to accomplish the end, was continued through the war, though it was never popular with them.

1783.   Instructions were given to the representatives to use their influence with the Assembly to obtain a remonstrance against the five years' pay granted by Congress to the officers of the Continental army.   The resolution passed by the town on this subject, was fiery, dictatorial and extravagant.   A single paragraph will show its bombastic character:

" For a free people just rising out of a threatening slavery, into free shining pospects of a most glorious peace and independence, now to be taxed without their consent, to support and maintain a large number of gentlemen as pensioners, in a time of universal peace, is, in our view, unconstitutional and directly in opposition to the sentiment of the states at large, and was one great spoke in the wheel which moved at first our late struggle with our imperious and tyrannical foes."

Further instructions were given at the same time to the representatives to urge upon the assembly the necessity of keeping a watchful eye upon the proceedings of Congress, to see that they did not exceed the powers vested in them, and to appoint a committee at every session to take into consideration the journals of Congress, and approve or disapprove, applaud or censure the conduct of the delegates.

At no period during the war were the people of Norwich alarmed with the fear of a direct invasion of the enemy, except at the time of the attack on New London, Sept. 6, 1781.   It was then rumored that Arnold, inflamed with hatred against the country he had betrayed, and harboring a particular spite to his native town, had determined at all hazards to march thither, and spread desolation through the homes of his ancient friends and neighbors. Preparations were, therefore, made to receive him; goods were packed, and women and children made ready for flight. The fiery patriots of Norwich wished for nothing more than that he should attempt to march thither, as it would give them a long coveted opportunity of wreaking their vengeance on the traitor. But the undertaking was too hazardous; Arnold, if he had the will, was too prudent to attempt anything but a sudden and transient descent upon the sea-board.

The last time that the militia were called out during the war, was in September, 1782. A detail of the circumstances will serve as a specimen of the harrassing alarms which had previously often occurred.

Benajah Leffingwell was then Lieutenant Colonel of the twentieth regiment, and at seven o'clock in the morning, an express reached him with the following order :

" To Major Leffingwell: I have certain intelligence that there is a large fleet in the Sound, designed for some part of the Main—would hereby request you without loss of time, to notify the regiment under your command, to be ready to march at the shortest notice—also send expresses to New London immediately for further news, and continue expresses as occasion may be. Your humble servant in the greatest haste, SAMUEL M'CLELLAND, Colonel.

Wednesday morning, six o'clock.

I have much more to say if I had time—I am on the road to New London from Windham, where express came to me in the night."

Before nine o'clock the whole regiment had been summoned to turn out with one or two days provisions, and be ready to march on hearing the alarm guns.

The regiment upon the ground that day, as the returns of the orderly book show, consisted of one field officer, thirty-five commissioned, do., and 758 men, in eleven companies, under the following Captains:

| | | |
|---|---|---|
| Joseph Carew, | Moses Stephens, | Jonathan Waterman, |
| Samuel Wheat, | William Pride, | Samuel Lovett, |
| Isaac Johnson, | Jabez Deming, | Jacob De Witt. |
| Nathan Waterman, | Alnor Ladd, | |

Orders at last came for them to march; they were just ready to start, when the order was countermanded; again an express arrived saying that the fleet appeared to be bound in, and orders were issued to stand ready; one hour they heard that the enemy was making preparations for a descent ; the next that the fleet was moving up the Sound. Finally the hostile ships having explored Gardiner's Bay, flitted out of the Sound, and the militia after two days of harrassing suspense, were dismissed to their homes.

# CHAPTER XXIX.

### GEN. JABEZ HUNTINGTON

WAS born at Norwich, in 1719. He graduated at Yale College in 1741, and soon afterwards entered largely into mercantile and commercial pursuits, and made a handsome fortune, principally in the West India trade. The central part of the town plot, was before the revolution the seat of considerable business. The street where Gen. H. resided, now so quiet and serene that every day wears the garb of the Sabbath, was then thronged with men and horses, and frequently blocked up with teams laden with country produce. Nearly 100 mechanics of more than a dozen different occupations, might then be numbered around the square. Gen. Huntington and his sons had large stores in this vicinity; forty or fifty merchant vessels at that time sailed from the port, and of these twenty, were owned and fitted out by Gen. Huntington, nineteen of them in the West India trade ; the other made voyages to *Old England.* The business of Gen. H. was mostly transacted in the town two miles from the port.

Gen. Huntington commenced his patriotic career in 1750, when he was chosen to the Colonial Assembly. For several years he presided over the lower house as Speaker, and afterwards was a member of the Council. On the breaking out of the revolutionary war, he lost nearly half of his property, either by capture of his

22

vessels, or from other circumstances connected with that calamitous period.

In the early part of the war, he was an active member of the Council of Safety, and Major General of the militia. His sons were all ardent patriots; two of them Jedidiah and Ebenezer entered into the army and served during the war. The exertions made by Gen. Huntington for his country, connected with the exciting events of the day and the pressure of private business, were destructive to his health; and in 1779 brought on a hypochondriac disorder, which gradually reduced him to a state of bodily imbecility and partial alienation of mind, which covered the last seven years of his life with a gloomy shadow. He died in 1786. His sons settled around him, establishing their homesteads in his immediate vicinity; though subsequent to the death of his father, Gen. Jedidiah removed to New London.

### GEN. JEDIDIAH HUNTINGTON

Was born at Norwich, in 1743, and graduated at Cambridge, in 1763, on which occasion he pronounced the first English oration delivered in that college at commencement. Settling near his father in his native place, he engaged with him in mercantile pursuits, but soon became noted as one of the Sons of Liberty, and an active Captain of the militia. He entered with spirit into all the measures of his townsmen in resisting oppression, and being raised to the command of a regiment, joined the Continental army with it in 1775. Two years afterwards, Congress gave him the commission of Brigadier General, which office he held with honor during the war, obtaining the confidence and attachment of Washington, and the grateful respect of his country.

In 1789, he was appointed by Washington, Collect-
or of the port of New London, to which place he
removed and resided there till his death in 1818.
Agreeably to a direction contained in his will, his remains were carried to Norwich and deposited in the
family tomb.

Gen. Huntington made a profession of religion when
quite a young man, and his conduct through life was
that of a consistent Christian.  He was a man of
prayer, active in the promotion of religious objects,
liberal in his charities, and a zealous friend of missions.  He was one of the first members of the American Board of Commissioners for Foreign Missions, and
continued active in its concerns till his death.

His first wife was Faith, daughter to Gov. Trumbull,
who died at Dedham, Massachusetts, in 1775, while on
the way with her husband to the continental camp at
Cambridge.  His second wife, sister to Bishop Moore,
of Virginia, survived him, and died in 1831.

### CAPT. ROBERT NILES

Was in the service of the State, during the whole
war, first as commander of the armed schooner Spy,
and afterwards of the Dolphin.  In the former vessel
he was employed to carry to France the ratified
copy of the treaty between that country and the
infant Republic.  Two other copies were sent out
by other conveyances, but both fell into the hands of
the British.  The copy conveyed in the Spy safely
reached its destination.  Capt. Niles was a native of
Groton, and born in 1734.  He died at Norwich, in
1818.

### CAPT. SETH HARDING,

Commander of the armed brigantine *Defence*, owned
by the State of Connecticut, was a citizen of Norwich.

In the early part of the war he was considered next
to Capt. Manly, the most successful of the American
cruisers.   He brought into New London several valuable prize vessels laden with ivory, mahogany, warlike
stores, wearing apparel, and West India products.
Whatever may now be the opinion of moralists with
respect to privateering, it is undeniable that it was at
that time regarded by the highest authorities in the
country, as a laudable and honorable business.   On
the 18th and 19th of June, 1776, Capt. Harding captured near the opening of Boston Bay, three British vessels
with recruits for their army in Boston.   His prisoners
amounted to 322, mostly Highlanders.   Among them
was Col. Campbell, of Gen. Frazer's regiment.

Capt. Harding afterwards commanded the *Confederacy*, a ship of thirty-six guns.   This ship was built
in the river Thames, a few miles below the Landing,
and sent to France after ammunition and stores.   Notice of the time of its sailing from France on the
return voyage, together with its destination, which it
was intended should be kept secret, having been
obtained by some persons inimical to the American
cause, it was by them communicated to the British
officers, who caused a fleet to be placed in ambush, at
the mouth of Delaware Bay.   The Confederacy with
its valuable stores fell into their hands.

### MAJOR NATHAN PETERS

Of Norwich, was an active soldier during the war.
He joined the Connecticut volunteers, on the news of
the battle of Lexington, and marched with them to
Boston.   He was engaged in the battles of Long Island,
York Island, Throg's Point, Princeton, Trenton and
Newport.

Happening to be at home on furlough in September
1781, when the British made a descent upon New

London, with characteristic ardor, he rushed to the scene of action, and was the first person who entered Groton Fort, after it had been deserted by the British troops. Hovering somewhere in the vicinity, he scarcely waited for them to embark before he cautiously entered the fort, and with his own hands extinguished the train which had been laid to cause an explosion of the magazine. In five minutes more the whole would have been a heap of ruins, under which the dead and dying would have been buried.

Maj. Peters died at Norwich, in 1824, aged 79.

### BENEDICT ARNOLD.

The biography of this celebrated traitor has been repeatedly and ably written. It is only intended here to give a few desultory sketches, which may be considered as the reminiscences of those who were personally acquainted with the family. His birth is recorded in the town book, Jan. 3, 1741. His parents had previously lost a son of the same name, and of their six children, only Benedict and Hannah lived to maturity. He was descended from the Arnolds of Rhode Island, an honorable name in that colony, where one of his ancestors, bearing also the name of Benedict, held for fifteen years the office of Governor. Two brothers of this family, Benedict and Oliver, coopers by trade, removed from Newport to Norwich, about the year 1730. The elder of the two, Benedict, or as the name is written in the Norwich Books, Benedic*k*, relinquished his occupation and engaged in trade and public affairs. He was an active, enterprising man, though passionate in his disposition. He appears to have served as collector, lister, selectman, constable, and militia captain.

His marriage to Mrs. Hannah King, whose maiden name was Lathrop, is recorded November 8, 1733.

22*

Mrs. Arnold was a woman of good exterior and estimable qualities. We learn from her grave stone, that she died in 1759, aged fifty-nine. She is there characterized as "A pattern of patience, piety, and virtue," and tradition allows that the truth is not exaggerated. The following is a literal copy (except in orthography) of a letter from her to her son Benedict, while he was at school in Canterbury. The original is probably still in existence.

"To Mr. Benedict Arnold, at Canterbury.
NORWICH, April 12, 1754.
    Dear child.    I received yours of the 1st instant, and was glad to hear that you was well; pray, my dear, let your first concern be to make your peace with God, as it is of all concerns of the greatest importance.
    Keep a steady watch over your thoughts, words and actions.    Be dutiful to superiors, obliging to equals, and affable to inferiors, if any such there be.    Always choose that your companions be your betters, that by their good examples you may learn.
    From your affectionate mother, HANNAH ARNOLD.
    P. S. I have sent you 50s.——use it prudently, as you are accountable to God and your father.    Your father and aunt join with me in love and service to Mr. Cogswell and lady, and yourself.    Your sister is from home."

It is lamentable to think, that the son of such a mother, and the recipient of such wholesome instruction, should have become a proud, obstinate and unprincipled man; leaving behind him a name and character infamous in the sight of his country, and spotted with violence, corruption and treason.

The house in which Benedict was born is still in a state of good preservation, though considerably enlarged since first built by his father. A few years since many parts of it exhibited marks of his mischievous childhood, in whittlings, brands, and hatchet cuts, upon the beams, planks, and doors. The letters B.

A. and B. Arnold were stamped upon it in various places. This house had a variety of occupants after the Arnolds left it. A man by the name of Laidley was its next inhabitant; and his wife, who had been long insane, dying suddenly and strangely, some supposed that her dissolution had been hastened by harsh treatment. She had been known to escape from the house to the adjacent woods in a state of frenzy, and those who assisted in her recapture stated that she was almost naked, and her body lacerated cruelly either by herself or others. A small room or closet in the house, with no aperture for air or light, and with a door only half the height of a person, was reported to be the place of her confinement, and these circumstances, probably exaggerated by rumor, obtained for the house a notorious and superstitious reputation.

In the year 1775, Deacon William Philips, of Boston, the father of Lieut. Governor Philips, removed his family to Norwich, and occupied the Arnold house, till after the British retired from Boston. Its next occupant was Mr. Malbone, of Newport, who also came to Norwich to seek a refuge from the bustle and violence of war. The misfortunes of this family, and the seclusion in which they lived, rather added to the fearful character which the house had acquired. It was said that seven of the name and all nearly connected, had died within the short period of eighteen months. About ten years before the family removed to Norwich, that is, in 1767, the brig Dolphin, of Newport, owned by one of the Malbones, and commanded by another, took fire off Point Judith, as it was returning from Jamaica, and was entirely consumed. Such was the violence of the flames, and the rapidity of their work, that all communication was cut off between the deck and cabin, and in the latter three ladies and two children perished.  Those on deck escaped in boats.  This, and other misfortunes connected with the family, had .made the name almost ominous of calamity.  The house was afterwards tenanted successively, though but for a short period, by several pure and noble-minded gentlemen, among whom were William Hubbard Esq. and Thomas Mumford Esq.  The occupants were changed so often, that public rumor ascribed it to the supernatural sounds and sights with which it was haunted.  At a subsequent period it was taken by a disbanded officer, whose late suppers, revels, and card-playing, added another kind of gloomy notoriety to the tenement, so that after his departure it remained tenantless for several years, till purchased and repaired by Mr. Uriah Tracy, to whose heirs it now belongs.

To return from this digression respecting the Arnold house to the Arnold family.  No one of the name in Norwich seems to have been a common place character.  Benedict, when a boy, was bold, enterprising, ambitious, active as lightning, and with a ready wit always at command.  In every kind of sport, especially if mischief was to be perpetrated, he was a dauntless ring-leader, and as despotic among the boys as an absolute monarch.  On a day of public rejoicing for some success over the French, Arnold, then a mere stripling, took a field-piece, and in a frolic placed it on end, so that the mouth should point upright, poured into it a large quantity of powder, and actually dropped into the muzzle, *from his hand,* a blazing fire-brand.  His activity saved him from a scorching, for though the flash streamed up within an inch of his face, he darted back, and shouted huzza! as loud as the best of the company.  It is remembered also, that having, at the head of a gang of boys, seized and rolled away some valuable casks from a shop-yard, to aid in making the usual thanksgiving bonfire, the casks were arrested on their way, by an officer sent by the owner to recover them; upon which young Arnold was so enraged, that he stripped off his coat upon the spot, and *dared* the constable, a stout and grave man, *to fight.*

At fourteen years of age he was apprenticed as a druggist to Drs. Daniel and Joshua Lathrop, and here he exhibited the same rash and fearless traits of character. A person who once remained in the shop with him during a tremendous thunder storm, related afterwards, that at every peculiarly loud and stunning report, young Arnold would swing his hat and shout hurrah! adding occasionally some reckless or profane exclamation. . Once during his apprenticeship he ran away, with the design of enlisting as a soldier in the British army; but his friends succeeded in finding him and induced him to return to his employment. Other anecdotes of his youth may be found in Spark's " Life and Treason of Benedict Arnold." Dr. Solomon Smith was the fellow apprentice of Arnold, and not Dr. Hopkins, as is stated in that memoir.

Miss Hannah Arnold, the sister of Benedict, was an accomplished lady, pleasing in her person, witty and affable. While the family still resided in Norwich, and of course when she was quite young, she became an object of interest and attention to a young foreigner, a transient resident of the place. His regard was reciprocated by the young lady; but Benedict disliked the man, and after vainly endeavoring by milder means to break off the intimacy, he became outrageous, and vowed vengeance upon him if he ever again caught him in the house. After this the young people saw each other only by stealth, the lover timing his visits to the brother's absence. One evening Ben-

edict, who had been to New Haven, came home un-
expectedly, and having entered the house without
bustle, ascertained that the Frenchman was in the
parlor with his sister.   He instantly planted himself in
front of the house with a loaded pistol, and commanded
a servant to assail the door of the room in which they
were, as if he would break it down.   The young man,
as Arnold expected, leaped out of the window ; the
latter fired at him, but it being dark, missed his aim.
The youth escaped, but the next day left the place,
choosing rather to relinquish the lady than to run any
further risk of his life.   Arnold afterwards met him at
the Bay of Hondurus, both having gone thither on a
trading voyage.   A challenge was given by one or the
other, and promptly accepted.   They fought, and the
Frenchman was severely wounded.

Miss Arnold was never married.   After the death of
her father she resided principally with her brother.
She died at Montague, in Upper Canada, in 1803, aged
sixty years.

The last exploit of Arnold during the war was the
burning of New London.   No act of his cast more dis-
honor upon his reputation.   Its contiguity to his birth-
place rendered it more than probable that he would
meet in mortal combat some of the companions of his
childhood and patrons of his youth.   It was truly a
fratricidal deed.

Oliver Arnold, brother to Benedict Senior, and uncle
to the traitor, at his death left a widow and five children, in straitened circumstances.   They had a small
house and garden, but nothing more.   To these relations, Benedict was always kind and liberal.   To one
of the sons, by the name of Freegift, he gave the education of a scholar, and designed him for one of the
professions; but the young man joined himself to the

Sons of Liberty, entered into the naval service, under
Paul Jones, and after fighting bravely, came home
with a ruined constitution, to languish and die. The
other son, Oliver, was of a roving disposition, and had
a peculiar talent at making extempore verses. A specimen of this talent, though trifling in its character,
may perhaps be acceptable.

In a bookseller's shop in New Haven, he was introduced to Joel Barlow, who had just then acquired considerable notoriety by the publication of an altered
edition of Watts' Psalms and Hymns. Barlow asked
for a specimen of his talent; upon which the wandering poet immediately repeated the following stanza :

> " You've proved yourself a sinful cre'tur' ;
> You've murdered Watts, and spoilt the metre ;
> You've tried the word of God to alter,
> And for your pains deserve a halter."

Oliver was also a sailor and a patriot, and cordially
despised the course taken by his cousin Benedict, in
betraying his country. Local tradition ascribes to him
the following acrostic on the traitor's name, and it is
even added that being on a visit to his cousin after the
war, and called upon by him to amuse a party of English officers with some extemporaneous effusion, he stood
up and repeated these lines. The composition itself,
however, contradicts such a report, as it bears no resemblance to other short and unstudied efforts of the
native rhymester, which have been preserved.

> " Born for a curse to virtue and mankind,
> Earth's broadest realm ne'er knew so black a mind.
> Night's sable veil your crimes can never hide,
> Each one so great, 't would glut historic tide.
> Defunct, your cursed memory will live,
> In all the glare that infamy can give.

> Curses of ages will attend your name,
> Traitors alone will glory in your shame.
>
> Almighty vengeance sternly waits to roll
> Rivers of sulphur on your treacherous soul—
> Nature looks shuddering back, with conscious dread,
> On such a tarnished blot as she has made.
> Let hell receive you, riveted in chains,
> Doomed to the hotest focus of its flames !"

### ROGER GRISWOLD

Settled in Norwich when first admitted to the bar, in
1783.  He married the daughter of Col. Zabdiel Rogers, and continued his residence in the place, until
elected a member of Congress in 1794.  He then removed to his native town, Lyme.  It is an interesting
fact that he came back to Norwich to die.  He was
elected Governor of Connecticut, in May, 1811, and
re-elected the succeeding year.  For several years, he
had been afflicted with a disease of the heart, which
at intervals caused him great suffering.  It increased
so rapidly, that in the summer of 1812, he was removed
to Norwich, that he might try the effect of a change
of air, and at the same time have the benefit of advice
from Dr. Tracy, in whose skill, as a physician, he had
great confidence.  But neither air nor medicine could
do more for him than alleviate the paroxysms of his
distress, and he died Oct. 25, 1812.  He was only fifty
years of age, having been born in 1762—a man of great
boldness and energy.  He was the son of Matthew
Griswold, one of the former Governors of Connecticut,
who held that office during the period that intervened
between Trumbull and Huntington.  His mother was
a daughter of Roger Wolcott, who was also a Governor of Connecticut.

# CHAPTER XXX.

Episcopal Church and Society.

TRADITION is the only source, from which anything has been ascertained respecting the first rise of the Episcopal church in Norwich. From thence we learn that the first church of England men in the place were Thomas Grist and Edmund Gookin, who were " allowed as inhabitants" in 1726. They resided upon the town plot. Mr. Grist was born in 1700, and in 1721, married Ann Birchard. Mr. Gookin was about the same age.

The year 1722 is the date given to the existence of Episcopacy as an order, in Connecticut, though it was first introduced by the Rev. Mr. Muirson, a missionary from the " Society for propagating the Gospel in foreign parts," at Stratford, in 1706. An Episcopal church was established at New London, in 1725, principally through the exertions of the Rev. Matthew Graves, who may also be considered as the founder of the churches in Norwich and Hebron. This gentleman was a missionary from the " Society for promoting Christian Knowledge," formed at London in 1698. It is not known how his acquaintance with Mr. Grist of Norwich, commenced, but he frequently visited him. Gradually, and at first, privately, a little band of ten or a dozen persons were collected on such occasions, among whom the ordinances of the church were administered. In this part of the town they never had

23

a regular minister or a house for worship, but the Gookin and Grist family, until their extinction during the present generation, were faithful and devoted adherents of the church. Mr. Grist himself lived to be very aged,—his three daughters died unmarried, Anna in 1812, aged 88 ; Hannah in 1815, aged 86, and Molly, in 1824, aged 83. Anna, the last of the Gookin family in Norwich, was also a spinster, and died in 1810, aged 80.

About the year 1732, the Rev. Ebenezer Punderson, a Congregational minister of Groton, declared for the Church of England, and crossed the Atlantic to be re-ordained. On his return, he organized a church in Norwich, Long Society, at the village of Poquetanuck, which has ever since existed, though it has always been small, and seldom able to support a pastor of its own. This church was formed about 1738. Mr. Punderson and Mr. Graves frequently preached at private houses in other parts of Norwich, and by degrees, a respectable society was gathered in Chelsea. A regular church organization took place about the year 1745. This infant church was founded and nourished by the united labors of Graves, Punderson and Seabury, of New London.

Jan. 7, 1746, a meeting was held at the Townhouse, to decide matters relative to the erection of an edifice " for the service of Almighty God, according to the Liturgie of the Church of England, as by law established."

> Rev. Mr. Punderson, *Moderator*.
> Capt. Benajah Bushnell, *Treasurer*.
> Capt. Isaac Clarke, ⎱
> Mr. Thomas Grist, ⎰ *Building Committee.*
> Mr. Elisha Hide.

Capt. Bushnell had previously presented ground for
the site, "at the north-east end of Waweequa's Hill,
near the Old Landing place," and a subscription was
presented, which had been circulated, and contained
eighty-seven names; the sum subscribed, £678. The
greatest amount by one individual, was £50, by Andrew Galloway. The three gentlemen who formed
the building committee subscribed £40 each. Mr.
Punderson afterwards collected in Rhode Island, £138,
and Capt. Bushnell in Boston, £178. All this was
probably Old Tenor money, or Bills of Credit, of reduced value.

The land and the church, when erected, were conveyed by deed to the committee, in trust—

" For the use of the ' Society for propagating the Gospel
in foreign parts,' and their successors forevermore, to be appropriated for an Episcopal church and church-yard for the
benefit of an Episcopal minister and members of said church,
and for no other use, intent or purpose whatsoever."

The consideration money was five shillings, and
possession and seisin were given, by delivering to the
Committee in the usual manner, " turf and twig."

In 1750, the church was in a condition to allow of
public worship. The number of pew holders was
twenty-eight. They built their own pews and held
them as their proper estate. The first church officers
were :—

    Capt. Benajah Bushnell, } *Wardens.*
    Capt. Joseph Tracy,   }
    Capt, Isaac Clarke,   }
      "   Thomas Grist, } *Vestry men.*
      "   Daniel Hall,   }
    Elisha Hide, *Clerk of the Church.*
    Phineas Holden, *Society Clerk.*

Mr. Punderson was the officiating clergyman.

In 1760, a subscription was raised for Mr. John Beardslee, " towards his inoculation and going to England for orders, that he may preach in the churches of England, at Norwich and Groton." An engagement was at the same time entered into with him, to pay the annual sum of £33, towards his support, when he should become their minister, which he did in the spring of 1763. The number of male communicants in the Chelsea church was, at this time, about twenty.

.The Groton church mentioned, is the one already alluded to in the village of Poquetannuck. That village lies at the head of a creek or cove, which runs out of the Thames about four miles below the Landing. It was early settled, being considered a fine location for fishing, building small sea-craft, and exporting wood and timber. It now contains about forty dwelling houses. A part of it lies in Groton, and it was within the bounds of that town that the Episcopal church was built. It has been generally dependent upon the Norwich church for the administration of the ordinances.

In 1767, a lot of land was given for a Glebe by Mrs. Zerviah Bushnell, and conveyed by deed to the " Society for propagating the Gospel in foreign parts." A glebe house was built, but we soon afterwards lose sight of Mr. Beardslee. In 1768, an agreement was made with John Tyler, of Wallingford, Conn., by which £60 sterling money of Great Britain, was advanced to him, to defray the expenses of a voyage to England to receive ordination ; he, on his part, engaging to return and officiate as their priest, at a salary of £30 per annum. The money was raised by subscription, and the list contains eighty names.

Mr. Tyler returned the next year, and became rector of the church. This gentleman had been educated

in Congregationalism, but after embracing the doc-
trines of the Church of England, he prepared for holy
orders, under the care of Dr. Johnson, of Stratford.

The persecution of the Episcopalians in our country during the revolutionary struggle, lies like a blot
upon the bright shield of patriotism. Whether
tories or not, they were all suspected of toryism,
and the clergy in an especial manner were obliged to
endure a thousand little domestic harassings, alarming
threats and destruction of property. Most of them
were forbidden to officiate as priests, either publicly or
privately, and their churches were shut up by order of
the magistracy. The church in Chelsea was closed
for three years, through fear of popular excitement.
In 1774, a subscription had been taken up for a porch,
steeple and bell, to be added to the church ; but the
project was suspended until 1780. No entry was made
on the records of the church from April, 1776, to April,
1779. But it is remembered, that during this time,
Mr. Tyler held divine service in his own house, and
was never molested in the performance. He was perhaps treated with greater indulgence than others, on
account of the well known benevolence of his character and the liberality of his sentiments. Family influence likewise was in his favor; his father-in-law,
Isaac Tracy Esq., being deacon of the Congregational
Church, and of unsuspected patriotism. Mr. Tyler
was never once personally abused during the conflict,
but he was frequently vexed with petty depredations
upon his property. At one time, he was afraid to drink
the water of his own well. The congregation at this
period had dwindled to a very small number. Often
the services were performed with an audience of not
more than fifteen or twenty persons.

Whether the title of " Christ's Church in Chelsea,"

23*

was held from the first is not known ; the designation
does not appear upon the records until 1785.

In 1790, a new church was built upon land given by
Mr. Phinehas Holden.  This was conveyed by deed,
not to the S. P. G. F. P. as the old one had been, but to
Trustees, " for the use of the Protestant Episcopal
Church of England."

One hundred and thirty pounds towards building the
church were raised, besides subscriptions of labor.   The
building committee were—

| | |
|---|---|
| Maj. Ebenezer Whiting, | Barzillai Davison, |
| Benajah Denison, | James Christie. |

In 1791 the owners of the pews in the old church
relinquished their rights, and here for the first time appear the names of persons now upon the stage of life,
viz : Christopher Vail and Cushing Eells.  The pews
in the new church were sold at public auction, and the
money applied to parochial uses.   There were thirty
purchasers to the pews, of whom not one now remains
alive.

May 19, 1791, the new church was solemnly " dedi-
cated to the worship of Almighty God according to the
liturgy of the Church of England, accommodated to
the civil constitution of these American States," by
the R. R. Dr. Seabury, Bishop of Connecticut.

> Ebenezer Whiting,   } *Wardens.*
> Ebenezer Huntington, }
> Jabez Huntington, *Society Clerk.*

Mr. Tyler's salary was at this time £60, and in 1794
it was increased to £80.  He had, moreover, liberty
of absence every fourth Sunday, at Poquetannuck,
and received a small stipend from the church there.

With the exception of the political jealousy during

the Revolutionary contest, the Episcopalians and Congregationalists of Norwich have never exhibited any acrimony against each other. On the contrary, social intercourse has been generally maintained, irrespective of denominational bounds, and the two sects have in many instances interchanged civilities, in a truly courteous and Christian spirit.

At a very early period we find that the Episcopal church employed the Congregational collector to collect Mr. Tyler's rates. Invitations have sometimes been cordially given to the Episcopalians to celebrate their festivals in the larger edifices of the Congregationalists, which have been cheerfully accepted; and in two instances at least, when the latter have been by sudden disasters deprived for a season of a place of worship, the doors of Christ's Church have been freely opened to them. One instance from the records may be given.

"At a legal meeting of the Episcopal Parish of Christ's Church, in Norwich, on Wednesday, Feb. 19, 1794, Thomas Mumford, Moderator,

Voted, that this meeting, taking into consideration that the Presbyterian church in this place, of which the Rev. Walter King is Pastor, are destitute of a convenient place in which to attend public worship, their meeting-house having been lately destroyed by fire, do consent to accommodate said Presbyterian society until Easter Monday, 1795, as follows: the Rev<sup>d</sup> John Tyler, our present pastor, to perform divine service one half the day on each Sabbath, and the Rev. Walter King, pastor of said Presbyterian congregation, to perform divine service the other half of said Sabbath, alternately performing on the first part of the day."

For this kind and considerate courtesy, the obliged party passed a vote of acknowledgment and thanks, which was inserted upon the records of both societies. The offer was accepted, and this amicable arrangement lasted for three months.

Mr. Tyler died January 20, 1823, in the eighty-first year of his age. He was an interesting preacher; his voice sweet and solemn, and his eloquence persuasive. The benevolence of his heart was manifested in daily acts of courtesy and charity to those around him. He studied medicine in order to benefit the poor, and to find out remedies for some of those peculiar diseases to which no common specifics seemed to apply. His pills, ointments, extracts, and syrups, obtained a great local celebrity. During the latter years of his life, he was so infirm as to need assistance in the performance of his functions. Mr. Clark was his colleague for three years, and Mr. Paddock the last year before his death.

Mr. Tyler was succeeded by the Rev. Seth B. Paddock, who officiated as Rector until the summer of 1844. Salary $800, together with interest on the sale of the Glebe house and lot, which was $100 more.

Mr. Paddock, after resigning his rectorship, took charge of the Episcopal Academy, in Cheshire.

The Rev. William F. Morgan was consecrated Rector in September, 1844.

In 1828 a new church was erected; the old one having fallen into decay, and its dimensions becoming too limited for the increasing audience. The whole cost of the new edifice, together with the organ and furniture, was $10,500. More than half of this was raised by voluntary contributions. The most liberal donors were Mr. Richard Adams and Mr. Jedediah Huntington. The former gave $600 and the latter $500. It stands a few rods west of the old church, between the middle and upper streets. It is built of stone, in the gothic style; its dimensions sixty-five feet by fifty-two. It was consecrated by the Rev. Thomas C. Brownell, the diocesan Bishop, July 29, 1829.

The deed of the Glebe houselot having been executed in favor of the S. P. G. F. P., it could not be alienated without taking some legal measures to obtain a
title.   A petition was therefore presented to the General Assembly, in 1835, who passed an act vesting the
property in the Society.

Mr. Tyler is the only one who has died Rector of
this church.   His monumental stone bears this inscription :

" Here lies interred the earthly remains of the Rev.
John Tyler, for fifty-four years Rector of Christ's
Church, in this city.   Having faithfully fulfilled his
ministry, he was ready to be dissolved, and to be with
Christ.   His soul took its flight from this vale of mis-
ery January 20, 1823, in the eighty-first year of his
age."

# CHAPTER XXXI.

Population. Inoculation. Division of the Ancient Town. Franklin. Newent. Bozrah. Long Society. Hanover. Portipaug.

CENSUS OF NORWICH, JAN. 1, 1774.

| | Persons. | Families. | Dwelling Houses. |
|---|---|---|---|
| First Society . . . | 1978 | 317 | 283 |
| West  do. . . . . . | 875 | 133 | 111 |
| Newent  . . . . | 641 | 98 | 92 |
| East . . . . . . | 1100 | 76 | 69 |
| New Concord  . . | 932 | 146 | 130 |
| Chelsea . . . . . | 1019 | 127 | 104 |
| Hanover . . . . | 323 | 53 | 44 |
| Eighth . . . . . | 453 | 74 | 68 |
| | 7321 | 1024 | 901 |

| | |
|---|---|
| Males under 10 . . . . . . . . . | 1099 |
| Females  do. . . . . . . . . . | 1054 |
| Males between 10 and 20 . . . . . . | 916 |
| Females  do. . . . . . . . | 749 |
| Males between 20 and 70 . . . . . . | 1468 |
| Females  do. . . . . . . | 1574 |
| Males above 70 . . . . . . . . . | 78 |
| Females  do. . . . . . . . . . | 94 |

In 1779, number of families in First Society 367; persons 2184.  In Chelsea 129 families, 1111 persons.

The whole population of the town as returned in the Grain Book of 1779, was 7187.  In 1780, 6541.  It is evident that these returns are very inaccurate.  At the latter date the population of the nine miles square was probably about 8000.

It is said that at the annual election for Governor, in 1786, 900 votes were given in Norwich for one candidate, viz: Governor Huntington. This, if it be a fact, illustrates the harmony of opinion that pervaded the eight societies, and shows the increased population of the place. Even in the present day, of almost un-limited elective franchise, it is rare to find a larger proportion of the inhabitants of a town voters.

These societies had, nevertheless, many local jeal-ousies, and vehement disputes on minor subjects. The Mason and Mohegan controversy with the State, at one time ranged the citizens into two adverse parties; conflicting opinions respecting points of ecclesiastical discipline, at various periods convulsed the churches, and almost rent them in twain: and one of the most bitter contentions that ever disturbed the town, was occasioned by a difference of opinion with respect to the regulation of swine, viz: whether they should be confined, or run at large. Elisha Hide Esq., then a young man, was very conspicuous in this controversy. He espoused the cause of *freedom,* and this eventually became the prevailing side. In 1760, a conflict was begun, with respect to inoculation for the Small Pox, which came very near being interminable. Individu-als had been agitating the question for many years, and it was now proposed to the town in this form, viz: Will the town approve of Dr. Elisha Lord's proceeding to inoculate for the small pox, under any regulations whatever. Passed in the negative. The subject was resumed again and again, with the same result. The popular feeling was excited, almost to violence, when-ever the faculty brought up the question. In .1773, we find Dr. Turner and Dr. Loomis opening a hospital for inoculation, on an island in the Sound, off Ston-ington, the citizens on the main land strenuously op-posing the erection of hospitals. In 1787, Drs. Marvin and Tracy made an effort to obtain permission to open a hospital, somewhere in the purlieus of the town, but in vain. They afterwards selected a beautiful and retired situation on the banks of the Thames, in that part of the Mohegan lands called Massapeag, and thither people resorted from all the neighboring towns to be inoculated. Public opinion was, however, gradually changing, and in 1792, a special meeting was warned to consider the subject, under the expectation that a vote would be obtained, to permit inoculation within the limits of the town. This expectation was disappointed; the opposition was vehement; a majority were in favor of the motion, but the law required two-thirds of the voices present, and it was lost. The yeas and nays at this time were carefully recorded. The conflict continued three years longer, but in 1796, a vote was obtained to open a house for inoculation, provided it be in some obscure and thinly peopled part of the town. After this there was no further controversy on the point.

The division of the town took place in 1786. This was accomplished in the most amicable manner. In full town meeting, on the question of petitioning the Assembly to have the town divided, there was but one vote in the negative. It was settled that the First and Chelsea Societies, should form the town of Norwich; Hanover, Newent, and a part of Long Society, a new town by the name of Lisbon; New Concord, Portipaug, West and Eighth Societies, should form the two towns of Franklin and Bozrah; and that East Society should be annexed to Preston, the middle waters of the Thames and Shetucket being the boundary. The division lines were harmoniously adjusted, and committees appointed from each of the new towns, to meet with one from Norwich to settle accounts, assume a just quota of the debts, take their part of the town's poor, &c.   The ancient town continued to have an annual meeting for several years, to see to those affairs of general concern, which had not been fully distributed or settled.

This division of the town was undoubtedly a wise and salutary measure.   But an historian who has hitherto considered the nine-miles square as a beautiful whole, cannot but sigh to see the integrity of his province destroyed, and may be allowed to linger awhile over those relinquished societies which will henceforward have a distinct history of their own.

### SECOND SOCIETY : WEST FARMS, OR FRANKLIN.

In the year 1718, the Second Church in Norwich was formed in that part of Norwich then called the West Farms, or North Society.   The settlements here were almost coeval with the Town-plot.   Many of the sons of the proprietors removed to farms which by repeated divisions of land made by the town, fell to themselves or their fathers ; hence the names of Lathrop, Tracy, Abel, Gager, Hide, &c., soon became diffused through the adjoining societies.   The Rev. Henry Wills was the first minister at West Farms.   In 1721 the church was favored with a great revival which added sixty-eight members to it; a large proportion out of a population that did not at that time exceed 400.   Mr. Wills was dismissed in 1749, in consequence of a division in the church with respect to Church government.   The Rev. John Ellis, his successor, was settled in 1752, and retained his charge about twenty-seven years.   The latter part of the time he was absent from his people, having joined the Revolutionary army as chaplain, with their consent.   Having decided to remain with the army, he asked and obtained a dismission from the church.   After the conclusion of the war, he preached

24

awhile at Rehoboth, Mass., but returned at length to his former people, and resided among them till his death in 1805. In 1745, upon the question of erecting a new meeting-house, a schism took place in this society. A party withdrew, and a new society was formed, which settled the Rev. Mr. Ives. This church however soon dwindled away, and was merged in that of the Separatists, which also in a few years became extinct. Mr. Ives removed to Munson, Mass., in 1758.

The meeting-house alluded to above, is still extant, though unoccupied, as the Society has recently erected a more modern and convenient edifice. It stands upon a high hill, looking out upon a rich and extensive prospect of forest and cultivated field. Within the walls, all is sombre, plain, and antique; the pulpit is at the side; it has an entrance in front and at either end; the pew frames and gallery resemble lace bobbins; the sound-board, bearing in large figures the date of 1745, the pulpit and pulpit window are carved and painted in different colors; the pulpit cushions are of gray velvet, with heavy black tassels, and when the wind comes in through the broken casements, they wave like a hearse pall. This description applies to it as it was in 1830. One must have seen it filled with its varied congregation, and surmounted with the thin and pallid face of its venerable pastor, and have heard his tremulous voice uttering the customary strains of exhortation and warning, in order to obtain the most striking impression of this old Puritan church.

Rev. Samuel Nott, third minister at West Farms, was ordained March 13, 1782. This venerable minister has preached his sixty-second anniversary sermon, and still performs all the duties of his office, though more than ninety years of age.

When the two Societies of West Farms and Portipaug were united to form a town, the proposition to give it the name of Franklin, is believed to have originated with Jacob Kingsbury Esq. This gentleman was Inspector General in the army of the United States, and served his country faithfully both in the army and navy for a period of forty years. He was a descendant of Deacon Joseph Kingsbury, one of the first pillars of the West Farms church. At the commencement of the revolution, he repaired to Roxbury, and entered the army as a volunteer, being then only eighteen years of age. He continued in the service until the close of the second war with the British, in 1815. He was a member of the old society of the Cincinnati. His death took place at Franklin, in 1837. He was then eighty-one years of age. One of his descendants, Lieut. Charles E. Kingsbury, a youth of eighteen, died at Fort Mellon, in East Florida, eleven days before him. So near together fall the green tree and the dry.

### EIGHTH SOCIETY, OR PORTIPAUG.

This is the society already mentioned, which broke away from the *Second* and established an independent church. It was not incorporated for many years. Mr. Ives was the first and only minister of the Congregational order.

A free church has since been erected here by the voluntary contributions of a few individuals. By the word *free*, is meant that it is open for all denominations of christians to occupy. It is however most generally in the service of the Methodists.

The Congregational church in Portipaug was constituted before that of Hanover, but the latter was first incorporated as an ecclesiastical society. Hanover is therefore numbered as the Seventh, and Portipaug as

the Eighth society. These ecclesiastical societies were
the original divisions or districts in use all over New
England in its earlier days. The great increase of
other denominations has rendered them obsolete.

Portipaug, spelt also Pottapange and Pettipaug, was
the Indian designation of the place. The name seems
to have been descriptive of a valley with a small
stream winding through it.

*Franklin*, which comprises these two societies is a
farming town, that in 1840 contained about 1000
inhabitants. The population has continued for a
number of years uncommonly stationary. In 1810 it
was 1161. In 1830, 1194. The extent of the town
is about five miles by four. It contains no considerable village ; and the only manufacturing establishment
of any importance is a woolen factory, on Beaver
Brook, near the Shetucket.

### NEWENT, OR THIRD SOCIETY.

The large tract of land lying between the crotch of
the rivers Shetucket and Quinebaug, was acknowledged by the English to be a part of the Mohegan territory. At an early period, it was inhabited by a band
of Indians tributary to Uncas, called by the first settlers
Showtuckets. A great part of this tract, given or sold
by Uncas to Capt. James Fitch, was commonly called
"the 1800 acre grant."

About the year 1694, Capt. Fitch sold out his right
to 1200 acres of this land to Joseph Safford, Richard
Smith, Meshach Farly and Matthew Perkins, all of
the town of Ipswich.

In 1695, Joseph and Jabez Perkins, of Ipswich,
made an additional purchase of 800 acres for £70,
and in 1700, Matthew Perkins sold out his previous
purchase to his brothers, the said Joseph and Jabez,

and about the same time, John Safford and Samuel Bishop, both of Ipswich, became planters.  The whole tract between the rivers, except what was expressly guarantied by the town to the Indians then residing upon it, was soon divided into farms, and leased out by indentures to various settlers.   Jabez and Joseph Perkins were accepted as inhabitants in 1701.   These two brothers continued to improve their land in common, until the year 1720, when they divided it equally between themselves, and after obtaining an acknowledgment of their title from the town, it was still further divided by deed among their respective sons, the daughters being each provided for by a portion of £50 in money.

This land was at first considered a very choice part of the nine miles square in respect to soil, but the farms have since very much diminished in value.   In 1725, the proprietors of the common and undivided land put an end to all controversy, by giving a quit-claim deed to Capt. Jabez Perkins, Lt. Samuel Bishop, Mr. Joseph Perkins and Mr. John Safford, of all the Indian land in the crotch of the rivers, and of all contained in Major Fitch's 1800 acre grant, for the sum of £75, money in hand, paid to said proprietors, provided that they shall allow the Indians to enjoy the said Indian land according to the town grant.

The ecclesiastical society in this place was organized in 1723, the town having previously appropriated sixty acres of land for the use of the first minister that should settle there.   The affairs of the society were entirely under the control of the Perkins family, as appears from the following entry:

" Jan. 17, 1720.   In town meeting ordered, that if the Perkinses at their return from Boston, do not bring with them a minister to preach in the crotch of the river, or satisfy the

24*

selectmen they shall have one speedily, the rate-makers shall put them into the minister's rates."

The Rev. Daniel Kirtland was the first minister. At his ordination, Dec. 10, 1723, the following ministers assisted :

Dr. Lord and Mr. Wills, of Norwich.
Mr. Mather, of Saybrook.
Mr. Estabrooks, of Canterbury.

The church agreed to profess discipline according to the Cambridge Platform. They professed to believe " that all organized church acts proceeded after the manner of a mixed administration, and could not be consummated without the consent of both elders and brotherhood."

Mr. Kirtland, after preaching nearly thirty years, became deranged, and his connexion with the church was dissolved on account of this calamity. He lived to the age of 72, died very poor, in 1773, and not having had any monumental stone, the spot which his remains occupy in the burying yard is forgotten and unknown. He had married, soon after his ordination, Miss Marcy Perkins, by whom he had two sons, Daniel and Samuel. Samuel, born in 1735, is well known as the faithful missionary of the Oneida Indians, and the father of President Kirtland of Harvard College. He was a pupil of the Indian school founded by Dr. Wheelock in Lebanon, and left Norwich in 1766, to go on the mission to which the remainder of his life was devoted. For forty years, his labors among the Aborigines were arduous and unremitted.

The Rev. Peter Powers, successor to Mr. Kirtland, was ordained Dec. 2, 1756, but relinquished his charge in 1766, on account of the insufficiency of his salary to give him a support, and for some years, they were without a minister, in a weak and scattered state. Something like a re-organization of the church took place in 1770 ; several of the Separates returned, and Dr. Joel Benedict, a man of fine classical attainments, was installed pastor. He remained with them thirteen years, and then obtained a dismission, on account of the niggardliness of his salary. He afterward settled in Plainfield, and acquired a distinguished reputation as a Hebrew scholar.

In 1780, Mr. David Hale of Coventry, was ordained at Newent. He was the brother of the accomplished and chivalrous Capt. Nathan Hale, who was executed as a spy on Long Island, by order of Sir William Howe. Mr. Hale was a man of very gentle and winning manners, of exalted piety and a fine scholar. He carried his idea of disinterested benevolence to such an extent, that if acted upon, it would overturn all social institutions. He thought it to be a man's duty to love his neighbor, not only *as* himself, with the same kind of love, but also to the *same degree*, so that he should not prefer, even in thought, that a contingent calamity, such as the *burning of a house*, or the *loss of a child*, should fall on his neighbor, rather than on himself. Mr. Hale supplied the deficiencies of his salary by keeping a boarding school. As an instructor, he was popular ; his house was filled with pupils from all parts of the county, but ill health and a constitutional depression of spirits, obliged him to resign this employment, and eventually his pastoral office. His mind and nerves were of that delicate and sensitive temperament, which cannot long endure the rude shock of earthly scenes. He returned to Coventry, and died young. Thus of four persons, successively ordained or installed over this church, not one died their minister. The Rev. Levi Nelson, the present pastor, was ordained in 1804, a man of whom it has been said that he never had an enemy ; a rare character to be given of any minister in these days of division, doctrinal disputes, favoritism and change.

The new society took the name of Newent, in fond remembrance of a town of that name in Gloucestershire, England, from which the ancestors of Joseph and Jabez Perkins originally emigrated.  The first of this family mentioned in the Norwich records is Daniel Perkins, who in 1682, married Deliver* the daughter of Thomas Bliss, of the Town-plot.  This connection may have led to the emigration of the family from Ipswich, though whether Daniel was the brother of Matthew, Jabez and Joseph, is not ascertained. The death of a Mr. Joseph Perkins is recorded in 1698.  This was perhaps the father of the Newent family, who may have come in his old age to reside with his sons.  Jabez married Hannah Lathrop in 1698.    Their sons were

| | | | | | | |
|---|---|---|---|---|---|---|
| Jabez, | born, | 1699 | Luke, | born, | 1709 |
| Jacob, | " | 1705 | | | |

It is from this line of the family, that the venerable Capt. Erastus Perkins, of Chelsea, is descended.   He was born February 17, 1752, and is still living.   His father Capt. Jabez Perkins resided in the Town-plot, and about the year 1750, brought home one day from the woods, two young elms, which he set out in such positions as would throw their shade over the shop that he then occupied.   These are now those lofty and wide spreading elms that nearly front the dwelling of Mrs. Daniel Coit.

---

* QUERY :—a mistake for *Dolinda?* See daughters of Thomas Bliss, page 99.

Joseph Perkins born in 1674, married Martha Morgan in 1700. His sons were

| Joseph, | born, | 1704 | Matthew born, | 1713 |
| John, | " | 1709 | William, " | 1722 |

Deacon Joseph died in 1726. His son Joseph, was a physician of large practice, and the father of two physicians each more noted than himself. The second, Dr. Joseph, devoted a long life to the duties of his profession in his native town. In the latter part of his life, he had some seasons of slight mental disturbance, and those who knew him well, always abstained from asking his professional advice, when he appeared without his knee-buckles; — such neglect being a sure indication that his mind was absent and unsettled. He died in 1794, having reached his ninetieth year.

Dr. Elisha Perkins, of Plainfield, was the celebrated inventor of the metallic Tractors. This was a method of curing diseases, by rubbing the patient in a certain manner with small pointed pieces of metal, steel or brass, which were thought to extract the pain by a kind of magnetism. The inventor not meeting with much success among his countrymen—the medical association of his native county discarding him from their fellowship as a quack—transferred the sphere of his operations to England. Here the invention excited considerable notice, societies were established in London and other places for the use of the Tractors in disorders of the poor, and reports were printed exhibiting numerous cases of cure. One of these societies established at Durham under the patronage of the Bishop, announced in 1805, the relief or cure of 200 diseased persons by the use of Tractors. Dr. Perkins soon afterwards died, and his Tractors have long disappeared from medical use.

Lieut. Samuel Bishop, and his brother John, were also emigrants from Ipswich. Samuel, the son of Samuel, was married in 1706 to Sarah Forbes. John, the son of John in 1718 to Mary Bingham. The descendants of these brothers are numerous.

### SEVENTH SOCIETY, OR HANOVER.

This society includes the south-west corner of Canterbury, and the south-east of Windham, but the main position of it, united with Newent, forms the town of Lisbon. It was incorporated as an ecclesiastical society in 1761, and a fund of £1600 raised by subscription for the support of the ministry. The meetings were held in private houses, near the centre of the society for several years. The church was gathered May 13, 1776, and a house for worship erected near that period. The Rev. Andrew Lee was ordained the first pastor, October 26, 1768. He exercised the duties of this office for sixty-two years alone, and though not a shining preacher, was highly esteemed as a sound divine and a useful pastor. His published sermons give evidence of talent and research. In 1830, the Rev. Barnabas Phinney was installed as colleague with Dr. Lee, who was then feeble and infirm, though able to preach occasionally. This venerable man died August 25, 1832, aged eighty-seven. Mr. Phinney was dismissed in 1833.

The Rev. Philo Judson, was installed his successor the same year, but in December 1834, was dismissed to Willimantic.

The present pastor is the Rev. James Ayres, formerly of North Stonington.

*Lisbon* is an irregular township, its boundary lines being mostly rivers. The inhabitants are principally farmers.

Population in 1800, . . . 1158
"        1810, . . . 1128
"        1830, . . . 1161
"        1840, . . . 1052

FOURTH SOCIETY : NEW CONCORD OR BOZRAH.

The Fourth Ecclesiastical society was formed in 1733. The Watermans and Houghs were some of the first settlers in this part of the town. Samuel and John Hough removed from New London, where the family had been residents since 1650. This was first known as West Society; that part before known as *West Farms* being then designated North Society. Permission had been given the planters in 1715, to form a parish by themselves, but being unable to support a minister, they were not regularly organized until eighteen years afterwards, when they took the name of New Concord, and were released from all obligation to support the ministry of the First Society, on condition of maintaining a gospel minister at least six months in the year.

The bounds between the two societies, were to be, *the river, the brook that runs out of it, the Cranberry Pond, the Cranberry Pond brook, the great swamp, the dark swamp, and the miry swamp.* It might be a difficult task, at the present day, to run the line from these data. The Rev. Benjamin Throop, the first regular minister, was settled January 3, 1738, and died 1785.

This Society afterwards became familiarly known as Bozrah, which name it retained upon being incorporated into a town in 1786.

Bozrah is four and a half miles long, and about four in breadth. Like other parts of the nine miles square,

it consists of a succession of hills and vallies, some of
them rocky and barren, others fair and fertile. "The
Woody Vales of Bozrah!" has been a familiar phrase
in the vicinity, from its having been the chorus of a
poem written by one of Bozrah's sentimental daughters. The chorus is perhaps the only relic of the production that survives.

This town has three houses of public worship, Congregational, Baptist and Methodist ; and two cotton
factories with villages adjoining, viz : Bozrahville and
Fitchville, both on Yantic river. The latter was built
by Nehemiah H. Fitch Esq., and his brothers in 1832.
It is five miles from Norwich city. Bozrahville is
eight miles from the city, on and near the dividing line
between Bozrah and Lebanon.

In 1786, the Rev. Jonathan Murdock was ordained
pastor of the Congregational Church in Bozrah. He
died in 1812. The Rev. David Austin was installed
his successor in 1815. This gentleman was a native
of New Haven, born in 1760, and fitted by an accomplished education and foreign travel, to become an
ornament to society, as well as by ardent piety, and a
lively and florid eloquence to be useful in the ministry.
He married Lydia, daughter of Dr. Joshua Lathrop, of
Norwich, and settled as pastor of the church in Elizabethtown, in 1788. The kindness of his heart and the
suavity of his manner endeared him to all who knew
him, while his zeal in the performance of his duties,
and his popular pulpit talents, made him successful in
his office, and extensively known as a preacher. It is
to him that Gov. Livingston alludes in the following
lines of his poem on Philosophic Solitude.

> " Dear A***** too should grace my rural seat,
> Forever welcome to the green retreat ;
> Heaven for the cause of righteousness designed,

His florid genius and capacious mind.
Oft have I seen him 'mid the adoring throng,
Celestial truths devolving from his tongue :
Oft o'er the listening audience seen him stand,
Divinely speak, and graceful wave his hand."

Mr. Austin was naturally eccentric, and had always something erratic and extravagant in his manner of thinking, speaking and acting. Unhappily his mind was led to investigate, too deeply for its strength, the prophecies ; his ardent imagination became inflamed, his benevolent heart dilated to overflowing, and his mental powers became partially deranged. He now appeared as a champion of the Second Advent doctrine, and held that the coming of Christ to commence his personal reign on earth, would be on the fourth Sabbath of May, 1796. On the morning of that day, he was in a state of great agitation, and one or two reports of distant thunder excited him almost to frenzy. But the day passed over as usual ; yet the disappointment did not cure the delusion of Mr. Austin's mind.

He now went round the country announcing the near approach of Christ's coming, and calling upon the Jews to assemble and make preparations to return to their own land. He declared himself to be commissioned as Christ's forerunner, a second John the Baptist, appointed to establish the new millenial church upon earth. His vagaries every day increasing, in 1797, he was removed by the Presbytery from his pastoral relation to the church at Elizabethtown. He then went to New Haven, where he erected several large houses and a wharf, for the use of the Jews, whom he invited to assemble there, and embark for the Holy Land. Having at last, in this and other plans, expended an ample fortune, he was for a while imprisoned for debt, and after being released from con-

25

finement, gradually became calm and sane upon all
points except the prophecies. He had no children,
and his wife had long before taken refuge in her
father's house, in Norwich. Here, too, Mr. Austin
returned after his wanderings, like the dove to the ark,
and after awhile the balance of his mind seemed to be
restored, and he began again to preach with acceptance
in various churches in Connecticut.

In 1815, he accepted a call to settle in Bozrah, and
from that time till his death quietly and regularly
preached the gospel of salvation. But though he performed all the duties of a pastor, and was much esteemed and beloved by his people, he continued still
to reside in Norwich, where he died, in 1831.

For elegance of manners, for brilliancy of conversation, for fervor of worship, for a large heart and a liberal hand, few men could surpass Mr. Austin. The
darkness that obscured his intellect on many points,
and which was never wholly removed, appeared not
to impair in the least those prominent traits, that lay
deep and shone through, to illustrate his character,
and to win for him the love and admiration of all who
came within his sphere.

### LONG SOCIETY.

The fifth ecclesiastical society was formed in that
part of the town which lay east of the rivers Shetucket
and Thames, then, as now, known by the name of
Long Society. The farmers of this side of the river,
in 1698, petitioned to be released from paying minister's rates in Norwich, which was granted, on condition of their paying in Preston. About twenty years
afterwards, permission was given them to form a distinct church, and sixty acres of land set apart for the
first minister who should settle there. The society

was not regularly organized till after 1740; but the Rev. Jabez Wight, who was the first and only minister ever ordained among them, commenced his ministrations some ten years earlier. Mr. Wight was born in 1701, married Ruth Swan, in 1726, and died in 1783. His pastoral charge extended over a period of fifty-two years, but the date of his ordination is not ascertained.

This society afterwards greatly declined. For many years they were not only without a pastor and any administration of the sacred ordinances, but without any regular religious instruction whatever. The meeting-house remained, and at long intervals a preacher's voice was heard in it, but the members of the church were dispersed or dead, and the communion plate had not been used for many years, when the Rev. Mr. Gleason, the Missionary of Mohegan, administered the sacrament, in August, 1837.

Several persons in Norwich city have recently taken great interest in the situation of this society; have established Sabbath and Singing schools there, obtained preachers, and cheerfully given their own services to advance the cause of religion.

Long Society, since 1786, has formed a part of the town of Preston.

# CHAPTER XXXII.

THE sixth ecclesiastical society was organized, at Chelsea, November 29, 1751.

> Capt. Dean, *Moderator.*
> Daniel Kingsbury, *Society Clerk.*
> Prosper Wetmore, *Collector.*
> Eleazer Waterman, } *Committee.*
> Nathaniel Backus, }

Capt. Jabez Dean was very active in promoting this measure, and in procuring ministers to preach to the new congregation. They began with hiring a minister only four months in the year, and taxing themselves 16*d.*, old tenor, on the pound to pay for it. They presented a memorial to the General Assembly to allow them to tax also the land of non-resident proprietors and ship-owners, which was granted. This mode of paying for ecclesiastical services soon became very unpopular, and in 1755 they declared that they would pay their minister by subscriptions and contributions. This also was found by experience to be a very uncertain and perplexing mode, and as soon as they had a regular minister they agreed to raise his salary in the usual way, that is, by society rates. They first secured the services of Mr. Elijah Lathrop, of Windham, and afterwards of Mr. John Curtis, who preached for them three or four years, from four to six months each year; they only hiring a minister a sufficient part of the year to prevent their being taxed towards supporting the ministry in the first society. Mr. Curtis boarded at Mr. Elderkin's tavern, where all the society meetings were then held: public worship was at private houses, in rotation with all those who had a room sufficiently large ; and it is said that at first, people were called together by the tap of the drum.

In 1755, Mr. Cleveland was hired, and paid whatever sum could be raised by weekly contributions. The same year a funeral pall, and bier, and burying ground were obtained. The burying ground was purchased of Mr. Jonathan Bushnell; it was a well-wooded lot, and the wood cut from it paid the whole expense.

In 1759, a vote was passed to call the Rev. Nathaniel Whitaker, of New Jersey, "provided he be regularly dismissed from his present charge." A salary of £100, lawful money, was offered him, with a settlement of £100, to be paid when the general list of the society should amount to £6000, exclusive of those churchmen's estates, who were excused from paying minister's rates. This invitation was accepted, and it is recorded, that in April, 1760, Mr. Whitaker, with his family and goods, arrived from the *Jerseys*, by water; the society paying £12 for the passage and freight.

On the 24th of July following, a church was organized, with the assistance of two neighboring ministers, Messrs. Wight and Throop, consisting of only six members, viz:

| | |
|---|---|
| Nathaniel Whitaker, | Nathaniel Shipman, |
| Nathaniel Backus, | Seth Alden, |
| John Porter, | Isaiah Tiffany. |

This last had been a member of the church in Lebanon. Seth Alden was a few years afterwards tried by a council of ministers, and excommunicated for drink-

25*

ing to excess.  A very strict personal inspection was
exercised by the church, over its members at this period.  At one time a charge was exhibited against one
of the members of the church " for going to see the river
break up on the Sabbath."  The offence, however, was
passed over with only a reprimand.  A young woman, in
a similar case, did not escape so easily.  She had spent
the night at a neighboring house, and returning home
on Sunday morning, lingered by the side of the Shetucket, to see the ice move down with the loosened
current, for which she was fined 5s.

Mr. Whitaker was installed February 25, 1761.  Mr.
Lord preached the sermon.  At this time, six other
persons, previously members of other churches, signed
the covenant, and united with the church, viz:

| | |
|---|---|
| Jonathan Huntington, | Jabez Dean, |
| William Capron, | Eleazar Waterman, |
| Caleb Whitney, | Ebenezer Fitch. |

Difficulties existed in the infant church with respect to the plan of discipline to be adopted; the
major part were in favor of a Presbyterian government, others were for the Congregational form.  The
plan at length drawn up and agreed upon, was thoroughly Presbyterian, and after the model of the
Church of Scotland; but Messrs. Backus and Shipman
expressed their dissent and recorded their protest, especially to one article which gave a *negative power*
to the minister.  A council was thereupon called,
which met the day previous to the installation and recommended that the Presbyterian plan should be laid
aside, and no human form adopted at present, but that
they should take the word of God for their rule and
directory, in discipline and manners, as well as faith,
and not use any platforms of human composition, for

their assistance in understanding this word until God should give them light, in a more explicit manner. Having settled a minister, immediate measures were taken to erect a meeting-house. Public worship had for some time previous been held at the tavern of Mr. Samuel Trapp; which was the house occupied by Benjamin Coit Esq., deceased. In the rear of this house the bell was fixed, being suspended from a scaffolding erected upon a rock.

The first vote of this society respecting a meeting-house was in 1752, when they requested leave of the town to erect one " on the highway that leads from Col. Huntington's Crammer lot to the highway near Asa Peabody's house." At the same time they appointed Benedict Arnold,* Jeremiah Clements, and Gershom Breed, a committee to attend to it. Funds were not forthcoming, and the project was at that time abandoned.

In 1760, Jonathan Huntington, Elijah Lathrop, and Ephraim Bell, were appointed a committee to build a meeting-house. It was with great difficulty that they obtained a convenient spot for a site. The streets and buildings had not then extended up the hill, and land was scarce and valuable. A small piece of ground was at length obtained of Jabez Huntington Esq., and the County Court ordered a stake to be erected on it as the Society's mark. This spot was considered too circumscribed, and the committee gave notice that the adjoining proprietors, Samuel Bliss and Daniel Tracy, *would not sell an inch.* The Court therefore ordered the stake to be removed. A warm controversy ensued, which greatly retarded the building of the church, but in 1764, another lot was purchased of Mr. Isaac Hun-

---

* Father of him who betrayed his country. He emigrated from Rhode Island, and took the freeman's oath in 1739.

tington, for 70s. the square rod, and permission obtained from the Court to set up the stake there.  A memorial was then presented to the General Assembly for
assistance in building, and a sum of money granted
from the treasury of the Colony for this purpose.
This church was erected in 1766, and stood on the spot
which Mansfield's row of brick buildings now occu-
pies.  The front was to the south.  The length thirty-
seven feet, the breadth forty-one.  The interior was
divided into thirty six areas.  A warm dispute arose
whether the pulpit should be placed on the east or
south side, but the party for the south prevailed.

After the outside of the edifice was completed and
the pulpit built, twenty-seven of the thirty-six spaces
for pews were sold for the sum of £300.  Two families were accommodated in each pew.  These being
finished, the bell was taken from its position on the
rock and hung in the steeple.  Joseph Smith was engaged to ring the bell and keep the house in order, for
a salary of twenty shillings per year, and thus the
church was made ready for public service.  Two
rooms were afterwards finished in the basement of the
house, and let out for storage.

It may be interesting at the present day to read a list
of the pew-holders, particularly to see who were associated in the same pew:

No.  1.   The Minister and his family.
     2.   Seth Harding and William Rockwell.
     3.   Sybile Crocker and Jonathan Lester.
     7.   Thomas Trapp, Jr., and Stephen Barker.
     9.   Jabez Dean and Elijah Lothrop.
    10.   John Tracy and Peter Lanman.
    11.   Joseph Trumbull and Jabez Perkins.
    12.   Ephraim Bill and Hugh Ledlie.
    13.   Ebenezer Fillimore, Jr., and Timothy Herrick.
    14.   William Coit and Simeon Carew.

No. 18.   Nathaniel Backus and Nathaniel Backus, Jr.
    19.   Abel Brewster and John Martin.
    21.   David Lamb and Moses Pierce.
    23.   Benajah Leffingwell and Ezra Backus.
    25.   Benjamin Huntington and Nathaniel Shipman.
    26.   Joseph Smith and Isaac Park.
    27.   Stephen Roath and Stephen Roath, Jr.

The omitted numbers were allotted to the space which remained unsold, until Mr. Judson's ordination. At that time, the remaining pews were built and assigned as follows:

No.  4.   Hannah Wight and Joseph Kelley.
    5.   Jacob De Witt and John M'Larran Breed.
    6.   John and Peter Waterman.
    8.   Benjamin and George Dennis.
    15.   Caleb Whitney and Joshua Norman.
    16.   Daniel Kelley and William Capron.
    17.   Prosper Wetmore and Ebenezer Fitch.
    20.   David and Samuel Roath.
    22.   William Reed and Zephaniah Jennings.
    24.   Joseph Wight and Lemuel Boswell.

In the mean time, Mr. Whitaker had become unpopular with a part of his people. In 1765, the dissatisfaction was so great, that a council was convened by mutual consent, to reconcile the two parties, if possible. Charges were exhibited to this council, against Mr. Whitaker, by Ephraim Bill, Prosper Wetmore, Peter Lanman, and the two Backuses, accusing him of neglect of duty as a clergyman. He on his part, accused *them* of violent language and unchristian conduct. The council came to no decision on any of the charges, and the breach was left as wide as before.

The same year the Connecticut Board of Correspondents for Indian affairs, made choice of Mr. Whitaker to go to Europe, in company with Occom, the Mohegan preacher, to solicit charities for the endowment of an Indian school. They offered to supply his pulpit during his absence, but when Mr. Whitaker laid the affair before his church, they refused to give their consent to his going, while he remained their minister. In the society meeting, the vote was a tie. The application was again repeated, and again refused. A council of advice was called, whose recommendation exactly coincided with Mr. Whitaker's inclination, viz. : that he should be allowed to accept the agency, without dissolving his relation to the church. This, the society refused—a strong party being unequivocally bent on effecting his dismission. A second council was called, who proposed that Mr. Whitaker should go to Europe as the Pastor of the church, but that he should relinquish his salary during his absence ; his people to have the privilege of settling another minister before his return, if they chose ; and if such an event took place, he was to be considered as dismissed. If he should return before the settlement of another minister, a council was to be convened, to decide whether he should continue with them, or be dismissed. This conciliatory proposition, which emanated from Dr. Lord of the First Society, was accepted.

Mr. Whitaker was absent about a year and a half. He returned in 1768, and resumed his functions, to the great grief of the dissentient members. A council was convened the next year, that advised him to ask for a dismission, which he did. The society refused by a vote of twenty-eight to nine. The majority of the church declared themselves averse to a separation, as seeing no sufficient reason for it, and earnestly desiring his continuance with them. A second council was called, which despairing of his future usefulness in this distracted state of the society, dissolved the connexion. Mr. Whitaker was a man of fine talents and prepossessing appearance. He had manifested great interest in the prosperity of Mr. Wheelock's Indian school at Lebanon, and in the welfare of the Mohegan Indians, his neighbors. On these accounts he had been selected as a proper person to accompany Rev. Samson Occom, to England, to obtain funds for that school. They carried with them a printed book containing recommendations, and an exposition of the state of Indian Missions in North America. Mr. Whitaker's recommendation from his church is as follows :

" The Church of Christ at Chelsey, in Norwich, in Conn : in New England, to all the churches of Christ, and whomsoever it may concern, send greeting :

Whereas it has pleased God in his Providence, to call our Reverend and worthy Pastor, Mr. Nathaniel Whittaker, from us for a season, to go to Europe, to solicit charities for the Indian Charity School, under the care of the Rev. Mr. Eleazer Wheelock, of Lebanon, and to promote Christian knowledge among the Indians on this continent :

We do unanimously recommend him, the said Mr. Whitaker and his services, to all the churches and people of God, of whatever denomination, and wheresoever he may come, as a faithful minister of Jesus Christ, whose praise is in the gospel through the churches ; earnestly requesting brotherly kindness and charity may be extended towards him as occasion may require ; and that the grand and important cause in which he is engaged, may be forwarded and promoted by all the lovers of truth.

Wishing grace, mercy and truth may be multiplied to you and the whole Israel of God, and desiring an interest in your prayers, we subscribe

    Yours in the faith and fellowship of the gospel,

By order and in behalf }   JONATHAN HUNTINGTON.
   said Church.  }   ISAIAH TIFFANY.
Norwich, Oct 21, 1756.

The delegates were eminently successful in their mission, both in England and Scotland. A large sum

was collected and deposited in the hands of trustees,
part of it for a projected college at Hanover, and part
of it for an Indian school. Some disagreement arose
between Whitaker and his Indian associate before
they left England, and they did not return together, though both reached home in 1768. Occom, in
his confidential correspondence, throws out some hints
with respect to Whitaker, which it is difficult to understand. Perhaps he suspected him of embezzle-
ment. Suspicions of his integrity appear to have been
excited in the minds of many of the noble patrons of
the charity in England. Whitaker was a worldly man,
and his conduct frequently irregular. While he lived
in Chelsea, he entered into trade, and attempted to
monopolize the vending of wine, raisins, &c. in the
Society. At least, this was one of the charges exhibited against him. It is said, that after his dismission,
he went to the South and died in penury.

We next find Mr. Punderson Austin preaching in
Chelsea: his perquisites were—his board at Mr. Gershom Breed's, paid by the society, [10s. per week,]
and what he could obtain from weekly contributions.

Mr. Ephraim Judson, of Woodbury, Conn., was the
next candidate, and after a short experience of his
ministry, a vote was obtained to call him to the pastoral office, *nem con.* He was ordained Oct. 3, 1771.
Sermon by the Rev. Noah Benedict. Mr. Judson was
a man of pleasing aspect, and had a full and flowing
eloquence at command, but he was greatly deficient
in energy and variety. He seldom used notes, and his
sermons were usually in the colloquial style of common
conversation; frequently using such familiar illustra-
tions as would only be necessary for the most illiterate
audience. For instance, in a sermon upon the Brazen
Serpent, fearing his congregation would not under-

stand what he meant, he repeatedly called it the *Brass Snake*. His expressions were sometimes very quaint and whimsical. Preaching at one time on the excuses made by the guests who were invited to the wedding feast, he observed that one had bought five yoke of oxen, and civilly entreated to be excused, but the one who had married a wife, replied absolutely, *he could not come*. Hence learn, said the preacher, that one *woman can pull harder than five yoke of oxen*. Mr. Judson once preached in the first Society, a sermon particularly addressed to young women, which, contrary to his usual custom, was *written out*, and elaborately finished in the style of Hervey's Meditations. To make it more impressive, he introduced a fictitious character of the name of *Clarinda*, expatiated upon her wit and beauty, and the number of her admirers, followed her to the ball-room, and other scenes of gaiety, and then laid her upon a death-bed with all the pathos of a romance.

In 1776, Mr. Judson was appointed chaplain of Gen. Ward's regiment, and with the consent of the society, was on duty with the army for several months. A dwelling house still standing on the burying ground hill, was built for Mr. Judson. An agreement was made, that if he remained with his people more than five years, the house was to become his own property ; if he left them before the expiration of that term, it reverted to the Society. As soon as the five years had elapsed, *i.e.*, in Nov. 1778, he asked for a dismission. The reasons he assigned were these : 1st, want of competent support : 2d, ill health ; 3d, negligence of the people in attending public worship. A council was called, who considering Mr. Judson's inability to study, and the great indifference which prevailed with regard to his ministrations, very few attending on public wor-

26

ship, dissolved his connexion with the church.  Mr.
Judson afterwards deeply regretted his folly in leaving
his people, and in a subsequent visit, made after the
settlement of another pastor, he preached to them, and
at the close of his sermon, asked forgiveness of the
church.  He confessed, with streaming eyes, that he
had done wrong, and many of the congregation were
also melted into tears by his frank confessions, his
penitence and apparent humility.  This, however
might have been done, partly for effect, for Mr. Judson
never preached many years in the same place, and at
length grew rich by repeated settlements—settlements
being then in vogue.

For several succeeding years, public worship seems
to have been at a low ebb in Chelsea.  Sometimes
they had preaching and sometimes not.  At one time,
Mr. David Austin preached to them for 40s. per Sabbath—subsequently, Mr. Zebulon Ely.

During this period also, they engaged the services
of Mr. Nathaniel Niles, a licensed preacher, who occasionally exercised his vocation, although he never
wished a settlement.  He established in Norwich during the war, a wire manufactory, but afterwards removed to New Hampshire, and became a civil magistrate, a farmer, and a judge of some court.  He is now
chiefly known as the author of the " American Hero,"
a sapphic ode, which was circulated and sung in Norwich, in those days of enthusiastic patriotism, and still
lingers in the memories of some old persons who have
never seen it printed.

Mr. Niles left behind him in Norwich the character
of a metaphysical preacher, fond of doctrinal points,
and shrewd in drawing lines of difference.  He was
fearless, however, in denouncing popular sins, and
calling upon men every where to repent.

In 1786, Mr. Walter King labored among them, and was successful in his attempt to revive the decaying interests of religion. The church was re-organized, and the covenant solemnly renewed by Jonathan Huntington, Ebenezer Fitch and twelve sisters of the former church. Seven others made a profession of faith at the same time, and these, with Mr. King, formed a church of twenty-two members, only seven of them males. Mr. King was called to office by a vote of the society, thirty-five against one, and ordained May 24, 1787. Sermon by Rev. Charles Backus. Mr. Judson, the former minister, then of Taunton, was one of the ordaining council. Mr. King's salary was £125 for the first year, and to be increased 40s. annually, until it should amount to £135, this sum to be the stated salary afterwards.

No office seems to have been more irksome than that of collecting the society rates for the payment of the minister. It was difficult to find any respectable person who was willing to serve as collector. In 1788, an agreement was signed by a number of gentlemen, and acceded to by the Society, that they would give in their names at the annual meeting, and one should be drawn from them by lot to execute this office, each engaging to serve whenever his name should be drawn. Another disagreeable office was that of Grand Juryman. In 1746, Benedict Arnold being chosen to this office, refused to serve, whereupon the town imposed a fine on all who for the future should in like manner refuse. This fine was often incurred.

The Rev. Charles Backus, who preached the ordination sermon of Mr. King, was born at Norwich, Nov. 5, 1749, and in early childhood was bereft of both of his parents, and with a patrimony insufficient for his education, was left to the care and generosity of his friends.

They liberally supplied the deficiency, and educated him at Yale College, where he graduated in 1769. He studied Theology with Dr. Hart in Preston, was ordained at Somers in 1774, and became eminent as an instructor in Theology, although he declined the professorship of Divinity, which was tendered to him by Dartmouth and Yale Colleges. He prepared between forty and fifty young men for the sacred desk, all of whom regarded their instructor with affection, admiration and reverence. He also sustained a high rank as a preacher. Dr. Dwight said of him—"I have not known a wiser man. He was excessive in nothing; firm in everything; pre-eminently upright and benevolent; always taking the direction of sound common sense; superior to the love of innovation, and to the rejection of it, when plainly recommended by truth and utility." He died in 1798. He had but one child, a promising youth, who left the world before either of his parents, in the 17th year of his age. His nephew, Dr. Azel Backus, who was also a native of Norwich, was the first president of Hamilton College, near Utica, N. Y.

On the division of the town, only two Congregational societies were left in Norwich, and Chelsea, from that period has taken rank as the *Second*.

# CHAPTER XXXIII.

THE war had a demoralizing effect on all parts of the country. Neither the institutions of religion nor education flourished ; but with the blessings of peace a very general improvement took place. Education began to be valued. The school founded by Dr. Lathrop overflowed with pupils. Here you might hear lessons from Dilworth's Spelling Book, and Curtis' Grammer—compositions read on the evils of land speculation, a hobby of that era as well as of some later ones, or the thirty-two points of the compass rehearsed by some tyro in navigation. Mr. William Baldwin was a noted teacher of this school. Other schools of a high character were soon opened in the town. A private establishment under the direction of Mr. Goodrich, called in boarders from abroad. The exhibitions of this school were deemed splendid, and great was the applause when Miss Mary Huntington came upon the stage, dressed in green silk brocade, a crown glittering with jewels encircling her brows, and reading Plato, to personate Lady Jane Grey, while young Putnam, the son of the old general, advanced with nodding plumes to express his tender anxieties for her, in the person of Lord Guilford Dudley.

Trumbull's book store and printing office continued to be the principal establishment of the kind in town. The assortment of books did not extend much beyond

26*

Bibles and school books; yet here you might find
Perry's Dictionary, Baron Steuben's Military Discipline, The Principles of Politeness, and the Economy
of Human Life. Also, "Gravity and Motion," a poem
for 4d., and " Cleveland's Hymns," for 9d. These
were indigenous productions, by one of the town's
*own.*

The sports of men and boys were of a rougher character than at present. Shooting at marks, horse-racing,
wrestling, and ball-playing were favorite amusements.
In the winter, sleighing parties innumerable kept the
streets alive with bells, and the taverns gay with ban-
queting. Strolling players were sometimes allowed to
perform in town. An advertisement of 1794, gives notice of the arrival " at Mr. Teel's Assembly Room," of
a party of Italian rope-dancers and tumbleis; and the
public were invited to call and see Clumsy the Clown
dance a hornpipe blindfold over fifteen eggs. Elections, training-days, and thanksgivings, were the customary holidays; and at these times a great variety of
athletic exercises gave vent to the restless spirits of an
active and energetic race.

The most distinguished of all festivals in New England has ever been Thanksgiving. It is always a day
of hilarity, though the first part of it is devoted to a
sermon. Family re-unions, bountiful dinners, weddings,
trials of skill in shooting, and evening bonfires, are
expected to grace the festival. The bonfires, indeed,
are only the work of boys, but the high hills in Norwich are a fine vantage ground, from which these tall
and vivid volumes of flame send forth a flood of light
over the woods and vallies, houses and streams below,
producing a truly picturesque effect.

Accidents have sometimes occurred on these festive
occasions. On the evening of thanksgiving day, 1792,

a large beacon fire had been erected as usual on Wa-weekus hill, at the Landing. A swivel was also dis-charged several times, which unfortunately burst, and one of the pieces, weighing about seven pounds, killed a young man by the name of Cook. It is said that the piece passed through his body, to the distance of thirty or forty yards, carrying with it his heart.

A considerable lustre was thrown on the town-plot, by its being the residence of the Hon. Samuel Hunt-ington, Governor of the State. He was not a native of Norwich, but for the last twenty-six years of his life made it his home. After the war, he built a new house, and lived in quiet dignity. A lively and happy circle of young people used frequently to assemble in this house, as visiters to the Governor's adopted chil-dren, or attracted by the beautiful Betsey Devotion, Mrs. Huntington's niece, and the belle of Windham, who spent much of her time here. After the social chat and merry game of the parlor had taken their turn, they would frequently repair to the kitchen, and dance away till the oak floor shone under their feet, and the pewter quivered upon the dressers. These pastimes, however, had little in them of the nature of a ball; there were no expensive dresses, no collations, no late hours. They seldom lasted beyond nine o'clock. According to the good old custom of Norwich, the ringing of the bell at that hour, broke up all meet-ings, dispersed all parties, put an end to all discus-sions, and sent all visiters quietly to their homes and their beds.

Mrs. Huntington was an affable but very plain lady. It is still remembered, that in a white short gown and stuff petticoat, and clean muslin apron, with a nicely starched cap on her head, she would take her knitting and go out by two o'clock in the afternoon, to take tea

unceremoniously with some respectable neighbor, the
butcher's or blacksmith's wife, perhaps.    But this was
in earlier days, before Mr. Huntington was President
of Congress, or Governor of Connecticut.

Samuel Huntington was born in 1732, and descended
in a direct line from Simon Huntington, one of the thirty-
five proprietors of Norwich.   Joseph, one of the sons of
Simon, removed to Windham, in 1687.   Nathaniel,
son of Joseph, was the father of Samuel, and by trade
a clothier.   He gave a liberal education to three of his
sons, but Samuel he designed for a mechanic.   He
accordingly learned the trade of a cooper, and after
serving out his time as an apprentice, continued to
labor for a short time as a journeyman.   This is only
one instance out of many in the annals of our country,
of persons who have risen to eminence from the hum-
blest stations.   Roger Wolcott, a distinguished Chief
Justice of Connecticut, rose from following the plow;
Roger Sherman was a shoe-maker.

Mr. Huntington's mind was naturally acute and in-
vestigating, and his thirst for mental improvement so
great as to surmount all obstacles.   From observation,
from men, and from books, he was always collecting
information, and he soon abandoned manual labor for
study.   He was self-educated—went to no college,
attended no distinguished school, sat at the feet of no
great master, but yet acquired a competent knowledge
of law, and was readily admitted to the bar.   He settled in Norwich, in 1760, and soon became useful and
eminent in his profession.   He frequently represented
the town in the colonial assembly, was active in many
ways as a citizen, agent for the town in several cases,
and forward in promoting public improvements.   He
was appointed King's Attorney, and afterward Assistant Judge of the Superior Court.   In 1775, he was
elected a delegate to the Continental Congress, and

served as President of that honorable body, during the
sessions of 1779 and 1780. While in Congress his seat
on the bench was kept vacant for him, and he resumed
it in 1781. He held various other important offices,
such as Chief Justice of the State, and Lieutenant Governor, and in 1786 was elected Governor, and annually re-elected by the freemen, with singular unanimity, until his death, which took place at Norwich,
January 5, 1796.

Mr. Huntington was of the middle size, dignified in
his manners, even to formality; reserved in popular
intercourse, but in the domestic circle pleasing and
communicative; his complexion swarthy, his eye vivid
and penetrating. One who was long an inmate of his
family said: "I never heard a frivolous observation
from him; his conversation ever turned to something
of a practical nature; he was moderate and circum-
spect in all his movements, and delivered his sentiments in few but weighty words."

His wife was the daughter of Rev. Ebenezer Devotion, of Windham, a charitable and pious lady, whose
memory is still honored in the neighborhood where she
dwelt. She died before her husband, in 1794. They
had no children of their own, but adopted and educated two children of his brother, the Rev. Joseph
Huntington, of Coventry, the author of " *Calvinism
Improved.*" These were Samuel and Fanny Huntington, who lived with their revered relatives as children
with parents, affectionately and happily. They were
present to soothe their last hours, to close their dying
eyes, and to place their remains side by side in the
tomb. They inherited from them, also, a very handsome property.

The daughter married the Rev. E. D. Griffin, President of Williamstown College: the son removed to

Ohio, in 1801 was chosen Judge of the Supreme Court, and afterwards Governor of the State for one term of office. He died at Painesville, Ohio, in 1817, aged forty-nine.

Gov. Huntington preserved to the last those habits of simplicity with which he began life. In the published journal of the Marquis de Chastellux, he several times mentions Mr. Huntington with marked respect. At one time, in Philadelphia, he went to visit him with the Chevalier de la Luzerne, the French ambassador, and observes, "We found him in his cabinet, lighted by a single candle. This simplicity reminded me of Fabricius and the Philopemens." At another time he dined with him, in company with several other French gentlemen of distinction, and adds : " Mrs. Huntington, a good-looking, lusty woman, but not young, did the honors of the table, that is to say, helped every body, without saying a word." This silence must surely be attributed to ignorance of the language of the gay cavaliers, and not to any deficiency of good manners or conversational power.

Mr. Huntington was always a constant attendant on public worship, and for many years a professor of religion. In conference meetings he usually took a part, and on the Sabbath, if no minister chanced to be present, he occasionally led the services, and his prayers and exhortations were solemn and acceptable. During his last sickness, he was supported and animated by an unwavering faith in Christ, and a joyful hope of eternal life.

This sketch cannot be better concluded, than with the earnest wish breathed by a contemporary panegyrist,—" May Connecticut never want a man of equal worth to preside in her councils, guard her interests, and diffuse prosperity through her towns."

# CHAPTER XXXIV.

THE spirit of enterprize revived in Norwich immediately after the Revolutionary war, and for twelve years,
reckoning from 1784, commerce flourished, and was
rich in its returns. The West India trade, especially,
offered a lucrative source of business. Very little flour
was then brought into Norwich; it was an export
rather than an import; more being manufactured in
the place than was necessary for home consumption.
Considerable wheat was raised in the state, even in the
eastern part, where it is now a very uncertain crop,
and less profitable than most others. The following
table of exports and imports for a period of fifteen
months, will exhibit in a clear light the industry and
enterprise which characterized this period. It is taken
from a newspaper of the day.

Exports and Imports of Norwich, from January 1, 1788,
to March 4, 1789, taken from the report of the Naval Officer :

## EXPORTS.

|  |  |  | £ | s. | d. | £ | s. | d. |
|---|---|---|---|---|---|---|---|---|
| 549 | horses, | value, | 12 |  |  | 6588 |  |  |
| 205 | mules, | " | 15 |  |  | 3075 |  |  |
| 205 | horned cattle, | " | 7 |  |  | 1435 |  |  |
| 321 | sheep, | " |  | 10 |  | 160 | 10 |  |
| 566 | hogs, | " |  | 15 |  | 424 | 10 |  |
| 1,903 | bbls. beef, | " |  | 40 |  | 3806 |  |  |
| 1,774 | " pork, | " |  | 60 |  | 5322 |  |  |
| 25,000 | lbs. butter, | " |  |  | 6 | 625 |  |  |

|  | | | £ | s. | d. | £ | s. | d. |
|---|---|---|---|---|---|---|---|---|
| 92,120 | " | cheese, " | | | 4 | 1535 | 6 | 8 |
| 6,600 | " | ham, " | | | 5 | 137 | 10 | |
| 16,000 | bu. | grain, " | | 2 | 6 | 2000 | | |
| 175 | M. | hoops, " | | | 70 | 612 | 10 | |
| 160 | M. | staves, " | | | 80 | 640 | | |
| 14,600 | lbs. | hayseed, " | | | 6 | 365 | | |
| 576 | bbls. | potash, " | | 5 | | 2880 | | |
| 25,000 | yds. | homemade cloth, | | 2 | | 2500 | | |
| 632 | hhds. | flax seed, | | 40 | | 1264 | | |
| 276 | tons | pressed hay, | | 60 | | 828 | | |
| 4 | bbls. | gingerbread, | 5 | | | 20 | | |

Total,                   £34,218   6   8

IMPORTS.

| | | £ | s. | d. |
|---|---|---|---|---|
| European goods, value | | 3909 | | |
| 1,500 hides, " 12s. | | 900 | | |
| 7,675 bu. salt, 1s. 8d. | | 639 | 11 | 8 |
| 112,625 galls. molasses, 1s. 4d. | | 7540 | | |
| 18,300 " rum, 2s. 6d. | | 2287 | 10 | |
| 1,271 lbs. bohea tea, 2s. | | 127 | 2 | |
| 20,700 " coffee, 1s. | | 1045 | | |
| 417,200 " sugar, | | 8344 | | |

Total,        £24,793   3   8

Shipping belonging to the port at this time.

| | | | | | | |
|---|---|---|---|---|---|---|
| Twenty sloops, | . | . | . | 940 | tons. |
| Five schooners, | . | . | . | 325 | " |
| Five brigs, | . | . | . | 545 | " |
| One ship, | . | . | . | 200 | " |

Total,   .   .   .   .   2010   "

In 1793, British privateers, began to seize American vessels in the West Indies, and for several years the commerce of New England suffered by these depredations. Vessels were captured, carried into British ports, and by the decrees of Admiralty courts, libelled

and condemned.  The merchants of Norwich shared
in these perplexities; many of their vessels were
seized, and an uncertainty cast over their commercial
projects.  Public meetings were convened to see what
could be done, and a memorial to Congress drafted
April 18, 1794.  A general spirit of arming in defense
of the country was prevalent, and many spirited resolutions passed in the larger towns.  In September of
that year, Brigadier General Joseph Williams reviewed in Norwich, the third regiment of cavalry, under
the command of Col. Elisha Egerton.  An approaching war with Great Britain was then seriously apprehended.

The storm blew over, and Norwich recovering from
this temporary shock, resumed her commercial importance.  Four or five vessels were sometimes to be seen
on the stocks at once.  Story's ship yard in West
Chelsea, launched ships of 200 and 300 tons burthen.

The increase of shipping for a few years after this
period, was very rapid.  In 1795, a list of vessels and
tonnage belonging to the place, was made out in order
to favor a petition forwarded to Government for the
establishment of a Post-office in Chelsea.  The following is a copy of this list taken from a draft in the hand
writing of Joseph Howland Esq., than whom no man
was better acquainted with the maratime affairs of the
place.

" List of Shipping belonging to the port of Norwich,
October 12, 1795.

|  | | | |  | | | |
|---|---|---|---|---|---|---|---|
| Ship | Mercury, | 280 | tons. | Brig | Union, | 130 | tons. |
| " | Columbus, | 200 | " | " | Endeavor, | 120 | " |
| " | Modesty, | 240 | " | " | Friendship, | 120 | " |
| " | Young Eagle, | 200 | " | " | Betsey, | 130 | " |
| " | George, | 364 | " | " | Charlestown, | 60 | " |
| " | Portland | 220 | " | " | Polly, | 180 | " |
| " | Charlotte, | 90 | " | " | Sally | 180 | " |

27

| | | | | | |
|---|---|---|---|---|---|
| Brig ½ Sally, | 60 | tons. | Sloop William, | 70 | tons. |
| " Betsey, | 90 | " | " Prosperity, | 90 | " |
| Schooner Polly, | 90 | " | " Polly, | 80 | " |
| " Allen, | 85 | " | " Negotiater, | 90 | " |
| " Elizabeth, | 75 | " | " Friendship, | 90 | " |
| " Chloe, | 75 | " | " Bud, | 35 | " |
| " Washington, | 65 | " | " ⅔ Betsey, | 45 | " |
| Schr. Shetucket, | 70 | " | " Mary, | 45 | " |
| Robinson Crusoe, | 120 | " | " Hercules, | 70 | " |
| Schooner Beaver, | 60 | " | " Juno, | 55 | " |
| " Jenny, | 70 | " | " Hunter, | 45 | " |
| Sloop Farmer, | 85 | " | " Patty, . | 35 | " |
| " Crisis, | 72 | " | " Nancy, | 70 | " |
| " Honor, | 65 | " | " —— | 65 | " |

Total seven ships, nine brigs, nine schooners, seventeen
sloops=forty-two. Total 4312 tons, of which only 210
tons is owned in the old Parish, and 4102 is owned in the
port or what is called Chelsea. The above does not include
a number of river packets, or four New York packets."

With the progress of time, the commerce of the
port has greatly declined; the articles exported are
now needed for home consumption; the maratime
interest is merged in the manufacturing, and what
shipping remains is employed in the coasting trade.

Among the enterprising citizens of this period, the
following ranked high. Dr. Elihu Marvin, Col. Zabdiel Rogers, Gen. Williams, Thomas Mumford, Joseph Howland and Levi Huntington. Mr. Mumford,
in his equipage, domestic establishment and table,
exhibited a lavish style of expenditure. He built a
new house on a large scale, and had one of the finest
gardens in the State, his head gardener having been
procured from Holland. The Howlands, father and
son, were extensively engaged in mercantile pursuits.
They afterwards removed to New York. Gen. Marvin
fell a victim to the yellow fever in 1798. This fatal
disease raged at that time with extreme violence in
New London, but Marvin, himself a skillful physician,

was the only victim to it in Norwich. Col. Rogers died in 1807, aged 72.

John M. Breed, Elisha Hyde, Roger Griswold, and Asa Spalding Esqs., were active as lawyers and public men. Griswold was conspicuous on political occasions. Breed was soon called to fulfill the duties of Mayor of the new city. Hyde was deeply interested in the land purchases on the Delaware and Susquehannah. Spalding was industriously engaged in amassing a large fortune. Yet it was then no easy matter to grow rich in the practice of the law. The price for managing a case before the common pleas, varied only from six to thirty shillings, and before the Superior Court from six to fifty-four shillings.

The work of building and repairing bridges, is one that has fallen heavily upon the inhabitants of Norwich. The period of the erection of several has been already noted. To Whiting's bridge over the Shetucket, succeeded one built by Nathaniel Giddings in 1757, which stood a few rods south of Samuel Roath's dwelling house. The land between this house and the bridge was granted to Mr. Stephen Roath, to improve for a corn-mill. The grant was made in 1761, and it was to last seventy years.

Gidding's bridge was soon condemned. In 1780, another was built on the same spot, under the joint direction of Norwich and Preston; £450, the avails of a lottery, was expended upon it. It was called the Geometry bridge, and was thoroughly repaired in 1792. The river is here 300 feet wide.

In 1817, Mr. Lathrop built the fourth bridge upon this spot, under the direction of the Norwich and Preston Bridge Company, which was incorporated in 1816. The expense was $10,000.

In 1767, the first bridge was built over the cove, where the wharf bridge now stands. The contractor was Mr. Gershom Breed. Great objections were made to the erection of this bridge, on the ground that it could not be made useful, from the high and precipitous hill on each side, particularly on the east. From Hyde's corner to the edge of the river, the declivity was then very abrupt, though the descent is now gradual. This is another instance, in which the work of levelling and filling up, has greatly altered the natural features of the scenery. Four years after the building of this bridge, the General Court granted a lottery, to raise money to refund to the undertakers the sum they had expended upon it, [viz: £60] to repair it, and make it wider. This bridge led to numerous meetings, plans and resolutions, in order to make it convenient and passable for teams, secure it from floods, have a good highway leading to it, make an addition on the south side, make two water-courses through it, appoint an overseer to receive wharfage, &c. For all these purposes, a second lottery to raise £300, was granted to the town in 1773.

The bridge at Lathrop's farm having been repeatedly carried away by the spring floods, in 1792, Norwich and Lisbon jointly erected a more substantial structure at this place, which was paid for by a tax. The spot is just above the junction of the Quinebaug, where the river is 212 feet wide.

In the year 1790, Middle or Main-street was opened in Chelsea, at an expense of £100, part of which was paid by the town, and part by individual subscription. This was a great improvement to Chelsea, though the plan was at first vehemently opposed by some of the owners of the ground. One individual erected a building directly across the western extremity, so as to close up the throat of the street, hoping thereby to put an end to the project.

About the same time, the highways of the town plot were also very much improved. Dr. Joshua Lathrop very generously gave $300 to be laid out on the old town street, "between the brook at the corner of the meeting-house plain, and the house of the widow Reynolds." William Hubbard Esq., was likewise a generous benefactor in this line. The road through " the Grove," from the Court-house to Strong's corner, was opened chiefly through his exertions. That very handsome street, the East Avenue to Chelsea, was also laid out by Capt. Hubbard, or rather straitened from the old road which was of a crescent form, the ends being at the store of Thomas Fanning Esq., and the house of Rev. Walter King. The same gentleman was likewise active in improving the road to New London, persuading some to give money, some labor, and some influence, until the object was accomplished. A company was incorporated in 1792 to make this road a turnpike, and erect a toll gate. This was the first turnpike road in the State. In 1806, it was extended to the landing, by a new road that began at the wharf bridge, and fell into the old road, south of Trading Cove Bridge. In 1812, another new piece of road was annexed to it, which was laid out in a direct line from the Court House, to the old Mohegan road.

The Norwich and Providence post road was made a turnpike in 1794.

The Norwich and Woodstock, extending from Norwich to Massachusetts line, in 1801.

The Norwich and Salem, leading to Essex on the Connecticut river, in 1827.

The Shetucket Turnpike Company to maintain a road through Preston, Griswold, Voluntown, and Sterling, to the east boundary, was incorporated in 1829.

About 1790 freemasonry began to be popular in Norwich. In 1794, Somerset Lodge was constituted with great pomp. The services were at the meeting-house in the town plot. Bishop Seabury preached a sermon in the morning, from 2 Corinthians v. 1.—" A building of God, a house not made with hands, eternal in the heavens." A grand procession was then formed, which passed through the town, accompanied by a band of music; dinner was served in a rural bower erected upon the plain, and in the afternoon the Lodge again proceeded to the meeting-house, and listened to another sermon, from the Rev. Elkanan Winchester, from Psalms cxxxiii. 1. " Behold how good and how pleasant it is for brethren to dwell together in unity."

A digression may here be allowed respecting Mr. Winchester and Universalism. The doctrine of Universal salvation, connected with a belief in the Trinity, and a purification from sin by a limited degree of punishment in another state, ending in actual pardon, and a final restoration to the favor of God, had at one period a considerable number of advocates in Norwich, though no regular society, holding to such principles, was ever formed. Allusion has been already made to the Separate meetings held in the town plot society. These, under Mr. Gamaliel Reynolds, gradually took the character of Universalism. In 1772, Mr. John Murray, the English Universalist, or " Great Promulgator," as he styled himself, came to Norwich, being invited thither by Mr. Samuel Post, the near neighbor and friend of Mr. Reynolds. He preached a number of times to large audiences, and gained many admirers. From this period his visits to the place were frequent.

The church in the town plot being in the charge of a committee of the society, who were not members of the church, he was allowed the free use of it. He also preached in the Episcopal church, under the charge of the Rev. Mr. Tyler, and held a public discussion with the Rev. Nathaniel Niles, in the Congregational church at Chelsea.

Mr. Murray was a man of wit and humor; fluent in speaking, with the manners of a gentleman. His social powers were highly esteemed in Norwich, and though he built up no society, he left an abundance of seed sown, the produce of which might be traced through the whole of that generation.

At a later period, Mr. Winchester, who was born in the vicinity of Norwich, often visited the place, and had many warm personal friends, particularly in the First Society. The Society Committee freely gave him the use of the meeting-house to preach in, and the same courtesy was extended towards him by the Rev. Mr. Tyler. The persuasive eloquence of Mr. Winchester operated less, perhaps, in his favor, than his unblemished life, and the affectionate simplicity of his manners. His knowledge of the scriptures was so minute, his memory so retentive and amenable to his will, that his friend, the elder Mr. Shipman, whose house was his home, when in Norwich, was accustomed to say that if the Bible were to be struck out of existience, Mr. Winchester could replace it from memory.

During the years 1794 and 1795, "Winchester's Lectures on the Prophecies," were published in Norwich. The work was issued in parts; the first two lectures were published by John Trumbull; the remainder by Thomas Hubbard. Mr. Winchester died at Hartford, in 1797.

# CHAPTER XXXV.

NOVEMBER 26, 1793, fifteen buildings were destroyed by fire in Chelsea. This was the largest fire ever known in Norwich. It raged from six to ten o'clock P. M., wind fresh from the N. W. It broke out in a store belonging to Messrs. Hubbard & Greene, of Boston, and was supposed to have been communicated through a fissure in the chimney, to some paper rags piled against it. The meeting-house, the dwelling-houses of Lynde M'Curdy, Levi Huntington, and Benadam Denison, stores occupied by Capt. William Coit, Coit & Lathrop, and Levi Huntington, were destroyed. Two persons were badly wounded. The loss was computed at £8000.

Mr. King's congregation being thus deprived of a house for public worship, assembled for three succeeding months in the Episcopal church, which, with true Christian hospitality, was tendered to them by the Trustees. A room was then fitted up for a temporary place of worship, and immediate measures taken to build another meeting-house. Mr. Joseph Howland and Mr. Thomas Fanning, owners of two lots of land on the hill, opposite the dwellings of the Rev. John Tyler and Dr. Lemuel Bushnell, offered these lots, together with £17, 10s., lawful money, in exchange for the lot on which the old meeting-house stood. This location being approved by the County Court as a suitable site for a meeting-house, the offer was accepted by the society. A lottery was granted by the General Assembly, to raise £800, and this, together with liberal donations from Thomas Shaw Esq. and Colonel Joseph Williams, enabled the Committee to commence building immediately. The dimensions of the new church were forty-two feet by sixty-two. It was completed so as to make the first sale of pews January 1, 1796. Precautions were taken to secure the building against fire, and among other regulations, the sexton was allowed to demand a quarter of a dollar for every foot stove left in the house after the meetings were ended. Mr. Lynde M'Curdy gratuitously ornamented the meeting-house lot with trees.

The sale of the pews for the first ten years produced from four to five hundred dollars annually,—for the next six years, reaching to 1812, on an average, about $650. Mr. King's stated salary was $450 ; but there was generally an annual gratuity added to this, of $100 or $150.

In the year 1810, very serious and unhappy difficulties arose in this church, which in the course of a few months greatly alienated the affections of the minister and his people from each other. The next year the Pastor, Church and Society, all united in calling a council, which met July 3, and consisted of the following persons :—

Rev. Joel Benedict, D. D., Plainfield.
" Elijah Parsons and Dea. Ephraim Gates, E. Haddam.
" Amos Bassett and Dea. Sylvester Gilbert, Hebron.
" Azel Backus, D. D. and David Bellamy, Bethlem.
" Calvin Chapin, Wethersfield.
" Daniel Dow and E. Crosby, Thomson.
" Dan Huntington and Dea. Chauncey Whittlesey, Middletown.

Rev. Lyman Beeeher and Hon. Benj. Tallmadge, Litchfield.
"   Noah Porter and Hon. John Treadwell, Farmington.

This council sat three days, the third, fourth, and
fifth of July, and voted to dissolve the connection
between Mr. King and the people of his charge.

Mr. King was subsequently settled in Williamstown,
Mass., and after a few years of labor there, died suddenly in his pulpit, while engaged in the exercises of
the Sabbath.

The Rev. Asahel Hooker was installed Jan. 16,
1812.   He died the next year, April 19, 1813, aged 49
years.   This excellent man was descended from the
Rev. Thomas Hooker, the first minister of Hartford,
and one of the most famous of our New England wor-
thies.   His first settlement was at Goshen, from whence
he was dismissed on account of ill health.   He was
distinguished as a theological teacher, and his death
was greatly lamented.

The Rev. Alfred Mitchell was ordained as the successor of Mr. Hooker, Oct. 27, 1814.   He was a son
of the Hon. Stephen Mix Mitchell, of Wethersfield—
graduated at Yale, and studied theology at Andover.
He was a man of retiring manners, but a faithful and
zealous preacher, and exceedingly beloved by his
church and congregation.   He died at the age of forty-
one, Dec. 19, 1831, uttering in submissive faith, as he
departed, "The will of the Lord be done."

These two last ministers lie interred in the burying
ground at Chelsea.   From the graves where they rest,
the eye can survey the scene of their labors, and almost
count the homes of that attached people, who listened
with such deep attention to their instructions, and who
followed them mourning to their tombs.

The Rev. James T. Dickinson, of Montreal, was

ordained April 4, 1832. Sermon by Dr. Taylor, of New Haven. July 30, 1834, Mr. Dickinson made a communication to the church, stating that he considered it to be his duty to become a foreign missionary, and requesting them to concur with him in calling a council to dissolve his connexion with them. The church, painful as it was for them to part with a young and beloved minister, duly appreciated his motives, and cordially acquiesced in his wishes. A council was called in August, who unanimously concurred in recommending the dismission of Mr. Dickinson. They expressed the highest confidence in him as a minister of the gospel, and affectionately recommended him to the fellowship of his christian brethren, wherever his lot might be cast. Mr. Dickinson received the appointment of missionary to China, from the American Board, and after spending a few months in the study of medicine, sailed for Singapore in the barque Rosabella, Aug. 20, 1835.

Rev. Alvan Bond, the present pastor, was installed as his successor, May 6, 1835. Sermon by Dr. Hawes, of Hartford.

The salaries of Mr. Hooker and Mr. Mitchell were $700 per annum. At the ordination of Mr. Dickinson, it was raised to $1000, and has since remained at that sum.

In 1829, the meeting-house was enlarged, and the square pews made into slips, at an expense of $2250. An organ was also furnished by subscription. After this alteration, the sale of the pews produced annually from $1000 to $1800. In 1832, the debt of the society, amounting to nearly $3000, was paid by subscription.

In the spring of 1844, the meeting-house was so much damaged by fire, supposed to have been kindled by an incendiary, that the society determined to build a new structure, instead of repairing the old. It is now partly completed; the material used is dark blue granite from a quarry in the vicinity; the style of architecture, Roman; estimated expense, $14,000.

A third Congregational Society was organized at the Falls in 1827, and a small brick church erected for a house of worship. Rev. Benson C. Baldwin ordained pastor, Jan. 31, 1828. This connexion was soon dissolved. Rev. Charles Hyde installed in 1830. A new church, for the use of this society, was afterwards erected on the Little Plain. Mr. Hyde continued in the pastoral charge about three years. His successors were Rev. J. W. Newton, ordained in 1834, and Rev. Thomas J. Fessenden. This society was always small and has since been merged in neighboring churches.

A Fourth Congregational church, which ought now to rank as third, was organized in the village of Greeneville, Jan. 1, 1833, with twenty members. A meeting-house was built the same year. Rev. John Storrs installed March 12, 1834. Dismissed April 7, 1835. Rev. Stephen Crosby elected pastor by an unanimous vote, in 1837, but never installed, on account of the stagnation of business at that period, which gave a temporary check to the prosperity of the place. He continued to officiate as pastor, till his death, in June, 1838. Rev. Alphonso L. Whitman, the present pastor was installed Dec. 4, 1838.

A Fifth Congregational church, consisting principally of a colony from the second, was gathered in Chelsea, June 1, 1842. Rev. Mr. Child was installed pastor Aug. 31, the same year. The society are now engaged in erecting an edifice for public worship, of Chatham free stone, in the gothic style, to have a tower in the corner 135 feet high. Estimated expense, $13,000.

BAPTISTS.

The earliest members of this denomination in Nor-wich, appear to have come from Groton, where the first congregation of Baptists in Connecticut was gathered. At least they imbibed their sentiments in that place. The first meetings were held about the year 1770, but the denomination increased very slowly, and though a small church was soon organized, they had no regular minister till 1800. On Christmas day of that year, Elder John Sterry was ordained pastor, and Mr. Dewey Bromley, deacon. The ceremonies were performed in the Congregational church at Chelsea. The first meeting-house was built in 1803, in West Chelsea.

Elder Sterry continued their pastor till his death in 1823. His successor was Elder William Palmer; and to him succeeded Rev. S. S. Mallery, who was installed July 9, 1834. Mr. Mallery remained with them but a few years, and since his dismission they have had the successive ministrations of Rev. Josiah Graves, Rev. Russell Jennings, and Rev. M. G. Clarke. The society is now small, and is a second time under the charge of Rev. William Palmer. The present meeting-house occupied by this society was erected in 1830.

A Second Baptist church was gathered in Chelsea in 1840, and Rev. M. G. Clarke installed their pastor. A meeting-house was built the next year. This church now consists of about four hundred members.

Norwich has given birth to two of the most eminent men of the Baptist church, in America:—Rev. Isaac Backus, of Middleborough, Mass., and Rev. Thomas Baldwin D. D. of Boston. These were both descended from the first stock of Norwich proprietors. Dr. Baldwin was born at Norwich in 1753. The venerable Dr. Lord, of the town plot, was his grand uncle. He remov-

28

ed in early life to New Hampshire, and there joined
the Baptist connexion.　At the age of thirty, he was
ordained an evangelist, and was for many years a faithful and laborious itinerant preacher.　He was afterwards invited to Boston, where he settled, and by indefatigable study and exertion, attained a high rank as a
preacher, and confessedly stood at the head of the
Baptist denomination in New England.

He died in 1825, aged seventy-one years.

The Rev. Isaac Backus, a distinguished Baptist clergyman, of Middleborough, Mass., was the son of deacon Joseph Backus, of Norwich, and born in 1724.
His mother was a strenuous separatist.　He was himself educated for a Congregational minister, but went
over to the Baptist communion, with the greater part of
his church, in 1750, and by his influence and writings
contributed greatly to the establishment and prosperity
of the Baptist cause in America.　He died in 1806,
aged eighty-two, having been a preacher nearly sixty
years.

### METHODISTS.

A grave-stone in the Chelsea burial ground is erected
to the memory of Mrs. Thankful Pierce, relict of Capt.
Moses Pierce, " the first member of the Methodist Episcopal church in Norwich, who like Lydia, first heard
the preachers and then received them into her house."
This lady, while on a visit to some relations in Tol-
land in the year 1796, met with the Rev. Jesse Lee,
a noted preacher in the Wesleyan connection, and
became deeply interested in his preaching ; and shortly
afterwards, on his way to Boston, Mr. Lee stopped at
Norwich, and preached the first Methodist sermon
there, in her house.　Other preachers followed, and
classes were soon formed both at Chelsea and Bean

Hill. At the latter place, Capt. James Hyde and Mr. William Lamb were the most noted among the early converts. In Chelsea, the society enjoyed for a while the fostering care of Mr. Beatty, a resident of the place, at whose house there was always preaching once a fortnight. But in 1804, Mr. Beatty, with several of his friends and their families, removing to Sandusky, the society seemed to be threatened with utter extinction, the only members of note that remained being two aged women—Mrs. Pierce and Mrs. Davison. They were however kept together, and their numbers enlarged, principally through the exertions of a young man, who became an exhorter, class leader, and finally a local preacher in their connection. This was Rev. D. N. Bentley, who for thirty years may be regarded as the main pillar of the Methodist church in Chelsea. In 1811, a new class was formed, and a chapel built on the wharf bridge, which was swept off and destroyed by a freshet of the river, in the spring of 1823. The next church was erected at the Falls village, and thither the members from the Landing resorted for public worship, forming but one church and society, till 1835. A large and convenient edifice was then erected in East Chelsea, and a separation took place. Previous to this, the society on Bean Hill had erected a church, and a fourth has since been built at Greeneville. These are all flourishing, though not large societies.

## UNIVERSALISTS.

The first organization of this denomination as a society was in 1820. A meeting-house was erected in 1822, in which services were held, though with frequent interruptions, for a few years. The society then very much declined. In 1838, a church was regularly organized, and a new edifice for public worship was completed in 1841, on the site of the old one. The position is beautiful, the structure a pleasing one to the eye, and finished in handsome style.

Since 1838, the church has been under the charge of three successive pastors. Rev. Henry Lyon, Rev. J. V. Wilson, and Rev. R. O. Williams.

It is understood that this society are Unitarians in doctrine, and believe that all punishment is confined to this life.

In 1844, a small Roman Catholic Church was built in Norwich, between Chelsea and Greeneville.

NORWICH CITY.

Norwich was one of the five cities incorporated by the Legislature, at the May session, in 1784. The boundaries included the First or Town Plot society and Chelsea.

The Mayor was at first chosen for an indefinite term. The succession is as follows:

1. Benjamin Huntington; elected July 13, 1784, and held his office till he resigned, 1796.

2. John McLarran Breed; elected April 18, 1796. Mr. Breed was a distinguished lawyer and an estimable man. He was descended from Allen Breed, who emigrated from England in 1630, and settled at Lynn, Massachusetts. Gershom Breed, the first of the name in Norwich, appears on the records as early as 1750. He engaged in commerce and merchandize, and was a useful and active citizen. His three sons were John McLarran, Shubael and Simeon, all now numbered with the dead. Mr. Mayor Breed died after a long and distressing illness, in June, 1798.

3. Elisha Hyde; elected June 11, 1798, and served till his death. Mr. Hyde was a lawyer of considera-

ble repute, and a man of great urbanity and
kindness of heart. He was born in 1751, and died
December 16, 1813. His wife was Ann, daughter of
Amos Hallam, of New London. They had two daughters but no son. His youngest daughter Ann Maria,
died soon after her father at the age of twenty-four.
Of this lovely and accomplished maiden, a memoir
was published by the companion of her youth—"who
from life's opening pilgrimage had walked with her in
the intimacy of a twin-being."[*]

4. Hon. Calvin Goddard; elected February 7, 1814,
and held the office until 1831. Mr. Goddard was born
at Shrewsbury, Massachusetts, in 1768. After being
admitted to the bar in 1790, he settled at Plainfield,
Connecticut. In 1801, he was elected a member of
Congress, and was re-elected a second and third time,
but resigned his seat in 1805. Two years afterwards,
he removed to Norwich, having purchased that beautiful seat which includes in its domain, the burial ground
of the Mohegan Sachems. In 1815, he was elected a
Judge of the Superior Court, and held it till displaced
three years afterwards by the changes consequent upon
a political revolution in the State.

Since the year 1831, the Mayor has been annually
elected.

5. Hon. James Lanman; elected June 6, 1831, and
held the office three years. Mr. Lanman's father emigrated from Plymouth, and settled in Norwich about
the year 1750. In 1764, he married Sarah Coit, of
Preston. His sons were James, Peter, Samuel and
Joseph. Mr. James Lanman engaged in the practice
of law in his native town, and filled several important
public offices, among which was judge of the Superior
Court, and Senator in Congress.

---

[*] L. Huntley, now widely known as Mrs. Sigourney.

28*

6. Francis A. Perkins; elected June 1834; served one year.

7. Charles W. Rockwell, June 1835 ; three years.

8. Charles J. Lanman,    "    1838; one year.

9. William C. Gilman,    "    1839 ;    "

10. John Breed,    "    1840 ; two years.

11. William P. Greene,    "    1842 ; one year.

12. Gurdon Chapman,    "    1843, and is now Mayor.

Whenever the commerce of the United States has been embarrassed, Norwich has suffered greatly. The year 1811 was a period of mercantile disasters all along the sea-board. A subscription was taken up in Chelsea that year, to aid the inhabitants of Newburyport in their greater distress.

The gloomy scenes of the war with England followed. Even the coasters and small craft in Long Island Sound were subject to great risks, and frequently captured. The commerce of Norwich was entirely destroyed; nor has the enterprize of the citizens since that period ever returned to this channel. It has sought out other sources of prosperity.

In May, 1813, the frigates United States and Macedonian, together with the sloop of war Hornet, were driven into New London harbor by a superior squadron of the enemy, and blockaded during the remainder of the war. The vessels were at length partially dismantled, and conveyed up the Thames river as far as Carter's or Walden's island, at the mouth of Poquetannok cove, within three miles of Norwich, and there laid up till the conclusion of the war. Great and well-founded alarm, for fear of a sudden invasion, at this time existed in Norwich, and at no time since its settlement has it been so seriously threatened. Had the British succeeded in their attack upon Stonington, there is little doubt but they would have made a sudden descent upon Norwich. A great number of merchant vessels were laid up in the harbor—three ships of war were in the immediate neighborhood—the many valuable manufactories of cotton, wool, flour, &c., that were carried on in Norwich—the ship-yards, the public arsenal, &c., all combined to fix the eye of the enemy upon it, and at the close of the year 1814, its situation was deemed very critical, and the minds of the inhabitants were filled with terror and anxiety. A petition was forwarded to the Commander-in-Chief for a military force to be stationed in or near the place, for its protection. But happily the treaty of peace put an end to these alarms.

The news of peace came so suddenly, that it threw the whole country into transports of joy; all was enthusiasm and ecstacy, and the rejoicings exceeded any thing ever before witnessed in America. The grateful tidings reached Norwich, February 13, 1815, and the citizens gave vent to their boundless joy in mutual congratulations, shouts, cannonades and illuminations: rockets flew up from the hills, salutes were fired from the ships in the river, and these were echoed from the fortresses at New London, and those again were responded to from the British blockading squadron at the mouth of the river, till the whole adjacent country was made glad with the tidings.

The winter had been distinguished as a season of severe frost; loaded sleds traveled on the bosom of the Thames in perfect safety; and for several weeks persons might skate all the way from Norwich to New London upon the river. But as soon as peace was proclaimed, preparations were made to revive business. With the first loosing of the waters, the small craft spread their light wings; the larger vessels that had taken refuge in the port were speedily equipped, the released ships of war proceeded down the river, and the whole ocean was again open to American enter-prize.

1818. A Constitution of the State of Connecticut was formed by a State Convention, at Hartford, in August. Previous to this the laws and government of the State had been based upon the Charter of Charles II., granted in 1662. The new Constitution was sub-mitted to each town separately, and being accepted by the majority, was ratified.

It was laid before the town of Norwich in October. The votes in favor of it were 194 ; against it 74.

The next subject which agitated the town related to the location of the courts. The inhabitants of Chelsea demanded that the sessions should thenceforward be held in their quarter of the town.

The contention on this subject continued many years, and reached its height in 1826 and 1827, when a strong desire to divide the town existed in the northern por-tion of it, and petitions to that effect were presented to the Legislature.

The question with respect to the location of the courts was three times brought before the General As-sembly, and fully discussed, and twice tried in the Superior Courts, the decision being each time in favor of their remaining where they were. But in the ses-sion of 1833, the Assembly voted to refer the whole subject to the representatives of the county of New London. These met in the City Hall, at Chelsea, September 19, and carried the question of removal, fifteen to eight. All opposition on the other side ceased from this time, and the transfer was made in peace. The struggle had continued about twenty-seven years.

The northern section of the town petitioned the Legislature to be separated from "the city," which was granted. The city limits since that period comprise only Chelsea and the Falls, with a section upon the river, extending to Trading Cove Brook.

The Town House was erected in 1829, at an expense of $9000.

September 25, 1833, the city of Norwich ceded to the county of New London the use of the City Court Room, and all the other rooms and appurtenances thereunto attached, for the use of the courts. The city also procured a lot and erected a jail, at their own cost, and ceded them to the county.

In 1838, the jail and jail-house, which was situated on the summit of the hill overlooking the port, were burnt to the ground. The fire originated in the cell of a prisoner confined for theft, and was kindled by him with a candle which he obtained from his wife. His design was merely to burn out the lock of his cell door, that he might effect his escape, but before he could complete his work, the fire got beyond his control; the light was discovered, the alarm given, and all the inmates rescued. But from the difficulty of obtaining water, nothing could be done to arrest the destructive element.

The buildings have been re-constructed on an enlarged plan, and though the taste which located such an establishment in the most conspicuous part of the city, may be questioned, yet the buildings themselves are pleasing objects in the perspective.

The city has also suffered severely from other fires. In 1833, the paper mill of R. & A. Hubbard, and a cotton factory and store belonging to Williams' Manufacturing Co., at the Falls, were destroyed by fire.

In the summer of 1844, a large factory was burnt at Greeneville.

In February, 1844, two extensive fires broke out within a few weeks of each other. By the first, four stores belonging to A. H. Hubbard, and Boswell's row, containing several stores and a dwelling house, all on Main street, together with a store-house on Shetucket street, were consumed. In the second, two three-story houses on Franklin Square were destroyed, together with several other buildings of less importance.

Norwich goes far before any other town in the State in the value of its manufactures. According to the report made by the Assessors to the Secretary of the State in 1839, the value of goods manufactured in the preceding year, was $1,150,205. The town next to it in manufactures is Manchester, which was estimated at $695,500.

### INCORPORATED MANUFACTURING COMPANIES.

" Thames Manufacturing Co., 1823 : for the manufacturing of cotton, woolen and iron : empowered to hold fifty acres of land : capital not to exceed $300,000, shares $500. In 1825, this Company was authorized to increase its capital to $500,000, and the quantity of land to 500 acres.

Quinebaug Manufacturing Co. : 1826 ; for making cotton and woolen goods ; capital not to exceed $1,000,000, shares $1000.

Shetucket Manufacturing Co, : 1826 ; for manufacturing iron : capital not to exceed $500,000, shares $500.

Yantic Manufacturing Co. : 1826 ; for manufacturing woolen and cotton goods ; capital not to exceed $30,000, shares $100.

Norwich Manufacturing Co. : 1828; for manufacturing cotton or woolen goods ; capital $100,000, shares $100 ; empowered to hold land not exceeding 500 acres.

Norwich and New York Manufacturing Co. : 1829 ; for manufacturing cotton and woolen goods ; capital $200,000, shares $500.

Norwich and Preston Iron Co. : 1829 ; for manufacturing castings, bar iron, nails, &c. ; capital $100,000, shares $500.

Greeneville Manufacturing Co.: 1833; for manufacturing woolen and other goods which may be deemed advantageous to the Company; not to occupy more than fifteen acres of land; capital not to exceed $50,000, shares $100.

### BANKS, &C.

Norwich Mutual Assurance Co : incorporated in 1795.

Norwich Bank: 1796. Capital stock not less than $75,000, nor more than $200,000; shares $100.

Norwich Marine (now Fire) Insurance : 1803. Capital not less than $50,000: shares $50. The name and character was changed in 1818; the object thenceforth being confined to insurance against losses by fire. Capital not less than $100,000 ; nor more than $300,000.

Norwich Savings Society : 1824.

Thames Bank : 1825 ; 2000 shares of $100. This bank succeeded to the business and privileges of the Norwich Channel Co. which had been incorporated in 1805.

Norwich Market, at Chelsea Landing : 1825. Capital not to exceed $10,000.

Quinebaug Bank: 1832 ; 5000 shares of $100 each. This bank was required to subscribe, as soon as organized, to the Boston and Norwich Railroad Company, $100,000, being one thousand shares.

Quinebaug Canal Bank was incorporated in 1827, but never went into operation.

Merchants Bank : 1833 ; 3000 shares of $100 each, with the privilege of increasing to 5000. A bonus was required of this institution, for the improvement of navigation in the Thames, not exceeding $30,000 ; afterwards altered to ten per cent. on the capital stock actually called in.

Merchants Insurance Co.: 1834. Capital not less than $100,000, nor more than $300,000 ; shares, $100. This company insures against disasters by sea, and losses by fire, on all kinds of mixed and personal estate.

Mechanics Society : for aiding destitute members and their families  Capital not to exceed $20,000.

POPULATION.

In 1830, the population was 5,170—in 1840, 7,239, of whom 4,200 were within the city limits. Males, 3,368, females, 3,871. The number of electors registered Oct. 15, 1844, was 1,383; which, allowing one in seven to be voters, would indicate a population at the present time not much short of 10,000.

NEWSPAPERS.

The second Newspaper established in Norwich, was " The Weekly Register." It was commenced in 1790, by Thomas Hubbard, on the town Plain. Six years afterwards, Mr. Hubbard removed to the Landing, and issued his paper under the designation of " The Chelsea Courier." It has been continued to the present time, with slight variations of the title, and now bears the name of " The Norwich Courier." Several other Newspapers have been commenced in the place, and through the influence of temporary causes, or the power of editorial talent, have obtained a transient share of public patronage, but after an ephemeral life have disappeared. Such was the fate of

The True Republican, by Sterry & Porter,

The Native American, by Samuel Webb,

Norwich Republican, by J. T. Adams.

The News list, in Jan. 1845, stands as follows :—

1. The Norwich Courier, published weekly and triweekly—by D. E. Sykes.

2. The Norwich Aurora, commenced 1836—by J. Holbrook ; now conducted by J. W. Stedman.

3. The Spectator, commenced in 1842—by J. Cooley.

4. The Norwich Gleaner, commenced 1845—by B. F. Taylor.

## MISSIONARIES.

The Foreign Mission Society of Norwich and vicinity, was organized in 1812. In October, 1844, it held its thirty-second anniversary.

In September, 1843, the American Board of Commissioners for Foreign Missions, held their annual meeting at Norwich. There was a peculiar appropriateness in the assembling of this great association at that place, as Norwich has always been distinguished, not only for her generous contribution of funds towards the support of missions both foreign and domestic, but for the more costly offerings of numerous sons and daughters to the promotion of the cause.

The following is supposed to be a correct list of the missionaries that have gone out from Norwich. About twenty of them were natives, and the others were for a considerable period residents of the town, before entering upon the duties of the missionary. Two of them, it will be seen, belong to an earlier period than the organization of the American Board of Commissioners for Foreign Missions. One is attached to a Methodist mission; one is an Episcopal clergyman in the employ of the Colonization society, and twenty-four have been in the service of the American Board of Commissioners for Foreign Missions:

| Year. | Names. | Mission. |
|---|---|---|
| 1766. | Rev. Samuel Kirkland, | Oneida. |
| 1761. | Rev. Samsom Occum, (Mohegan,) | " |
| 1812. | Rev. Samuel Nott, Jr., | Mahratta. |
| 1812. | Mrs. Nott, (Roxana Peck,) | " |
| 1819. | Rev. Miron Winslow, | Ceylon. |
| 1819. | Mrs. Winslow, (Harriet L. Lathrop,) | " |
| 1820. | Mrs. Palmer, (Clarissa Johnson,) | Cherokee. |
| 1821. | Rev. William Potter, | " |
| 1825. | William H. Manwaring, | " |
| 1826. | Mrs. Gleason, (Bethiah W. Tracy,) | Choctaw. |

29

| Year. | Names. | Mission. |
|---|---|---|
| 1827. | Rev. Jonathan S. Green, | Sandwich Islands. |
| 1827. | Mrs. Gulick, (Fanny H. Thomas,) | " |
| 1833. | Mrs. Smith, (Sarah L. Huntington,) | Syria. |
| 1833. | Mrs. Palmer, (Jerusha Johnson,) | Cherokee. |
| 1833. | Mrs. Hutchings, (Elizabeth C. Lathrop,) | Ceylon. |
| 1833. | Mrs. Perry, (Harriet J. Lathrop,) | " |
| 1833. | Rev. Stephen Johnson, | Siam. |
| 1835. | Rev. James T. Dickinson, | Singapore. |
| 1835. | Rev. William Tracy, | Madura. |
| 1835. | Mrs. Hebard, (Rebecca W. Willimas,) | Syria. |
| 1836. | Mrs. Cherry, (Charlotte H. Lathrop,) | Madura. |
| 1836. | Rev. James L. Thomson, | Cyprus. |
| 1839. | Mrs. Sherman, (Martha E. Williams,) | Syria. |
| 1839. | Mrs. Brewer, (Laura L. Giddings,) | Oregon. |
| 1839. | Mrs. Cherry, (Jane E. Lathrop,) | Ceylon. |
| 1840. | Rev. Joshua Smith, | Africa. |
| 1843. | Miss Susan Tracy. | Choctaw. |
| 1844. | Miss Lucinda Downer, | " |

### RAIL ROAD.

The Norwich and Worcester Rail Road Company was formed in 1832; the Legislatures of Connecticut and Massachusetts each granting a charter for that portion of the road which lay within their respective States. These two companies were united by the said Legislatures in 1836, the whole capital amounting to $1,700,000. The length from the steam-boat landing in Norwich, to the depot at Worcester, is fifty-eight and nine tenth miles, eighteen of which is in Massachusetts. The materials used, and the workmanship were all of the best kind, and it is believed to be a road of as solid and durable construction as any in the country. It was first opened through the whole distance, in March, 1840.

Just beyond Greeneville in Norwich, the road forms a curve of 1,000 feet radius along the banks of the Shetucket, affording a fine view of the river, the bridge and adjacent country. Three miles from the city, at the Quinebaug Falls, the company were met

GREENVILLE. FROM PRESTON.

by an immense mass of rock lying across their contemplated route. Here a deep cut was channeled for a considerable distance through a friable rock, but reaching at length a bed of solid granite, a tunnel was excavated 300 feet in length, and twenty in width. The height from the bed of the tunnel, to the summit of the rock above, is about 100 feet. Sitting in the car and gazing upon the scenery, you suddenly find yourself gliding into the bosom of frowning cliffs, and enveloped in subterranean darkness. You come out slowly, grinding along the edge of a precipice, with the ragged, foaming, contracted river below you on one side, and a barrier of cliffs on the other.

The road for many miles keeps near the Quinebaug, which has every where the same characteristics, chafed and noisy, the banks bold, the bed rocky, and the edges disfigured by boulders brought down with ice in spring floods, and lodged along the water course.

The section of the road from Norwich to Jewett City in Preston, was the most laborious and expensive of the route. The course was winding, the radius short; the earth encumbered with rocks; the contractors lost money, and were obliged to throw themselves upon the company. The tunnel alone cost nearly $30,000.

A large depot or station house was erected at Norwich, contiguous to the steam-boat landing, two stories high, and 200 feet in length. It is situated just at the spot where the Shetucket contracts its course, turns a quarter round, and glides into the Thames. Here the company purchased a small rocky promontory called the Point, pulled down the buildings which covered it, blew up the rocks, filled the shallows, and constructed the station house, together with a wharf and a solid stone wall.

During the severe flood in the spring of 1841, a bar was formed in the channel of the Thames, by an accumulation of sand brought down the Shetucket, 360 feet in length, which it was found very difficult to excavate, so as to leave the channel of its former depth. In consequence of this bar, the steamboats which had before this occasionally grounded in the river, were now frequently delayed two or three hours upon their route. This obstruction, together with the serious inconvenience arising from the ice in the winter season, induced the company to extend their road from Norwich along the bank of the river, seven miles to Allen's point, near Gale's ferry, where it is supposed that no serious obstruction will ever be presented by the ice. This part of the road was completed in 1843, and in regard to its location and scenery is altogether of a novel character.

The Shetucket is spanned by a lofty bridge, after which the route is directly upon the brink of the Thames, being channeled along her banks and running over her coves and streamlets by bridges and causeways, affording views varied and picturesque in the highest degree.

The Norwich and Worcester rail road having been constructed at a period of pecuniary pressure in the country, unexampled in its severity and continuance, it is no matter of surprize, though it certainly is of regret, that the public-spirited band of men who commenced the undertaking and completed it under such discouragements, should have suffered severely in a pecuniary point of view by the measure. It is not often the case in this world, that they who expend their zeal and energies upon a great work, are the persons that reap the most benefit from it. They plan, and execute, and toil on with unceasing ardor to complete an undertaking and then are swept aside, or pass away, while others enter into their labors, and enjoy that which costs them nothing. There is nothing discouraging in this; it rather ennobles measures which otherwise would be but sordid ; teaching the generous mind to enter upon its beneficial task, whether personal advantage accrue from it or not ; to do good, and pursue noble ends by noble means, without too solicitously expecting a reward, or indulging regret if it be withheld.

### HEALTH, LONGEVITY, DEATHS.

Norwich may be called a healthy town. Though surrounded by running streams to a greater extent than most places, it contains no stagnant waters or marshy grounds. Fevers and chills are of rare occurrence, and there seems to exist no causes for disease that are not common to the changeable climate of the State.

The first three or four generations in this place were distinguished for longevity. Dr. Lord said in his old age : " When I first came here, there was a beautiful sight of venerable, aged fathers, and many of them appearing of the right Puritan stamp, the hoary head found in the way of righteousness." And he adds, " there is now some greater number of the aged, from seventy and upwards, than there was at that time." For want of accurate public registering, we have but few data on which to form any estimate of the proportions of diseases and death. Dr. Lord stated in his half-century sermon (1767) that 1000 persons had died in the first society in fifty years—average number, annually, twenty—extremes, fourteen and thirty—112 of the whole number lived to be seventy or upwards, and one over 100 : 390 died under fourteen years of age. At that

29*

period, there were forty living at the age of seventy or upwards.

Dr. Strong, in 1828, stated that the number of deaths in the society, for the preceding 50 years, amounted to 1450, averaging twenty-nine annually ; extremes, sixteen and sixty-three.   The inhabitants for each period cannot be exactly ascertained, but probably it would not be far from the truth, to estimate them at a medium, during Dr. Lord's ministry, at 1600, and during Dr. Strong's, 1800.   Perhaps the variation has been even less.   Good judges say that the population of this society has been nearly uniform for 150 years ; emigration and death keeps the balance in equipoise.

According to the above estimate, the proportion of deaths in this society is about one in sixty or seventy, which is the usual proportion in all the healthy parts of New England.

From 1787 to 1827, a period of forty years, Dr. Strong married 365 couple ; probably during that time, not more than half a dozen marriages took place which were not solemnized by him.   These marriages average nine or ten per year.   In the year 1796, he united twenty-four couples.   From '87 to '97, 144 couples, averaging fourteen per year.

To illustrate the general health of the town, the following fact may be noticed.   Dr. Strong built the house in which his son Henry Strong Esq., now resides, and lived in it fifty years with his family.   He had three children, and usually kept two or three domestics, and yet his own death in 1835 was the first that had ever occurred in the house.

A remarkable instance of longevity, viz., that of Mrs. Lathrop, who died in 1732, at the age of 103 years, has already been mentioned.   The following instance is mentioned in Dwight's Travels: "Ann Heifer, a widow at Norwich, Conn., died March 22, 1758, in her 105th year."

Aged inhabitants of Norwich, present at a political festival, in 1840.

| | | | |
|---|---|---|---|
| Erastus Perkins, | aged 89 | Ichabod Ward, | aged 80 |
| Samuel Avery, | " 88 | Newcomb Kinney, | " 80 |
| Seabury Brewster, | " 86 | Benjamin Snow, | " 77 |
| Christopher Vail, | " 82 | Nathaniel Shipman, | " 76 |
| Bela Peck, | " 82 | Zachariah Huntington, | " 75 |

Only one person, it is believed, has been killed by lightning in the town. This was a young woman, sister to Thomas Leffingwell, the third of that name, who was struck dead by the descent of the electric fluid, while in the act of closing a window. The event occurred in the old Leffingwell house, in the Town-plot society.

The number of suicides, for the whole period, cannot be ascertained ; but from the number of instances collected, it is estimated that they may amount to fifteen or twenty. The list comprises people in all conditions of life, and both sexes :—one was a respectable woman, a wife and mother ; three or four were disappointed in love, but the majority were hard drinkers or persons of immoral habits.

The first suicide in the town, if we may credit tradition, was Micah Rood, a man respecting whom several legends have been preserved, somewhat contradictory, and only partially harmonizing with the brief notices that may be gathered from the records. The following is as connected a statement as can be made out of these various accounts.

Thomas Rood, the father of Micah, was one of the first farmers that settled in Norwich. It is not improbable that he came upon the ground with the first proprietors. He had a farm four or five miles from the town plot, in that part of the town which is now Franklin. His second son, Micah, possessed in 1715, a comfortable farm "near the saw mill." The tradition is, that he introduced upon this farm a peculiar variety of the apple, of an early species, fair outside, and excellent flavor. One tree in particular, by assiduous cultivation, had become large and productive. By what means he fell into poverty is not known. His old age was rendered miserable by the combined influence of want, and a depression of spirit, amounting perhaps to insanity.

The following record is copied from a slip of paper found among the town books.

"Norwich, Sept. ye 13, 1726.
Att a Town meeting Legalley warned This Town Desier the Present Selectmen to Agree with some sutabele parsen to keepe Micah Rood and his wife and the Town ingaege to pay what ye Selectmen shall agree for—Voted.—"

Tradition says that Micah was intemperate and dishonest, and that in a fit of remorse he hung himself upon his favorite apple-tree. Since which period, says the legend, every individual apple from this stock has been tainted with a speck of blood. It is an undoubted fact that the apples of this neighborhood, locally called *Mike* apples, received their name from him, as having been propagated from a tree upon his farm. It is true also, that this species of apple, generally exhibits somewhere in the pulp, a small red speck, resembling a tinge of fresh blood. This, connected with the suicide of Micah Rood, affords sufficient matter for a tale of superstition.

It is strange that the commission of crime, which ought to make men afraid to die, should so often lead to self-murder. Yet notwithstanding this aggravation of their guilt, there is always something that awakens our sympathy in the fate of the suicide. Take, for instance, another case that occurred in Norwich, in which the victim was a poor negro slave, named Jock.

He used occasionally to attend the new-light meetings, and had one or two seasons of being very religious. He courted a neighboring servant girl of his own color, but at length thinking himself ill used by her, in a fit of jealousy and anger, he one night took a gun, loaded it with bits of an old pewter spoon, which he cut up for that purpose, for want of bullets, went to the house where she lived, looked in at the kitchen window and saw her sitting by the fire with her master's child in her arms. He leveled his piece, fired and hit her in the shoulder. Immediately thereupon he fled to a swamp in the neighborhood, where he remained till driven out by hunger. He was then seized and confined in jail. The boys under his window one day told him that the woman whom he had shot, was dead; and that very night he hung himself in prison. His body was given to the elder Dr. Turner for dissection, and his bones formed into an anatomical figure, were long kept in his office, an object both of terror and curiosity to the ignorant and the children of the neighborhood. If obliged to pass the place a little after night-fall, they were sure to imagine that they saw Jock's ghost.

But it is not only the stings of a tormenting conscience that lead to the commission of suicide. Few minds, without the aid of strong religious faith, can sustain a great calamity. Whenever therefore some uncommon misfortune crosses their path, they become desperate, loathe life, and seek relief in the grave. A more recent case of self-destruction that occurred in Norwich, is of too interesting a nature, not to be minutely detailed.

Albertus Siraut Destouches, a French gentleman of

polished manners and respectable standing in society, settled in Norwich about the year 1790. He was a native of Bordeaux, had been educated at Leyden, in Holland, and after seeing much of life and manners in the old world, he removed to Demerara and engaged in commercial pursuits. From this place, he came to Norwich, where he entered into the mercantile line, purchased a handsome house, and married a widow lady of respectability. Being afflicted with a very painful disorder, he gradually withdrew from all business, and in a great measure from society. He had a large library, and endeavored to divert his mind with books, but so acute were his sufferings, that he was driven to despair, and life rendered odious to him. It was long, however, before he could convince himself that it would be justifiable in him to commit self-murder. He consulted various authors, and often conversed on the subject. At one time he endeavored, by high bribes and the most affecting entreaties, to prevail on one of his domestics to kill him, having a kind of natural repugnance to the taking of his own life. While wavering in his mind whether suicide might not be justified by the laws of God, he addressed the following note to the Rev. Dr. Strong, of the first society. It will be given with all its peculiarities of idiom and circumstance.

From my bed, March 30, 1796.

Reverend Sir.—

Having not the advantage of being particularly acquainted with you, nothing but your public character and known disposition to oblige, would have emboldened a poor sick man to apply and entreat your reverence for the favor of granting me a little of his precious time for a short visit, as not being able to do it myself. Fettered in my bed, stranger, without friend or relation and actually as waving between sickness, pain, distress, misfortune and despair, I hope you will not

refuse him that favor, and acquaint verbally by the bearer when may expect, when granted.   In expectation of which I remain,                     Reverend Sir,
                    of your Reverence
                        the Humble Servant,
                        ALB. SIRAUT DESTOUCHES.
Reverend Mr. Strong, present, up town."

In the interview with Dr. Strong, which succeeded, the fitness of religion to sustain the soul under all earthly trials, was the principal topic of discourse, and M. Destouches permitted his visiter to retire without laying before him the peculiar subject that engrossed his thoughts.   This led to a second more extended letter, of which the following is an exact transcript.

      " Reverend Sir,
   As nothing but your kindness and your principles of human-ity only, authorizes me to disturb you again, and to intrude upon the precious time which your public character prescribes to devote to those only, whose similarity in their manner of thinking do coincide or agree with yours, permit, Dear Sir, that a poor unfortunate sufferer, who has no other claim or protector than the humanity and, (if I dare say it) the most rigid moral,—trouble you again with this billet.
   When last week you did me the favor of visiting me, how-ever good it did me, as I did not touch the point or subject I desired, I will expose now briefly the main part of it, the rest being become, by my low situation now useless.
   I hinted to you, dear Sir, in our last interview, how unfor-tunate I have been here since my arrival, in matter of con-cern, and I related you, and you was yourself witness of my suffering, but since that time, I did experience an increase of pain (however now a little abated) which my strength does not permit to bear very much longer.   Strength and hope of recovery are gone, and nothing is remaining but a most dis-tressing death which is the only end I have to expect, if I do not prevent it by an immoderate use of opium.
   But, Dear Sir, though I find in my distressful situation, reasons to justify such an attempt, which the remembrance of all my other misfortunes, and the consciousness of my own un-usefulness, any longer in the society corroborates, a

certain doubt holds me back, and none of my books give me any satisfactory account pro nor contra. Paley's Moral Philosophy, Hume's and Montaine's Essays tell me not enough. You would oblige me much if to the revelation which speaks magisterially to the will only, you could procure me some arguments to illustrate my reason in so dark a matter, when nature has lost its influence upon our senses. Not daring to expect yourself for the answer, a few lines upon the paper may satisfy.

Reverend Sir, your most Humble Servant,

ALB. SIRAUT DESTOUCHES.

Wednesday Morning."

Dr. Strong after the reception of this letter visited the unfortunate sufferer repeatedly, and being now aware of the leading purpose of his mind, employed every argument that reason or religion could suggest, to divert him from its execution. But in vain—his resolution grew stronger as his frame grew more feeble. He became convinced that the act was lawful, and often declared that if his sufferings should increase beyond what he felt that he could endure, he should seek a violent relief. On leaving him one day, Dr. S. obtained from him, after much persuasion, his word of honor, that, at least, he would not commit the deed until he had seen him again,—holding out the idea that he would make the subject a matter of particular study, and hoped then to be able to produce arguments to convince him that he ought not to destroy himself. Having obtained this promise, and fearing that another interview would be as unsatisfactory as the former had been, he purposely kept out of the way of the sick man. Sometime afterwards he was called to attend a funeral, which obliged him to pass the dwelling of M. Destouches. He drove quick, in order to escape observation, but before he could get past the house, the unfortunate gentleman raised the sash of his chamber window, and waved his hand expressively, as if to say, "I see you," closed it again, and instantly shot himself dead. Upon the walls of his room was written several times, in imperfect English, with a pencil,—"'Tis more as I can bear."

M. Destouches in his will left the greater part of his books, which were mostly of an infidel character, to a gentleman in Leyden, (Holland.) His executors took great pains to fulfill his wishes, but they could never hear from the legatee, or learn whether he was living or dead. The matter was referred to the Legislature of Connecticut, who ordered the books to be deposited in the library of Yale College, until called for by some person duly authorized to claim them.

Only two executions have been ascertained; these both took place on Long Hill, overlooking the town plot. The first was soon after the settlement of Dr. Strong, who preached the execution sermon. The criminal was a man of the name of Dennis, who killed a comrade by a sudden stroke, in a quarrel. He seems to have been condemned by a sentence too rigorous; as the fatal blow was dealt in a state of passionate excitement, and the victim was well enough to walk the streets for a fortnight afterwards.

The other was in 1816. An ignorant mulatto, named Miner Babcock, about twenty years of age, stabbed his step-father, in a quarrel. They had frequently fought before, with fists and hard words, but this time Miner drew out his jack-knife, and in the scuffle, the old man, who was much the worse character of the two, received a wound, of which he died. Miner was hung upon the same spot where Dennis suffered. Both of these scenes collected a large concourse of spectators from all parts of the State.

The village of Greeneville was established on the

30

purest code of morals; not a foot of land was sold but upon condition that no ardent spirits should be vended upon it. Yet in its very infancy it received a foul blot upon its fair fame, from an act of atrocious villany which occured in its precincts. A man by the name of Sherman, a native of Rhode Island, killed his wife and child in the most barbarous manner; the child, on its mother's bosom, receiving one of the deadly blows aimed at the wife. It is supposed that he committed the crime in a fit of anger, inflamed by intoxication, for though, from the tenure of the lands in Greeneville, he could procure no intoxicating liquor there, yet it was thought he had inflamed his veins with the deadly poison in a neighboring society, from which he returned that evening. He was tried and executed at New London.

FRESHETS.

The annual breaking up of the ice in the rivers around Norwich, and the consequent overflowing of the waters, frequently occasion great damages. Mills and bridges are swept away, meadow lands devastated, fences destroyed, and individuals, as well as the public, sustain serious losses. Some parts of the town are, from their situation, peculiarly exposed to these ravages. The narrow and winding outlet of the Shetucket, and the high banks that restrain it on the south, naturally tend to throw the accumulated swell of the river over the flat part of Chelsea. Only a few of the most remarkable of these floods can be here noticed.

In June, 1778, a great freshet was produced by rain, without the aid of snow or ice. For two days, (tenth and eleventh of June,) the rain poured down without intermission, with all the vehemence that is displayed in a violent thunder shower. The rivers rose with great rapidity, to an almost unprecedented height, and caused great damage in and around Chelsea.

The most alarming freshet of these rivers that has occurred within the memory of any now living, was in 1807. A heavy rain fell upon frozen ground and rushed towards the rivers. The ice began to break and move in the night, and the rise of the waters was so sudden and terrible as to cause great alarm and consternation. The bells were rung, and expresses sent to different parts of the town for assistance. The current swept over East Chelsea, and covered Main street up as far as the store of Mr. Charles Coit. A temporary embankment was formed at this place, by placing the mast of a vessel across the street, securing it by heavy stones, then placing rails and timbers upon it, and filling in hay and straw to stop the leakage. The waters slightly trickled over this breast work, but it kept off the main body until it subsided, which was in the course of a few hours.

In September, 1815, at the equinox, a most destructive gale of wind was experienced on the coast of New England. At Chelsea the tide rose to an unprecedented height. Several stores on the wharves were swept entirely away, and others injured. On the wharf bridge the depth of water was five or six feet; beating over it with such fury as to carry off the market and a store adjoining. The market drifted up the river and lodged on the east side of the cove, thirty or forty yards above the bridge. All the shipping in the harbor was driven ashore, knocking in the sides of stores, and lodging almost in the streets.

In March, 1823, the sudden rise of the river swept off several buildings from the wharf bridge: among them was the Methodist chapel, which passed down the river into the Sound before it broke into parts. This incident gave rise at the time to many jocular reports. The newspapers in some places published that it bore off both pastor and flock, and that they were heard singing as they passed New London. They reported also that it had landed whole on one of the islands, and that services would be performed there in future. A schooner from Providence, then in the Sound, asserted that it came driving by them in the night with lights in it.*

To show the force of the water in this flood it may be stated, that the Yantic was considerably deepened in some places, by the removal of large stones. One that weighed more than a ton, and which had been placed in the bed of the river many years before, to support a foot bridge, was raised, carried up into a meadow, and thrown against a large tree. An oil-mill was swept off, with a considerable quantity of flax-seed in it. By the middle of May several meadows adjoining the river were covered with young flax.

### MISCELLANEOUS REMARKS.

Norwich abounds in springs of clear and soft water. Wells on the side hills generally require to be dug to the depth of twenty feet, and on the plains forty feet or more. In some few places the water is hard, and this probably arises from some mineral property of the earth through which it passes, as the town does not produce clay, which is the substance that most frequently prevents water from uniting with soap. There are some instances of wells that are alternately hard and soft, varying as different springs flow into them, and prevail at different seasons. Those springs which are reached by blasting the superincumbent rocks, are almost invariably pure, while those which pass through earthy strata, are apt to be tinctured with these ingredients.

---

* This incident gave rise to a little poem, by Brainerd, called " The Captain." Though but a fragmentary production, it is very graphic and highly finished.

The rock formations in and around Norwich, are all primitive, consisting of gneiss, hornblende and granite; of inferior quality for building, and of little use except for walls, cellars and wells.

The valleys between the hills appear to form parts of an irregular alluvial plain. The late Daniel L. Coit Esq., a gentleman of intelligence and accurate observation, conjectured that this plain might have been at some distant period the bottom of a lake, which by the recession of the waters, or other violent cause, had been much changed in its aspect. This plain appears in an unbroken form between the town and landing, but it extends in an irregular and broken condition to Bean Hill, and it appears also on the west side of the Yantic, and on the south-west of the cove below the falls. It is distinguished by sand, loose gravel, and rounded small stones, entirely different in geological structure from the hills adjacent, and intimating a secondary formation. No rocks similar to those which mark the hills, are found on the plains, and the termination of the two regions is in some spots so abrupt, that Mr. Coit supposed some violent cause must have produced this effect, and that probably the bed of the Yantic, if not of the Shetucket, was once as elevated as the plain, and the lake received its waters. The point of land, east of Mr. R. Hubbard's dwelling-house, seems to have been left by an eddy passing round the hill, and rushing into the basin below. It is worthy of note that the Great Plain, Sachem's Plain, and Chelsea Plain, are all on the same water level.

On the north side of Waweekus Hill, the descent is gradual, and rocks are scattered along the declivity. This primitive formation continues to the north, the rocks being occasionally found in the lots, even after the ground has become level, until it meets the allu-

30*

vion in the third lot in the rear of the residence of Gen. William Williams. Beyond this there is not a rock to be found through the plain, and the earth a foot or two below the surface is composed of gravel and rounded stones.

The well at the dwelling-house of the late Rev. Mr. Mitchell, the first opened on the plain, was dug forty-two feet, and through the whole of this depth, the earth was composed of gravel and rounded stones, from the smallest size to those of one or two pounds weight, without a drop of water until they reached the depth of thirty-seven or thirty-eight feet, after which water was very abundant. The gravel was undoubt-edly too loose to contain water, which was not found until the alluvion was pierced through and the primi-tive formation reached, on which it rests. It is believed that similar appearances have been presented in digging all the other wells on the plain.

The scarcity of stone on the plains, formerly led to the cultivation of prim hedges, as being less expensive and more elegant than any other fence, and at one period many fields and gardens were surrounded with these beautiful hedges. Almost every homestead between the Arnold house, and the wharf bridge, was adorned with them, so that they were considered one of the peculiarities of the town. But from some causes, not well ascertained, there was a general failure of prim [Ligustrum vulgare, Lin :] throughout the coun-try, about the period of the revolutionary war, and it has since been comparatively a rare shrub. Popular opinion sportively attributes the decay to the fact that the Rogerene Quakers were whipped with prim withs; and it was long maintained that the shrub could never again be made to flourish in the soil. It is not known that this deluded people endured any flagellation in the

town subsequent to that of 1726, and the hedges flourished in all their beauty for forty years afterwards; so that it
is difficult to conceive how this idea orignated. However that may be, some recent experiments show that
this mysterious sympathy with Quakerism has become
extinct, and Norwich may yet recover her ancient reputation in this line.

Few towns are better accommodated with gardens
than Norwich, or receive greater returns for their cultivation. The soil is suitable for the production of most
kinds of fruit and vegetables. It is more moist on the
sides of the hills than on the plains, and they bear the
drought better, but are more backward. Home lots
that are well attended, produce fine crops of grass.
Fruit is abundant; though plumbs and cherries are
often much injured by insects, and almost all fruit-
bearing trees have suffered from their ravages. There
is a small insect that deposites its eggs in punctures
upon the young branches; and when the maggot is
hatched, it feeds upon the wood and eats its way out,
leaving a swollen excrescence, which destroys the fer-
tility of the branch. Such at least appears to be the
process. But a still greater enemy to the garden, is
the rose slug, which has vastly increased during the
last half century, and has been very destructive both
to fruits and shrubs.

Within a few years the vergaloo pear has very much
degenerated, but the cause is not ascertained. The
canker worm has not been very troublesome since the
year 1794, at which time it was very injurious. In the
month of June of that year, there was a remarkably
cold and tedious storm, which seemed to drive them
away for that season; for they were very numerous on
the trees the day before the storm, and none to be
found after it. The storm could have only operated in

hastening their departure for the season.   Dr. Dwight
supposes them to have received their death blow
throughout this region, in the month of March, 1795,
while in the miller state.


### DESCRIPTIVE SKETCH.

Norwich consists of an assemblage of villages along
the banks of the Yantic and Shetucket, with a broad
extent of woods and barren heights, interspersed with
farms moderately fertile, spreading like wings to the
N. E. and S. W.   The villages are six.   The most
northern is a small manufacturing village, called Yan-
ticville, and consisting principally of families connected with the large flannel and carpet factories under the
agency of Erastus Williams Esq.   There is one quite
ancient house in this group, formerly owned by Elijah Backus Esq., and still the residence of the family.

Bean Hill, now called Westville, was the northern
limit of the Town Plot; many of the descendants of
the first settlers reside here on the old homesteads;
Hydes, Backuses, Huntingtons, &c.   There is a Methodist Church, a pottery and satinet factory in this part
of the town.

The *Town*, a central section, locally so called, is
principally built around an undivided square, occupied
by the burying yard and some fine meadows.   This
was once the principal seat of business, but now forms
a delightful residence for persons withdrawn from the
active pursuits of life.   The inhabitants have been
from the first settlement, distinguished for sobriety,
love of order, good sense and intelligence.   The site
on which it is built is very/irregular and much broken,
consisting of a narrow, picturesque valley, following

the windings of the Yantic. Here, upon the Plain, stands the First Society meeting-house; no other sect or denomination have ever had a house for worship in this part of the town. The court-house, since the removal of the courts to the Landing, has been occupied for a school, the old jail was taken down, the post-office transferred to another location, the taverns shut up, and the peace and quiet of the "Happy Valley" now broods over this charming plain, once the seat of so much activity and business.

Between the Town Plot and the City, but included within the limits of the latter, is that beautiful part of Norwich called the Little Plain: the *Mohegan Plain* would be a more appropriate designation, since this spot appears to have been the favorite resort of the Mohegan Sachems—beloved and venerated by them above all others, and chosen for their last resting place, where removed from all inferior society, they might repose among their kindred in royal seclusion. The eastern side of the plain is skirted by a rocky woodland ridge; the western is bordered by the upper part of the Falls Village. On the north-west, where it approaches the Yantic, and the low meadows called Noman's Acre, a rural cemetery has been recently laid out. It was consecrated in July, 1844; the services being performed by a union of all denominations of Christians in town. The location is beautiful, and when " the young trees shall entwine their roots with the sacred dust," and overshadow the grassy mounds and sculptured monuments of the future dead, it will be an ornament to the city, and a hallowed place of resort to its inhabitants.

On this plain, and in its vicinity are many elegant private mansions—a small, but tasteful church, and the Indian burial ground shaded by a grove of trees, between whose shafts rises the granite obelisk that commemorates the name of Uncas. The corner stone of this monument was laid by President Jackson in 1833. The obelisk was contributed by the ladies of Norwich, and the whole enterprise completed and commemorated July 4, 1842.

It is not known for how long a period before Uncas, the Mohegans had brought their sachems to this place for interment, but it is generally supposed that at the time of the settlement, the graves covered a couple of acres, and that the whole plain was originally chosen for the royal cemetery. If the dust of the old Sachems could rise up bodily from their graves, said an aged man, I have no doubt but we should see them ascending here and there, far towards the centre of the plain.

The Falls Village lies in a hollow bend of the Yantic, just where it rushes over the rocks through a winding channel into the cove of the Thames. It is wholly of manufacturing growth, and with the exception of an ancient woollen factory and oil mill, and Mr. Elijah Lathrop's dwelling-house, has been entirely built since 1822.

Chelsea, now Norwich City, is singularly romantic in its situation. Its very streets are declivities, and its buildings are in tiers one above another. It is built just upon the point of land where the Shetucket meets the Thames; its lower streets have either been won from the water, or blasted out of the rock. The first view of it from the river below is very striking; it appears and disappears in the windings of the river, as if a drop curtain had shut it out from view. As you approach it by water at night, the lights from the houses high up the hill, seem to be suspended in the air. Chelsea has now seven churches.

Leaving the extreme point between the rivers and

tracing the Shetucket towards the east, we should have found, at the close of the last century and the beginning of this, a low miry place little better than a swamp, and considered by the citizens the least desirable of all their suburbs. This place was swept over every spring by the Shetucket, which deposited there all its ice, mud and rubbish. It was commonly called Swallow-all. The brook that runs through it bears that designation in the town records so long ago as almost to render it *classic*. Yet both the origin and the orthography of the name is doubtful. If derived, as some say, from the swallows, who used to make their holes in the high banks adjoining, it should be written Swallow-Hall. But if, as is most probable, the name is derived from the situation as the receptacle of the Shetucket, the popular designation is correct.

This tract is now changed in almost every feature. The river is restrained by embankments within proper limits; the brook has almost disappeared; the low and marshy spots have been filled up; the rail-cars pass like flying caravans along the brink of the river; two respectable churches have been built in the valley; and almost every trace of the ancient Swallow-all is obliterated from the fertile gardens and pleasant mansions of East Chelsea.

Pursuing our course for about half a mile along the Shetucket, we come to Greeneville, the youngest of the Norwich group of villages, and owing its existence entirely to the Water Power Company.

This company was incorporated in 1829, for the purpose of preparing a certain portion of the waters of the Quinebaug and Shetucket, for use to manufacturing establishments. Their capital is $80,000.

They purchased four hundred and sixty acres of land, extending nearly three miles in length each side of the

Shetucket, in Norwich and Preston.   They built a dam
of solid and costly masonry, and dug a canal wider
than the Erie, (forty-five feet wide and nine feet deep)
and seven-eighths of a mile in length.   Four factories
were very soon erected between the canal and the
river, and leased out upon productive terms.   Other
mill seats have been sold and leased, but they have
still on hand a large amount of water power unsold,
sufficient, it is supposed, to carry in the whole sixty
thousand spindles.   The water is abundant even in the
dryest seasons, and the company claim that there is
none to be found in the union, taking the advantageous
position and other facilities into consideration, which
is worth intrinsically more per thousand spindles than
this.   The village of Greeneville was laid out by this
company, and the land sold and leased on advantageous terms.

Greeneville is noted for its excellent common schools;
and where education and mental improvement receive
a proper degree of attention, the chief objection to large
manufacturing establishments is obviated.   The population, consisting perhaps of fifteen hundred persons,
comprises but one school district.   They have two neat
and convenient school-houses, built upon a modern
plan, and the schools are kept without interruption
from year to year, and funds are annually provided
sufficient to bring the means of instruction within the
reach of each individual.

In the eastern part of Norwich, in a bend of the Shetucket, is a plain, which ever since the settlement of
Norwich, has gone by the name of Sachem's Plain.   It
is so called in the first grants of land made in that
quarter, and the traditions both of whites and Mohegans concur in saying, that here the Sachem Miantino-

moh was captured by Uncas, and to this place being brought back, here he was slain and buried.

On the 4th of July, 1841, a considerable concourse of people, young and old, principally from the village of Greeneville, celebrated by a festival, the erection of a monumental stone to the memory of the Narragansett chief. It is a block of granite, eight feet high, and about five feet square upon the base. It is placed as near to the spot where he was buried, as could be ascertained, and bears this inscription :

MIANTONIMOH

1843.

This monument was erected principally through the exertions of William C. Gilman Esq. It was consecrated by prayer and libations of pure water from a neighboring spring, where perhaps the Sachem had often slacked his thirst, and cooled his heated brow, on his marches through the wilderness towards the seat of his rival, Uncas.

The prosperity of Norwich being based upon substantial grounds, must necessarily be of an enduring character. A large tract of country finds it a convenient port through which to transact business with New York. Agencies are established for the sale of manufactured goods of various kinds, and even of the raw material, and an extensive trade, wholesale and retail, is carried on in coal, lumber, groceries and dry goods. It is easy of access, midway on the great thoroughfare from New York to Boston, and business can be done here in a cheap, safe, and expeditious manner. Its own manufactures are varied and important, employing a large number of minds and hands, and its rivers and streamlets afford an almost inexhaustible supply of water power, by which they may be increased to any number and amount.

We may also enumerate among the sources of prosperity, the excellent schools of Norwich, the picturesque beauty of its scenery, the affability, ardor and liberality of its inhabitants, and the readiness with which they enter into plans of improvement, and concur in all attempts to make the routine of life happy, and mend the manners as well as the heart. From year to year the inhabitants have a variety of temperance and Sabbath school festivals, agricultural shows, meetings of societies, and out-door parties. The beautiful plains of Norwich have been the scene of many of these innocent festivities. And in this connection, the name of one of the most liberal promoters of such scenes may be mentioned, Charles Rockwell Esq.; a gentleman who has done much in various ways to benefit his native town, and whose countenance, encouragement, and active aid are never withheld, when the cause of religion is to be advanced, the wants of the poor relieved, the minds of the ignorant enlightened, and the hearts of children made happy.

## STATISTICS OF MANUFACTURES.

The following Statistics of a few of the manufacturing establishments of Norwich, was obtained from the proprietors themselves. The list is far from being complete, and is in fact but the commencement of one ; but further statements were not obtained in time for this publication.

| NAME. | KINDS OF GOODS. | HANDS. | AMOUNT ANN. |
|---|---|---|---|
| Shetucket Co. | Cotton (colored goods,) | 200 | about $175,000 |
| Chelsea Man. Co. | Paper, (various kinds,) | 100 | 260,000 |
| R. & A. H. Hubbard, | Paper, | 50 | 100,000 |
| Culver & Mickle, | Paper, | 10 | 30,000 |
| Wm. H. Pease, | Paper, | 9 | 25,000 |
| Kennedy, | Cotton Mill, | 50 | 75,000 |
| Wm. H. Coit, | Carpets, | 35 | 38,000 |
| Wm. A. Buckingham, | Carpets, | 40 for labor, | 10,000 |
|  |  | value, | 48,000 |
| Falls Mills, | Cotton, (colored goods), | 150 | 100,000 |
| N. H. Eddy & Co. | Satinet, | 20 | 30,000 |
| Norwich Foundry, | Foundry & machinery, | 35 | 25,000 |
| Kennedy & Tillinghast, | Cotton, | 65 | 75,000 |
| Adams & Kennedy, | Twine, | 20 | 30,000 |
| J. W. Shepherd, | Sash and Blind, | 20 | 30,000 |
| Rogers & Baker, | Sash, Blind and Doors, | 12 | 35,000 |
| Henry Allen, | Bedsteads, | 14 | 10,000 |
| Yantic Man. Co. | Flannels, | 110 wool, | 150,000 lbs. |
|  |  | make | 500,000 yds. |
| C. W. Rockwell's Mill, | Cassimers, | 50 | $100,000 |